PRAISE FOR *A Sanctuary of Trees*

"Back in 1929, J. Russell Smith published his classic *Tree Crops: A Permanent Agriculture*. At the time, and mostly since, hardly anyone seemed interested in reading about, let alone doing, farming that includes trees as part of an appropriate, resilient agriculture and even suggesting that such agriculture is a love of country. I didn't expect to ever see a book like Smith's again, yet now we have Gene Logsdon's *A Sanctuary of Trees*, a renewal of all those classic ideas cast in the context of today's, and hopefully, tomorrow's world."

—Frederick Kirschenmann, author, *Cultivating an Ecological Conscience: Essays from a Farmer Philosopher*

"Logsdon peels away the storied layers of our forests and beckons us to rekindle our connections with our most constant companions—trees. This book belongs as much in the hands of educators as it does on every homesteader's handmade bookshelf. Seldom are reminiscences so forward looking . . . but that is ultimately Logsdon's hallmark as an author."

— Philip Ackerman-Leist, professor, Green Mountain College, and author, *Up Tunket Road*

"*A Sanctuary of Trees* is a beguiling, companionable read, full of sharp-eyed wonder, genuine humility, and a thousand nuts of useful wisdom: when and how to build a plank road; how to not get killed felling an old tree; how to get lost, and found; and—if you read his book as Logsdon walks his woods—how to live a long, alert, insatiably engaged life. This one's a keeper."

—David Dobbs, author, *Reef Madness,* and coauthor, *The Northern Forest*

"Gene Logsdon does it again! This time he is out past the gardens, beyond the meadows, and deep into the groves and woodlots he has known and loved. What he brings back is a lover's report on a life-long affair of his. He is still contrary, thank goodness, more respectful of forests than of forestry; but *A Sanctuary of Trees* is a wonderfully woodsy book, neatly wrapped around a personal memoir. Reading it, we watch Logsdon casually learn about sassafras, chain saws, mistletoe, log houses, cordwood, birdsong, and a hundred other bits of vital forest lore. In private life he may be a tree hugger, and this narrative is seductive enough so that any thoughtful reader will probably develop similar symptoms."

—Ronald Jager, author, *Eighty Acres, Last House on the Road,*
and *The Fate of Family Farming*

"I am more enamored with Gene Logsdon than ever after reading *A Sanctuary of Trees*. Without melodrama, angst, or anything resembling shock value, this lush autobiography details Mr. Logsdon's relationship with—of all things—trees! Trees. How sane and civilized it is. I learned so much from this grounded and completely wonderful book."

—Janisse Ray, author, *Ecology of a Cracker Childhood,*
and *Pinhook: Finding Wholeness in a Fragmented Land*

A SANCTUARY OF
TREES

OTHER BOOKS BY GENE LOGSDON

Fiction:

Pope Mary and the Church of Almighty Good Food
The Last of the Husbandmen
The Lords of Folly

Nonfiction:

Holy Shit: Managing Manure to Save Mankind
Small-Scale Grain Raising
The Contrary Farmer's Invitation to Gardening
The Pond Lovers
The Mother of All Arts: Agrarianism and the Creative Impulse
All Flesh Is Grass: The Pleasures and Promise of Pasture Farming
You Can Go Home Again: Adventures of a Contrary Life
Good Spirits: A New Look at Ol' Demon Alcohol
Living at Nature's Pace: Farming and the American Dream
The Contrary Farmer
The Low-Maintenance House
Gene Logsdon's Practical Skills
Organic Orcharding: A Grove of Trees to Live In
Two-Acre Eden
Getting Food from Water: A Guide to Backyard Aquaculture
The Gardener's Guide to Better Soil
Successful Berry Growing
Homesteading: How to Find New Independence on the Land

A SANCTUARY OF
TREES

Beechnuts, Birdsongs,
Baseball Bats, and Benedictions

GENE LOGSDON

Chelsea Green Publishing
White River Junction, Vermont

Project Manager: Patricia Stone
Developmental Editor: Ben Watson
Copy Editor: Cannon Labrie
Proofreader: Eileen M. Clawson
Indexer: Linda Hallinger
Designer: Melissa Jacobson

Printed in the United States of America
First printing April 2012
10 9 8 7 6 5 4 3 2 1   12 13 14 15 16

Our Commitment to Green Publishing

Library of Congress Cataloging-in-Publication Data

Logsdon, Gene.
    A sanctuary of trees : beechnuts, birdsongs, baseball bats, and benedictions / Gene Logsdon.
        p. cm.
    ISBN 978-1-60358-401-2 (pbk.) — ISBN 978-1-60358-402-9 (ebook)
    1. Trees. 2. Trees—Utilization. 3. Trees—Ecology. 4. Trees—Folklore. 5. Nature in literature. 6. Philosophy of nature. 7. Human-plant relationships. 8. Human beings—Effect of environment on. 9. Country life. I. Title.
QK475.L64 2012
511'.52--dc23

                                    2011052013

Chelsea Green Publishing
85 North Main Street, Suite 120
White River Junction, VT 05001
(802) 295-6300
www.chelseagreen.com

Contents

ACKNOWLEDGMENTS

MY THANKS to publisher Margo Baldwin at Chelsea Green and all the folks there who have so enthusiastically and astutely turned my verbal meanderings into readable text, especially Ben Watson, Patricia Stone, and Cannon Labrie.

Also thanks to Dennis Barnes, Bryan Hoben, John Fichtner, and Max Roth for allowing me to use their sensitive and unusual photographs to show so well the many-sided blessings of a woodland culture.

Advice and information from Wendell Berry, Wes Jackson, David Kline, Brad Roof, Brad Billock, Otto Binau, John Fichtner, John Watkins, John Gallman, Andy Reinhart, Jan Dawson, Danny Downs, Keith Downs, Morrison Downs, Donnie Downs, Jimmy Downs, and especially my siblings, Marilyn, Giles, Jenny, Berny, Rosy, Teresa and Gerry, has been especially helpful.

None of this would be possible without the love and close participation of my wife, Carol; our children, Jenny and spouse Joe Cartellone, Jerry and spouse Jill; and grandchildren Becca Cartellone and Evan and Alex Logsdon, all of whom have shared the work and joy of living in a sanctuary of trees.

CHAPTER 1

Discovering Tranquility

WE ARE ALL TREE-HUGGERS. The reasons are not just sentimental or even environmental in the modern sense. We have relied on trees for food and shelter since way before we decided, without much evidence, that we were "*Homo sapiens.*" Our primate predecessors took to the trees for safe haven, and so do we, even today. Russ, a friend who farms not far from me, likes to tell how he escaped an angry bull by climbing a tree in his pasture. Ever since then he has referred to that arboreal refuge as the Tree of Life.

The most endearing example of our love of trees is Central Park in New York City. Over the years all sorts of schemes by what I call privateers have been brought to bear to "develop" parts of Central Park. Rarely has that ever succeeded, even when huge amounts of money and power were brought into play. The public will not be swayed, will not allow encroachments into its lovely forest in the city. Not even the sacred commandments of our mightiest religion, capitalism, have swayed the people. Central Park may not be the most "economic" use for that land. Too bad. Go practice your money religion somewhere else and leave the park alone.

When I was barely old enough to be called by that misnomer, *Homo sapiens*, we depended on trees even more than our primate ancestors did. Trees kept us from freezing to death. We cut firewood in the winter, and in other seasons, when the work of planting and harvesting slacked off, we split the log chunks into kindling and cut up waste wood—rotted-off fence posts, old boards, rafters and siding from deteriorating or torn-down barns and sheds, fallen tree branches—anything that would burn. We heated with wood because we were too poor to buy more extravagant fuels. We could have afforded lump coal, I suppose, but like wood, that would still have required manually feeding the fire day and night. If we had to do that anyway, might as well burn something that did not require out-of-pocket cash.

I was born into the wood culture and wood fuel economy at the tail end of it. Dad had worked out a deal with the neighbor who owned the woodlot adjacent to our land, allowing him to cut wood "on the half"; that is, half of what he cut went to the landowner. (Later on, Dad would buy the woodlot.) I had to go to school for the first time that year, so I know it was 1937, and I was irritated because I missed out on the tree felling. My sister, a year younger, gloated because, not yet in school, she could take my place as Dad's right-hand helper in the woods. I suppose if either of us had been old enough to do much work, we would have preferred school, but I doubt it. So when Dad hauled a load of log chunks or split firewood to the cellar with the wagon and a team of horses, she got to ride along while I sat fidgeting in school. We had no idea that finer folks, who burned coal, gas, or oil, thought we were poor.

Burning wood because we were poor meant that we were really rich in real values. We stayed just as warm as the wealthiest oil baron while the woodland provided many other things that barons can only pine for (damn those puns). The woodlot gave us morel mushrooms that we loved to hunt; maple sugar and syrup; ginseng (the poor man's Viagra?); fried squirrel and stewed rabbit (hasenpfeffer); sassafras tea and sassafras root beer; pawpaw custard, if you could stand it; persimmon cider; hickory nut cookies and black walnut cake; raspberry shortcake, blackberry cobbler, and elderberry pie. I could go on and on.

The woodland also provided all kinds of opportunity for play: hunting and trapping sports, hockey sticks, homemade bows and arrows, baseball bats (my cousin Virgil turned one on his lathe for his son), gunstocks (my brother would later make excellent ones), walking sticks, and wild grapevine swing sets. One of my very earliest memories of happiness in the woods was a day when I was recuperating from a mild concussion; I'd fallen off the sliding board at school. I had been in bed for about a week, reading adventure stories of Indians, pioneers, and Robin Hood. I really adored Robin Hood (still do) and his proficiency with bow and arrow. It was one of those rare warm days that can come in late February, and I was headed for Snider's Woods to make a homemade bow and arrows for hunting rabbits. The reality of this adventure was not nearly as glorious as my imagination depicted it, but I did find an ash sprout for a bow growing off a tree trunk where Dad had previously cut wood for the furnace, and several other sprouts that were straight enough for arrows. I did not flush any rabbits out of the brush piles to practice my aim on that day, and when I shot my arrows at trees instead, I usually missed. I was only a little disappointed to learn that using a bow and arrow requires consummate skill, first in the making, and then in the shooting. Just the idea that a potent weapon could be made directly from the woods, a weapon the poor could use to get food and to stop the rich from oppressing them, struck me as most appealing. I was already a revolutionary, based purely on instinct plus the influence of Robin Hood. The woodland was my salvation: it could provide hideouts and the means to defend myself.

Still convalescing from the concussion, I grew a little dizzy, so I sat down on the south side of the woods, closed my eyes, and soaked up the sun. Something about the unnatural warmth of that late winter day made me think that I was about to burst into bloom. I can feel that sun to this day, and the surge of radiant joy that I felt. That was the first time I knew my place in life was in the embrace of nature and the tranquility of the woods. That kind of tranquility, rendering me utterly serene, was what I needed in life more than anything else except food. It *was* a kind of food. Time after time in later days, I would choose this tranquility over money, glory, or office, but it would take me thirty years to claw my way back permanently to my own sanctuary in the woods.

Rather than going to the lumberyard we went to the woods for fence posts, pen and yard gates, hayricks, barn siding, structural lumber, ladders, milking stools, feed troughs, roof shingles, tomato and bean stakes, furniture, shelves, wooden tableware, wagon beds, wagon tongues, truck racks, shop benches, tool handles, cow stanchions, doghouses, corncribs, chicken coops, smokehouses, outhouses, woodsheds, and ready-made hooks to hang everything from hats to horse thieves. If you managed the woods correctly there was, in addition to firewood and lumber, an occasional high-value log good enough to sell for veneer.

Then there were the intangibles, like that sun on the south side of the woods in February, or the song of a wood thrush at twilight in the spring. In summer, the trees provided a shady respite; in winter, a break against the wind. And in all seasons the woods became a sanctuary for meditation as awe-inspiring as any rose-windowed cathedral.

Show me a coal mine that can do all that.

Nor did our wood economy end there. For one thing, while it may not be provable by science, a BTU from a wood-burning stove feels warmer than two BTUs from any other kind of heat this side of hellfire. We also made secondary use of these BTUs to heat water by running the water pipes around inside the furnace firebox. There was always a big kettle of hot water on the kitchen woodstove too. Mom would leaven the cistern water in the tub with a steamy addition from the kettle to take the edge off the cold water. She cooked with wood heat, and, wonder of wonders, the food was just as tasty as any from an electric or gas range.

It was my job, before electricity, to keep the woodbox full of kindling—pieces of dry split wood, no more than two inches thick, that would catch fire quickly in the stove. Mom could feed kindling into the stove very cleverly, controlling the temperature under cooking pots and frying pans almost as accurately as an electric or gas stove would do later. She would refer to a three-stick fire for oatmeal in the morning or a six-stick fire under a slab of beef for supper.

Dad would make kindling with a hatchet, chopping through splits of oak or ash that he set on a tree stump, striking down with the hatchet in his right hand, a thin piece of wood falling off with every stroke, till he had reduced the chunk all to kindling. We had lots of tree stumps around to use for benches and chairs. There was even one on the floor of the barn, which got covered with hay every summer and uncovered every winter. That's how close our farm was to the primeval forest that went before it. When Grandpa Rall built the barn, he just built it over the big stump, knowing it would rot away in time. No use doing work nature would do for you.

Chopping kindling was easy work, Dad pointed out, if the wood was very straight-grained oak, especially red oak, which split so easily he liked to joke that he could do it with the edge of his hand. He could split off pieces almost as straight and even as sawn wood. He showed me how the "old-timers," as he called them, could rive shingles off squared chunks of oak wood using the same technique. He did it with his hatchet, setting it on the top end of the wood about an inch in from the edge and driving it down into the wood with the butt of an axe. He could rive off clapboards an inch in thickness from a six-inch-squared chunk that were almost as even and uniform as sawn shingles. "Old-timers had a special tool, a froe, to make shingles," he told me. "You shingled the roof just the way you do now with bought shingles. You laid them on the roof, row by row going up from the bottom edge of the roof to the peak, lapping the second row over the first and the third over the second and so on to cover the cracks." Then he stared at me and added: "Good to know this. Might have to do it again some day." Another pause. "Oak is best, but it has to be free of knots. Shingle oak is the best of all."

I tried my hand at the job. Splitting kindling *was* easy. Actually sort of fun. Splitting out six-inch-wide shingles was harder. "It's easier with a froe," Dad said. "If I had one I'd show you. The froe is L-shaped, the handle at right angles to the blade. When you drive the blade down into the wood and it doesn't go through easily, you can twist down on the handle like a lever to pop the shingle loose."

And so I learned some of the art and skill of the old wood culture we were still living in then. I carried the phrase "shingle oak" around in my head for the rest of my life because for reasons I can't explain, odd notes about trees have always stuck with me.

We were energy-independent but at the time didn't realize there was value in that fact. The second that Mr. Edison's disciples raised the cross of electric salvation before our eyes, we left the sawdust trail and embraced it. First came stoker coal, which made possible an automated way to feed the furnace. Actually, first came electricity to run the motor on the stoker. I still wonder if many of us would not have kept on heating with wood if someone had found a way to feed cordwood into a furnace automatically. Then came oil. Then natural gas. Then propane. Electric heat got into the act too. Anything that relieved us of the job of feeding the fire manually was heavenly. Then everyone could go forth and get jobs to pay for the privilege of push-button heat.

Not everyone was happy even then. Rather than pay a lot of money for automatic warmth, some people started going to Florida in winter to escape the cold, which of course cost more than paying for fuel to stay warm at home. An elderly neighbor and friend now passed away, Jerome Frey, used to love to point out to me the weakness in that kind of thinking: "I was never so cold as when I went to Florida one winter and the temperature went below 50 degrees," he would often say to me. "They aren't equipped to handle anything under 70 degrees down there." He never went again.

But that's not the greatest irony of almighty progress. With all the modern, advanced, high-tech, expensive, automatic, luxurious, gleaming, push-button heat, I was never really warm in winter again until I went back to heating with wood.

I would like to leave it go at that and simply write the rest of this book about the tranquility that I've found living in a grove of trees, but there are grimmer reasons why some of us should be thinking about wood these days. There may be no true tranquility without it. When the electric current goes off in the middle of winter, our comfortable, carefree lives turn off with it. We may have to turn to wood for the same reason my father did long ago. In terms of energy today, *everyone is poor.* No matter how much money we think we have, or rather how much the Federal Reserve prints for every occasion, we are entering an era when there's simply not going to be enough push-button heat to go around.

Lest that sounds paranoid, consider this. The big power companies, like American Electric Power that serves our area, let it be known recently that they have been looking into burning wood to generate electricity. Some of these power companies own thousands of acres of woodland and, if shortages of other fuels did occur, well, why not consider wood? I doubt that they could do that with enough efficiency to make it pay, and evidently they must have reached that conclusion too, because in most cases they have shelved the idea, *for now.* But if giant utility companies even considered the possibility of generating electricity with renewable wood, it certainly makes sense for individual homeowners, at least those of us in rural areas, to be thinking about wood for home heating because we can do it quite efficiently if we have a grove of trees, or have friends who do.

I keep thinking about the forest devastation going on in third world countries where the land looks empty and barren because the trees around villages are being stripped away for home fuel. Efforts are only beginning there to bring in high-efficiency stoves that increase tremendously the BTU output per acre of forest. Nor, as far as I can find out, are there ongoing studies, experiments, or actual forest studies in these countries to grow plantations of high BTU fuelwood trees like black locust that can be coppiced every ten years. (More on coppicing in chapter 11.) The people too often are too busy killing each other. Of one thing I am sure, as I will try to demonstrate in a later chapter: the cost of energy from such forests would be far less than producing ethanol from corn.

We are all painfully aware that fuel prices are rising. Electricity, oil, gas, and even coal prices are climbing. What are you paying today to stay warm? What were you paying ten years ago? Twenty? When we moved to our own woodland retreat some forty years ago, our electricity cost us 3.5 cents per kilowatt-hour. Now it has gone as high as 11 cents and everyone knows that's not the end of it. Oil and gas have risen similarly. If this occurs while our economic wizards assure us that inflation is under control, whatever will happen when it is obvious to everyone that it is not under control and never was? Wood for home heating may not be practical for cities, but out in the countryside it can save money and save oil and gas for areas with more concentrated populations.

Trying to figure precisely how much your own firewood and labor are worth as substitutes for fossil fuels is difficult because, as we shall see, there are so many variables. From my experience, an able-bodied person should be able to turn logs and tree branches into cordwood with a chainsaw and a maul at the rate of one cord in five hours after the log is on the ground. I see figures that say it takes longer than that. At age seventy-nine, I work up a cord's worth in about eight hours, taking frequent rests. I have a hard time figuring out if my labor is a cost or a profit. Working up firewood is my afternoon recreation on warmish days in late fall, early spring, and winter. I enjoy being out in the woods. I think that these interludes are more effective in gaining peace of mind than $100-an-hour sessions with a psychiatrist and more healthful physically than $50-an-hour sessions at an exercise center. I enjoy even more those occasions when neighbors come by and talk awhile, giving me an excuse to rest even longer.

But I shall pretend to be very correct in the accounting and bookkeeping department. Let us say it takes six cords of wood to heat a moderately sized, well-insulated, three-bedroom house through a northern Ohio winter. Masonry heaters along with sufficient insulation and perhaps a bit of passive solar heat can reduce that amount significantly, as we shall see, but let's be conservative and say six cords. If you know what your fuel bill is now when you are heating with oil, gas, or electricity, you can easily figure the value of wood heat to replace fossil fuels.

I daresay we are talking about an average home heating cost today of somewhere around $2,500 a winter, to use figures as loosely as the feds do when talking about deficits. If it takes six hours to work up a cord of wood, or thirty-six hours for six cords of wood, your labor is worth $70 an hour. Kind of a nice wage for spending a few peaceful hours in the woods trying to figure out why your friends think you are crazy. If you are old and crusty like me and need a part-time job, you can hardly find a retirement position, except maybe lolling around as a retired general in the Pentagon, that will pay better.

Your chainsaw will cost you about $50 a year over its lifetime if you take care of it. Chainsaw blades will cost maybe another $30 a year unless you are good at sharpening them yourself, in which case about half that. You'll need a pickup truck, but if you are living in a sanctuary of trees, or contemplating doing so, you surely have one already. Yes, there's a little gas and oil involved. So okay, you only make $40 an hour. Of course, using horses to haul the wood to the house might lower the costs more. And with horses, you could drag logs out of the woods without cutting truck lanes through the trees.

Another way to compute value is to compare your wood's BTU output directly with the alternate fuel you now use. A cord of air-dried white oak firewood is equal in heat output to somewhere around 300 gallons of No. 2 fuel oil.

How big a grove of trees do you need to provide this kind of lucrative part-time work indefinitely? That question will be exhaustively addressed later on, but just to get your brain in forward gear, I can assure you from experience that five acres of more or less mature woodland can in some cases supply you with three winter months of heat every year without depleting the annual supply of wood. With ten acres, you will not only get all the firewood you need until death do us part, but logs or lumber to sell or use yourself. So what are you waiting for?

What you are waiting for is the same thing I waited for until I was forty years old, I suppose. It took that long for me to arrange my life so that I could live the way I wanted to live it. (It took me until I was thirty to even understand how I wanted to live.) With a whole lot better planning and insight, I could have moved to the woods at age twenty-five or even sooner, but I was not smart enough to figure things out that early in life. Smart is probably the wrong word. It really doesn't take a whole lot of brains to find a sanctuary of trees to live it, just awareness that you can do so if you want to badly enough.

I am not suggesting that deforestation is not a serious problem worldwide. Lester Brown, in his *Plan B 3.0: Mobilizing to Save Civilization* (New York: Norton, 2008), describes the situation very well. Developing countries have been losing forests at the rate of 13 million hectares a year. But then he goes on to say something quite surprising to many people. "Meanwhile, the industrial world is actually gaining an estimated 5.6 million hectares of forestland each year, principally from abandoned cropland returning to forests on its own and from the spread of commercial forestry plantations" (p. 87). While the world is still losing forestland, it is true only in those parts where wood is the principal or only fuel, and efforts to make growing and burning it more efficiently are not yet in place.

The situation today is best described by that old saying about not being able to see the forest for the trees. There are woodland possibilities at least in the United States waiting for you almost everywhere that rainfall is sufficient. But because we early on denuded so much of our land of its pristine stands of trees (and have been repenting that ever since), we tend to think that there is a shortage of woodland sites for tree sanctuaries. Not so. In most of the United States, you can't take fifty steps with your eyes closed and not bump into a tree. We have culturally closed our eyes to that reality. We don't see little nooks and crannies of one or two acres overgrown with second- or third-growth trees and brush as being excellent opportunities to develop little sanctuaries. (And of course these kinds of tree groves are almost totally overlooked by geographers trying to estimate the amount of forest in this country.) It is not difficult to find bigger groves too, and if you can't, it is almost as satisfying to plant a grove and watch it grow to become your sanctuary.

We still have a lot of remnant woodland in the United States for at least three reasons. The first is that the forest is very resilient, much more so than human civilization. It is awesome to see those jungles of trees in South and Central America hiding the ruined buildings of resplendent but long-forgotten cities. Trees spread just like weeds, given any chance at all. Many of us think that trees have to be deliberately planted, when in reality we just have to let nature take its course. If you don't think so, don't mow under the trees in your yard. Most of our trees in their natural habitat will seed themselves thickly the very first or second year. If we parked the lawn mowers, every yard in the eastern United States would return to forest in twenty years. I've watched this happen on abandoned farmsteads (see figure 10 in the color insert). Given about thirty inches of annual rainfall or more, trees will come marching in. Parts of New England and the South are on their third or fourth regrowth of timber. Maine, Vermont, and New Hampshire have been cut over at least twice, and today, eighty percent of the land there is still forested.

The second reason there are more trees, not less, than a century ago, is that even here in the Corn Belt, where level farmland is so much more productive than in hilly New England, we are just about at the end of the happy, sappy bulldozer era of turning everything a tractor won't fall off into giant baseball diamonds for corn. There just isn't any more land that can be profitably cleared for corn and soybeans. For whatever else that means, the forest remaining still amounts to thousands upon thousands of acres, in ravines, river- and creeksides, steep hillsides, floodplains, and even on the best ground where property owners hold tree groves more sacred than corn. Also trees are growing up between housing tracts on vacant land too difficult to develop, or on land waiting to be developed.

A quick way to grasp what is going on is to study land development in New England in the 1800s and 1900s. There is an excellent map drawing in *Eric Sloane's America* (written and illustrated by Eric Sloane and published in 1954), showing a typical landscape in New England in 1800 and another a century later. The 1800 sketch shows a solid patchwork quilt of farms and farmhouses with only a few trees. Every acre at that time of small, horse-worked farms was utilized for farming because, with hand methods, every acre could be so utilized. But a hundred years later, only the more profitable, more easily farmed acres remained in cultivation. The rest of the land was in urban housing or had returned to woodland. This very same kind of development has now gone on in the Midwest. In 1900, all the rural land was committed to farming. Every bit of it. As my neighbor Albert Rall used to boast, the hunting on his farm was very poor because he used every acre for livestock or crops. Now, a hundred years later, significant parts of this landscape are returning to woodland because it is not profitable for today's kind of farming with its large-scale machinery and very narrow ranges of profit. Small acreages of rougher land near creeks or in ravines was profitable pasture in 1900 but in 2000 is not enough to fence and graze profitably. It is going back to trees. It would go back faster except that many landowners can't stand to see land go to "brush," which is the beginning of a new forest, and so they mow and mow and mow these remnants at great expense of time and money. One of my friends was so obsessed with this kind of neatness that he tried to keep every foot of his creekside land in grass and lost his life when his tractor turned over into the creek. Had he left that "brush" alone, it would be woodland today and he would be here to enjoy it.

The land behind or between subdivisions that does not lend itself to more houses is often used by people living nearby as their own little parks. Such land, and there is quite a bit of it, is treasured mainly for the privacy and beauty it affords for the adjacent homes. Its potential for tree crops and food, if managed correctly, has not been realized yet. In many cases the amount and value of wood growing there could be doubled or tripled.

I know one person who did realize the potential. He grew up in a subdivision right next to land of this kind and, remarkably for this day and age, he built a neat log house for his family on some of that land, *using the trees right there that had seemingly no commercial value.* When I asked him which tree species made the best log cabin logs, he said: "The ones that are handiest to the cabin." This is the kind of "suburban forest industry" just waiting for other enterprising people to take advantage of.

The third reason the trees are on the increase is what is being called urban farming and urban forestry. If you fly over a residential area of almost any city—and especially any village, even in the Plains, where trees are not particularly natural—you seem to be flying over woodland. There are trees everywhere because people plant them around their homes. We all love trees, even if sometimes they fall on our houses. We go right on planting more. That is good. There are all kinds of equipment and skilled tree cutters now who can handle big trees around houses just fine. The next move, and it is already happening in some progressive communities, is that the residents of a suburban area get organized and draw up a plan and program for forest improvement of their woodland sanctuary. They manage their trees not only as individual lawn ornaments, but as collective forest products.

There is a good reason, other than for home heating, that we should be thinking of bringing more wood back into our daily lives. Plastics have replaced wood for hundreds of uses where wood would be just as practical. We know now that many common plastics are releasing harmful chemicals into the air and into our foods and drinks. The culprit is BPA—bisphenol A. The Plastic Culture that has replaced the older Wood Culture is dangerous to our health, but if we would regain the knowledge about wood lost in that cultural shift, we could easily use wood as a replacement for many plastic products. There must now be a return to our primeval roots, and it is happening. There will come a time when every grade-school kid will again be able to tell a hickory tree from a walnut, a maple from an oak. We will master again the basic skills of making basketry from wood instead of those horrible plastic sacks, making table woodenware, wooden tool handles, wooden machinery parts, and wooden toys. It is not as though the knowledge has been forgotten. There is an army of woodworkers out there ready to respond to an army of consumers. The Longaberger Basket Company in Ohio is a classic example of just how successful using wood to replace plastic can be.

There is one more reason those of us who love tree sanctuaries should treasure our woodlands. Perhaps we don't want to heat entirely with wood. Perhaps we don't want to make beautiful turned bowls out of black cherry or baseball bats out of heartwood ash. But let us say it is January and the temperature is falling toward zero. An ice storm knocks out your power. Blizzard winds close the roads. Suddenly, the very essence of what "home" means has been taken from you. You are no longer secure. You are in fact facing dire insecurity, the danger of freezing not only your water pipes but your arteries. There is nowhere to turn for rescue. If you have some wood in the garage and a stove standing by, it can quickly be perking away contentedly, the teakettle singing and a pot of soup warming. Tell me: what is that kind of tranquility worth? It is not measurable in money. It is priceless.

Chapter 2

Babes in the Woods

Keeping a sanctuary of trees is a journey of constant discovery. The keeper comes on board usually after the trees have been on the road, so to speak, for decades or centuries. This ancientness is utterly beguiling to tree lovers. Even if knowledgeable about forestry in general, they usually have no notion of what has transpired in the past in their grove, or in the place where they are seeking to buy a grove. Just to think about how, a century or more ago, Native Americans or immigrant settlers might have stood under the same oak tree you are standing under today inspires awesome daydreams.

There is no specific, particular knowledge about how trees got to where they are growing or why they remain. Who and what kinds of people and other creatures walked here, lived here when these trees were just sprouting? Before they sprouted? This kind of knowledge appears all the more intriguing now that anthropologists and archaeologists are convinced that what the first Europeans found in America was not a natural "forest primeval" or wilderness but, at least partly, a human-managed forest. This conclusion greatly alters how we should view the woodland we choose to live in. If we are to manage it "correctly," we must take into account not just the botanical and biological environment of the place, but how its natural history may have been influenced by humans, animals, and insects. Only then can we begin to define what "correctness" might be.

I am fortunate to know at least a little of the past two hundred years of my woodland because, first of all, I grew up in it, and because I still live in it eighty years later. More than that, the land round about has always been owned or managed by my kinfolks, so I have had the good fortune to learn from ancestors what happened here for a hundred or more years before I was born. My pioneer forebears knew personally people who had been acquainted with the Wyandot Indians who lived here until 1842. Some of the folklore of these woodlands that was passed down to me is centuries old.

Growing up, my siblings and I spent at least as much time in these groves as we did in our cultivated fields or in the barn and barnyard, and, if sleeping time is not counted, even in the house. None of the woodlots belonged to us at first, and the fact that five of them now do strikes me as nearly miraculous.

But the explanation is logical enough. We loved those tree groves so much that, as adults, we were willing to go to quite extraordinary lengths to own them and thereby keep away the bulldozers that obliterated so many other tree groves in our county. Our favorite grove we called Adrian's Woods on the western border of the farm, named after the relative who owned it. Many a day we played there with our cousins for hours. Kerr's Woods, to the south, belonged to "two old ladies in Columbus" and was farmed by Adrian and his brother Raymond, and before that by great-uncle Dave. The eight-acre grove just to the north of us my father bought after the previous owner, Ralph Snider, died. Many years later, after I had spent much time in other faraway woodlands, my wife and I came back here and acquired a fourth woodlot about two miles from the home farm where we have lived now nearly four decades. A fifth woodlot is part of my brother's farm. There are several other woodlots in the same area that I roamed while growing up. Today, old pastureland near these groves is also growing back to woodland. These woodlots have been my lifelong college of what I call "deep forestry."

This education actually began with a grove on the east side of the home farm that did disappear, in the forties, to the bulldozer. This was the first woodlot to vanish in our farming community, which is probably why I remember it so well. When the farm on which the grove stood was sold out of the Rall family when I was about nine, the first thing the new owner did was to cut down the woodlot. He could hardly be blamed, I suppose. It was such a nondescript little scrap of land, as far as it could be from the roads that methodically mark every mile square in our county. It was being used mostly as a trash dump, a common fate of woodlots in those days. The new owner said he just wanted to "square up the farm," an excuse often used to cut down groves in our flat, checkerboard-square, Corn Belt landscape, where everyone is a straight shooter and always makes "square deals" and never (horrors) runs in circles. The geometry of squares and rectangles rules our way of thinking. Everything must always set square with the world.

There were a few giant trees in the grove that were no doubt worth some money, or at least they would be today. My oldest sister and I, who witnessed the end of the grove, were not at first dismayed because Dad said that logging off the trees would encourage morel mushrooms to grow there. Hunting morels in the spring was our most exciting pastime. The spongelike fungi are hard to see on the woodland floor and seem to pop up where you have just looked. Morel hunters know what I mean.

But I remember the disappearance of that grove so well for a reason that is hard to put into words. The stumps remained for a couple of years afterward, and the burdock grew rampantly in the sunlight that now reached the woodland floor. Someone said that burdock roots could be harvested and sold, but we had, then, no knowledge of how to find buyers for such products. We did indeed pick a big sackful of morels there, though.

Then one spring day when I walked back to "Nelson's sawed-off woods," as my sister still calls it, after Nelson Rall, the previous owner, to hunt for more morels, there was nothing there except black soil. The area had been transformed into farmland. I stood there transfixed at the total absence of the tree stumps and the new seedlings that had already started to grow back. I tried to figure out exactly where the biggest oak stump had stood, where we had found the most morels. It just seemed impossible to my boyhood mind that this remote little retreat of mine had so totally vanished into thin air. Poof! There was something evil about it.

I became at that moment a defender and savior of woodlots. Heightening my resolve, my elders were upset at the disappearance of "Nelson's sawed-off woods" too. The Ralls (my mother's family— there were at least fourteen nearly contiguous Rall family farms in the neighborhood) were, with one or two notable exceptions, extremely traditional and conservative in their farming philosophy. No one at that time was accustomed to such sudden disappearances of tree groves because no one had grasped yet the power of bulldozers. And a sacred rule of rural life had been violated. I can still hear Adrian saying to his brother Raymond—bellowing it actually, because he always italicized important announcements by shouting: "A farmer must reserve ten acres of every hundred for a woodlot." I never forgot that, mostly because the longer I lived, the more I became convinced that he was right.

I have often wondered about my attraction to wild nature, particularly woodland. If anyone were ever foolish enough to sequence my DNA, I wonder if they would find a tidbit of genetic scrap that was supposed to have dropped off along the way, like the primate tail shriveled and finally dropped off the human butt, so they say. This stray gene might tie me closer to the sanctuary of the trees than is true of most people. Or is it possible that everyone possesses this genetic grist and they just have not had the opportunity to express it? Perhaps this is the gene that guarantees the continued existence of the human race. We who have it will save humanity, not through any intelligence or wisdom, but because we can't help it. Or maybe we are the ones headed for extinction and the humans who can graft iPads to their tailbones will survive.

Our tree groves grow in an area of fertile farmland, the kind that normally is the first to see its trees cleared away for cultivated fields. The topography of the land is mostly flat with only small slopes backing away from the creeks that curl between the level cornfields. These trees are what remain of the old-growth forest that covered this land two centuries ago. They protect little pockets of virgin soil *never* touched by the blundering, bludgeoning point of the plow. In other words, the trees are not themselves the only treasure here. Perhaps in these remnants of primeval soil there live microbes, or unique combinations of microbes and mycorrhizal fungi, that give to food grown on them a vital healthfulness that is being lost in farmed soils. Maybe that is why the Indians' medicinal plants really did work sometimes. If so, the microbiological life of this soil may be capable of "reseeding" the depleted soils in the fields around the woodlots, should humans ever come to their senses, just as the trees still growing there are fully capable of reseeding the fields around them with more trees.

There were quite extensive stretches of wetland prairie not far away from our groves (some remnants still remain) that as far back as I can trace were free of trees. Between the prairie and the forest, and more often on little hillocks within the prairie where the land was naturally well drained enough for trees to grow, there were stretches of savanna with stands of oak trees, called "islands" by old-timers. These savannas, where extensive, are also called "oak openings," and some of them still exist as preserves and parks in northern Ohio and elsewhere. Natural history indicates that there was almost constant war between the prairie, the savannas, and the deep forest. Fire ruled this war. The thick prairie grass in the fall was prone to great fires, some intentionally set by the Indians, most caused by lightning. The fires killed all the trees except for bur oak. For a while, the oaks would advance, then the grass would advance. The savannas were the no-man's-land between the two armies.

The landscape of field and tree grove asserted itself after the prairies and the great forests were mostly gone, and it remains across middle America as far west as the Great Plains even today, wherever concentrated farming operations and the traditional love of woodlands bump heads. The bulldozer boys would like to knock down all the trees on the more level land, but there is enough sacred regard for groves in the bosoms of many rural people still today to keep some woodlots intact, even on good farming land. These groves, easy to see from highways because they stand out like islands in the corn, have mostly been neglected after the days when wood was necessary for heating fuel. Needless to say, they can sometimes be bought if you are willing to pay a little more than the going farmland prices. When a farm is sold these days, the wooded areas are almost always sold separately because they are much in demand by tree-sanctuary lovers. Tree people can outbid the farmers for the woodlands because they don't have to buy the whole farm and can pay more for the woodland than farmers can justify.

Woodland Indians back in the dim light of prehistory were the first keepers of the forest where these groves still remain, and they were no doubt managing the trees much more than the white settlers realized. Bob Chenoweth, in his fascinating book titled *Black Walnut* (Champaign, IL: Sagamore Publishing, 1995), gives ample botanical and even archaeological evidence that black walnut and white oak groves were planted and managed by humans in prehistoric times, because neither species will sprout and grow up on its own in dense forest. Where groves of these species are found, you can rest assured that at one time it was in a sunnier part of the forest, kept that way by Native Americans in the aftermath of a fire or windstorm.

I would give anything to be able to roll back history and talk to the Wyandots who lived among our trees before us. Our biggest white oaks behind the house today were sprouting when the Indians still lived here in 1842. Once, in Kerr's Woods, I was helping Raymond and Adrian round up their sheep in the fall. At one point, Raymond reached down and pulled up a plant from the woodland floor, peeled back the root, and started chewing on it. Then he started shivering and tears welled up in his eyes. "It makes you do that," he said calmly. "Indian turnip. Tastes awful but cleans you out good. The Indians knew." I was wide-eyed at his strange behavior, but as children will do, I soon accepted the experience as just part of everyday life. But I never forgot. Many years later, walking in Kerr's, I suddenly remembered that incident and decided to check old Raymond out. I remembered the cone of red berries on top of the stalk of that "Indian turnip" and knew by then that it was what is colloquially called jack-in-the-pulpit (*Arisaema triphyllum*). I looked it up in an old medicinal herb book. Sure enough, the plant was called, in pioneer times, Indian turnip, and the root, although "quite poisonous when fresh" according to the herbal, was commonly eaten by the Indians after boiling. How did Raymond know? This knowledge surely came to him from oral tradition. There is in fact quite a bit of family folklore that claims there is Wyandot blood in the Rall family. What I saw Raymond do, I feel sure he had seen his father do, who in turn had seen his father do it. That would have been my great-grandfather, and *he* had learned it from people, perhaps the Taylors for whom he worked, who were living here before the Wyandots were forced to leave. One of the Ralls married a Taylor. The only problem was that someone along the way forgot to tell my ancestors that they were supposed to boil the roots first. Whenever I see a jack-in-the-pulpit in my tree groves I think of Raymond, and I hear the footfalls of the Wyandots.

The Indians were of course masters of the woodland. They knew all about hickory nuts and walnuts and sweet acorns that could be ground into bread flour. They boiled maple sap and built cabins and longhouses out of logs and tree bark without benefit of saws, hammers, and nails. On the prairie lands five miles south of our groves they conducted fire-ring hunts annually. The tall grass was set ablaze in a circle, forcing deer within the ring of fire into an ever-smaller concentration where they were easier to kill. One of these ring hunts is described in some detail in a precious early history of our county, *Atlas of Wyandot Co., Ohio from Records and Original Surveys*, published by Harrison & Hare of Philadelphia in 1879. Most counties have atlases like this, and because many of them have been reprinted, they are more easily available now. Ours contains priceless information about what the county was like before white settlers "improved" the landscape. It also contains plat maps of all the townships, so that ownership of any tract at that time can be tracked. These atlases are of special interest for those trying to put together a history of their tree sanctuaries.

What does this have to do with understanding woodlands? Everything. The ring-hunt account mentions that the Indians would wait until rain was threatening so that, hopefully, the fire would be extinguished before it burned off too much grass outside the circle. The hunters would have noticed early on (who knows how many centuries they were doing this?) that when the fire did spread too much outside the ring, it would go through the trees on the higher land in the prairie. The bur oaks and sometimes other white oaks would survive the fire. This knowledge was not lost on the Indians. Fire became not only their way to corral deer but a tool to open, or keep open, sylvan glades for the food trees they desired, but which wouldn't grow in dense forest shade.

Every year, starting about 1820 but in earnest after 1870 when my ancestors arrived here, pioneers nibbled away with their axes at the trees around their cabin clearings to make fields. More importantly for our family's tree groves today, Dave Harpster, after whom the nearby village is named, and a few other shrewd pioneers looked at the prairie and saw opportunity. Here was land that did not have to be cleared. The prairie was being ignored by the "sodbusters" because it was mostly too wet to farm without substantial drainage. But Harpster figured it would make good sheep and cattle range. He bought up some five thousand acres of it—the government was practically giving it away—and became known eventually as the Wool King of the World, even in the banking houses of New York City. He set the tone of local farming at that time. Others saw what he did and took sheep farming one step further. R. N. Taylor, who in 1870 owned much of the land that was later owned by our family, was one of them.

Clearing land of trees was a slow and onerous task. The job was not over when the trees were cut and disposed of. The forest is extremely resilient and, as was often said jokingly, in about the time a pioneer took to sharpen his axe, new trees would be sprouting back up again. Cleared glades in the forest would quickly bounce back with a new stand of saplings before the stumps could all be cleared or burned away. The farmer, wanting cornfields, needed a way to keep his land clear of this new growth that sprang up in the sunlight while he was getting rid of the old trees. That's where sheep came into the picture. Cows would eat off new growth too, but sheep would do it better and would, on that scant diet, produce wool. For ranchers like R. N. Taylor, who didn't own as much prairie as Harpster, sheep became the rotary mowers of their day. Much better in fact. Mowers do not grow a wool crop every year.

Using sheep to keep cleared land free of regrowth until the plow could take over, or to keep pasture lands too hilly to plow clear of trees, became standard practice in our area. Sheep became the weed eaters and brush killers of that time, keeping pastures looking like golf courses and wooded areas like parks. Sheep were a necessary part of almost every farm until about 1950. Not by accident did the sport teams in our high school get the nickname Rams. (When the girls' teams came along, they were called Lady Rams!)

My great-grandfather and his brother hired out to R. N. Taylor when they emigrated from Germany and from him learned the ways of sheep. Over time, the Ralls acquired the Taylor lands and continued to raise sheep on the uncultivated parts of their farms. More land was cleared, but some squares and rectangles of old-growth forest remained, because, as Adrian said, they were supposed to remain. Grazed by sheep, the woodland returned an income over and above the income from the wood. But grazing effectively prevented the next generation of trees from growing. Or so it seemed. Because no new trees were coming along, and because the white oaks and hickories lived longer than other species, the foresters said that oak-hickory was our "climax" forest—that woodland here would end up in a more or less permanent stand of these two species if left to its own devices. I am quite sure now that there is no such thing as a climax forest, yet the foresters still teach it. For instance, the oak-hickory "climax" grove behind our house has transformed itself over the last forty years into a maple "climax" grove.

Even if the sheep were bad for the groves, they made of the woodland a wonderful playground for children. There was no underbrush. Also, without new competition coming along, the white oaks and hickories seemed to produce much more bountiful nut and acorn crops than they did in ungrazed woodland. Large buckeye trees grew in Adrian's Woods. We gathered the buckeyes, built a fire, and threw them into the flames, where they popped explosively. Who needed firecrackers?

There were black walnut trees in Adrian's and Kerr's too. We hunted squirrels and trapped raccoons and muskrats. Fried squirrel was much tastier to our way of thinking than wild rabbit. My father insisted that young raccoon, plentiful in the woods, were good eating too, but he never persuaded my mother to cook them. Coon hunting was nevertheless a favorite neighborhood occupation. We had a saying: "When it's dark, the coon hunters own the woods."

The three groves contiguous to our farm served different purposes for us, actually. Kerr's was more for gathering nuts and hunting squirrels. Adrian's was mostly for playing pretend games. I was Uncas, the Last of the Mohicans. Or sometimes I was the Deerslayer or the Pathfinder. I avidly read the Leatherstocking tales by James Fenimore Cooper, wordy as they were, until finally I began to imagine that I was a Mohican. I'm still wondering. Since the Logsdons fought in the French and Indian War, how do I know if maybe I bear some DNA from the Mohicans? Science has just discovered that some of us even possess Neanderthal DNA. The chances that I am the Last of the Mohicans are certainly better than that.

Snider's Woods was never grazed because it was never Rall land or, as far as I can tell from the old maps, Taylor land either. So there was always a good growth of that evil stuff the Ralls referred to as "bresh" in Snider's—thorns and thickets under the younger trees. Where Dad had cut firewood there was an especially splendid growth of "bresh"—mostly black raspberries, and even some rare yellow and red ones. We reserved Snider's mostly for hunting morels, however. Just as the nut trees flourished better in the open Kerr's Woods, so morels seemed to be more plentiful in the denser Snider's Woods. Dad eventually moved the old brooder house where Mom had raised chicks for years from near the house to the woodlot. There it became our cabin in the woods where my sisters and brother spent much of their growing-up time when I was far away in other woodland adventures. We were all a bunch of woodrats, I guess. Oddly, one of the very first articles I ever wrote for a magazine was about that brooder-house cabin in the woods.

Snider's Woods gave us another lesson in deep forestry. In the very center of the woodlot there was a raised oblong bed, measuring about 100 feet by 50 feet. It was hard to make out amidst the fallen leaves and underbrush, but around it a shallow ditch had been dug. It was here, we learned, that old Mr. Snider cultivated ginseng to sell. Ginseng needs a shady place to proliferate, and making a raised bed probably provided for better drainage. We thought of ginseng then about the same way society views marijuana today. Growing it was not illegal actually, but we decided there must be something as shady about it as the forest floor it grew on. We certainly thought there was something shady about Mr. Snider, probably unfairly, and avoided him. Now I dearly wish I could have talked to him about ginseng. There were still a few ginseng plants growing in his woods just a few years ago. Wild woodland ginseng fetches a very fancy price, perhaps because it requires eight years from planting to harvest. Just another of a long list of projects I always planned on but never did.

By the time I was thirteen years old, I had mastered at least the basic idea of how a woodland culture might flower today, even if I did not use such a fancy term for it. It was not that I knew very much, but my experiences had opened my mind to the possibility of a life drawing sustenance directly from the trees. I knew that I could stay warm in winter with wood. I knew that this material could be shaped into tools and toys and furniture and barns and houses. I knew that a tree grove was full of food of all kinds. I knew there were medicines there much cheaper than those in a drugstore, and perhaps just as effective. I tried chewing on willow twigs to stop a headache as folklore directed. It didn't seem to work, but I found out later that willow bark does contain salicylic acid, the active ingredient in aspirin. I learned that tree shade on a hot day could be much more comfortable than air-conditioning and that a cold day was much less cruel on the lee side of the woods. Most of all, I learned how lucky

I had been to grow up among the trees. That was reason enough to have my own grove, if ever I became a father myself. I would have a place for my children to play and learn there's more to life than the make-believe of television.

Then I made probably the stupidest decision of my life, only to have it turn out to be the smartest thing I ever did. I decided to listen to my teachers when they suggested that I should study to become a priest. Looking back now, the real reason I went along with the idea, or at least the real reason I stayed in the seminary as long as I did, was a little detail my teachers didn't appreciate. The high school prep-seminary where I chose to go was situated on four hundred acres of woodland. My cousin Ed, who was my frequent companion in the woods, decided to go too. We thought about those four hundred acres and decided it might turn out to be fun to study for the priesthood.

Chapter 3

Going to School
in the Forest

I stopped walking so that the rustle of leaves my feet were stirring up would not drown out other sounds. But there was nothing else to hear except a bit of plaintive birdsong far off and a whisper of wind in the trees. I was standing deep in a forest I knew to be at least four hundred acres in size because that's how much woodland belonged to the seminary where I was going to high school. But the expanse of trees stretched well beyond that, covering the surrounding knobby hill country so characteristic of southern Indiana. Much of it was too steep to farm. To my boyhood mind, this was heaven. Perhaps I could walk all day in one direction and never see another human. I could shout out profanities as loud as I could and no one would hear me, maybe.

"Damn!" I yelled, just to hear what it sounded like with the volume turned up. The only answer was the echo of my voice drifting through the trees.

"Hell and damnation!" I tried again. The leaves on the trees barely quivered.

I was in a mood for what I considered, at age fourteen, to be ornery language. I had been in the seminary now for two months. My homesickness was so acute I sometimes felt like I was going to vomit. I had always gone to the woods to nurse my sorrow, and here at the seminary that was easy to do. The forest grew almost up to the walls of the school buildings, dormitories, priests' residence, library, chapel, barn, and other outbuildings. Slipping away, I felt a kind of wild comfort. No one in the whole world knew exactly where I was.

That day I had wanted to explore my new sylvan Shangri-la to the fullest, and this was the first chance that had come to me—a Sunday afternoon called Visitor's Day when students whose homes were nearby could enjoy visits from their parents. My parents were too far away, which made me feel all the more sulky.

I walked on for another few minutes and then stopped abruptly. Among the enshrouding trees ahead was an indication that I was not in pristine wilderness as I wanted to believe. Hunkered down under the trees was a log cabin, a magical sort of thing to me, as I had known them only in adventure books and not in real life. Obviously other humans had been here before me. As I gingerly edged forward, ready to flee at any sign of life, it became clear that this was an abandoned cabin. The clay chinking between the logs was falling out, the chimney was cracked and crumbling at the top, and there was a generous covering of leaves on the roof. The logs were all round, none hewn or sawn flat-sided, again indicating possible pioneer times. But the roof was covered with tar paper, which suggested something more recent. Closer inspection revealed that there was only one room to it, with a porch in front. Inside was a crude fireplace only.

I sat on a bench made of branch wood on the porch, overwhelmed by the spirit of the thing. Log cabins meant to me Indians, bears, wolves, pioneers warming themselves before the hearth, Daniel Boone, Abe Lincoln—the entire ambience of frontier times when humans and trees confronted each other with nothing more between them than an axe. A log cabin symbolized the embrace between civilization and nature, humans literally wrapping the trees around them as they might draw on a coat and hat. This was how the initial partnership between American life and the trees was formed, it dawned on me, and so it continued, even to the present, with humans desiring to live in log houses long after such houses had been outdated by technology.

Then, about a hundred yards away, I found a second cabin. It was not as well put together as the first one but was similar in size and construction. I was curious even then about how the cabins were put together. My only previous knowledge of log construction, from reading novels of pioneer life, had led me inadvertently to think that building this way was something complicated, requiring special knowledge. What I inspected now said otherwise. Where the logs crisscrossed at the corners, they were notched. That was logical enough. The notches held the logs in place and also allowed them to fit closer to each other on the walls so that less chinking was necessary between them. Anybody should be able to figure that out and put up such a building with an ax, chisel, saw, and a stand of trees nearby.

The roof raftering was a little more complicated, but it was easy to see how it was put together too. Small logs, about five inches in diameter, had been used instead of two-by-fours, their ends notched into cut-out stair steps up the slant of the gable end trusses. Wherever logs crossed they were notched to hold them in place. Seeing it, I could grasp how easy it would be to imitate. Anyone with will and energy could do it.

From my previous reading, I knew that pioneer cabins had clapboard roofs, not tar paper, and, from my days of making kindling as a younger boy, that hand-rived shingles or clapboards were not all that difficult to make. But how they were actually installed I learned from an old book:

> The clapboards were rived or split out of straight green oak timber about four feet long, eight to ten inches wide and an inch thick . . . a froe was used for this purpose with aid of a wooden mallet to drive it into the block of wood prepared for the boards. The end of the block was inserted into a forked log so as to form a pry to aid in the splitting with the froe, the handle of which served as a lever to aid in the splitting. The clapboards thus made were laid in rows across the horizontal rafters overlapping upon each

course several inches and being placed lengthwise up and down. They were not nailed but kept in place by weight poles, as they were called, consisting of round logs eight to ten inches in diameter, laid across the roof the whole length. These poles were kept in place by split blocks laid endwise between them on the clapboards, the lower pole being fastened with wooden pins driven into auger holes bored in the lower log. (From Martin Welker, *Farm Life in Central Ohio Sixty Years Ago*, vol. 4, tract 86 [Cleveland: Western Reserve Historical Society, 1895], p. 34.)

It occurred to me as I studied these two sylvan cabins here in the seminary woods, that they could be built without purchasing anything except the tools to work the wood, in this case an ax, a froe, and an auger and bit. Didn't even need nails. If a froe were not available, in a pinch, clapboards could be split with an ax. And pioneers knew how to bore holes with burning sticks. Or a roof could be made entirely of straight saplings notched to the rafters and pushed tightly against each other, cramming the cracks with moss or bark. It would leak, maybe, but clapboards sometimes leaked too, according to the old accounts. I only vaguely realized it at the time but the log cabin was teaching me an important lesson. *A person did not have to have a bunch of money to build a house. Just lots of trees.*

I took a new friend, Bryan, to see my great discovery (see the photo he took of me back then on this book's cover.). We would gather there often over the next four years, using the better cabin as our secret clubhouse, as boys are wont to do. We would spend almost as much time there away from the seminary classrooms as we were allowed. The school classrooms taught me about human society; the woodland classroom taught me about nature's society. To my surprise, only a few students found the cabins and the woodland around them as fascinating as we did. Most of our classmates seemed uncomfortable in the woods, wary, ill at ease. That knowledge provided me with another lesson in woodland culture. The "ramparts people," as I would come to call those of us who liked to live somewhat removed from so-called civilization, were a minority. Most of the students who spent four years at the seminary rarely walked deep into the woods.

Bryan and I liked to sit on the roof of our forest classroom in the fall, just back from summer vacation, and gather up the beechnuts that fell there from the huge tree that grew close by. The beechnuts were hardly bigger than peas and were difficult to see or collect on the forest floor. On the roof, we could scrape up a handful at a time. I wondered if that's why the builders had located their cabin under a beech tree. Eating them was slow work that required cracking the nut between one's teeth and then picking out the meat, sort of like eating sunflower seeds. They were very tasty, though, and worth the effort. Another lesson: *The forest always has food if you know where to look.*

Who had built the cabins remained a mystery for some time. Older students seemed to know nothing about them, and teachers seemed unwilling to talk about them. When we finally learned the history of the cabins, some of that aloofness was understandable. The Franciscans had started the seminary about a decade earlier, during the Great Depression. At that time, they were so poor they could not raise enough money to feed the students, and so some of them were sent home. The ones who stayed built the first log cabin and probably ate a lot of beechnuts. When times got better financially, those boys who had gone home were allowed to return if they wished. For reasons never exactly spelled out, but probably just because boys will be boys, a gang rivalry built up between the ones who had stayed and the ones who had returned. The former would not allow the returnees into their log cabin, so the latter built a second cabin. So bitterly were the two groups divided that the rector of the seminary finally closed both cabins and forbade the students from visiting them. Supposedly the order was still in effect, but by that time, some ten years later, it was no longer enforced.

I found this history extremely significant, not because of the story itself, which was really just about boys and their clubhouses, but because still in the 1930s there were high school students who knew how to build log cabins and did it. In just ten years' time, cultural attitudes had changed enough that most of the boys coming into seminary did not even like the environment of the woods, let alone want to build log cabins there. The Second World War had come and gone, and with the end of it also came the end of the old agrarian society in which even boys knew how to build log cabins. From then on, house building came at the mercy of the money economy, with the result finally that millions of people could no longer afford a house.

There were more woodland lessons to learn, in which the school curriculum and the woodland classrooms sometimes overlapped. Among the trees new to me here was the American persimmon. When not fully ripe, these persimmons were extremely astringent. Just biting into one puckered and numbed the mouth and tongue painfully. And I was not by far the only one in the seminary to have learned that lesson. Like all boarding schools, ours had an initiation rite. Freshmen were forced to eat a green persimmon. Probably because I was small and childlike for a high school student, the sophomores mercifully forced me to take only one bite. But from then on until after frost when persimmons start tasting good, I hid out in the woods every evening during recreation period if I saw sophomores gathering to wreak more punishment on freshmen. In hiding, I saw one boy pummeled by upper classmates until he ate a whole green persimmon and vomited. Here I was learning another lesson: *Beware of any society that encourages ritual cruelty, especially one involving green persimmons.* Actually, if one believes the old herbals, unripe persimmons are good for a variety of medicinal purposes, so maybe I should view the seminary initiation more positively.

At any rate, once a persimmon is ripe, after a frost or two, the scene changes. The fruit tastes quite sweetish and sometimes hangs on the trees even into spring if there are not many raccoons and opossums around. The longer it hangs, the sweeter it gets. The taste doesn't quite compete with that of peaches and apricots, but for boarding school boys, always believing themselves on the verge of starvation, they were a treat. I imagined that back in the thirties, when food was scarce at the seminary, the boys ate lots of them. Maybe that was how the initiation rite got started. I once ate a persimmon that had hung all winter on a tree and had dried up into something reminiscent of a dried apricot. It was quite delicious. Many years later, on a visit to the University of Maryland, I was treated to persimmon ice cream, also very delicious. Another way to eat persimmons is to mix them with honey and cook them a bit. (See chapter 15 for a recipe for persimmon pudding.) The pioneer's delight was to find a bee tree when persimmons ripened.

The pawpaw was also a new discovery for me. Bryan called them "wild bananas" because they were yellowish, longish, and tasted faintly like bananas. Our biology teacher, who occasionally took his classes on walks in the woods as part of his instruction, singled out the pawpaw's long and elegant leaves, like nothing else in the woods. I remember the day he pointed the tree out to me, so well in fact that I also remember the date: March 3. It was warm for that early in the year, even in southern Indiana, and I remember distinctly experiencing that same feeling of contentment and bliss that I had felt as a child on that late February day in Snider's Woods back home. I could feel the sap rising in my veins and in all of nature around me. I was at home in the woods, and I was wholly happy.

Thinking back now, I realize how fortunate I was to have had a teacher who understood that the best way to learn about reality was to encounter it face to face, not by reading from a book in a classroom. He said the pawpaw was really a tropical tree and that it was still a matter of debate how it had gotten this far north, and on into Michigan in fact. He told us about a butterfly of great beauty, the zebra swallowtail, whose larva lived only on pawpaw leaves. He must have been a very eloquent teacher because thereafter Bryan and I spent hours in the woods hunting for the zebra swallowtail. When we finally found one, we understood. Black and white and red, the butterfly had two tails or tresses hanging down from its abdomen, longer than the rest of its body. It was as striking as any tropical butterfly in the illustrated books, and we figured we knew why. It was a tropical butterfly, just as the pawpaw was a tropical plant. If prehistoric humans brought the plant north with them for its food and medicinal value, then it was logical that the butterfly had come along too. Another lesson: *The trees did not necessarily get here in the woods on their own initiative.*

Another teacher-priest introduced us to more forest lore. His nickname was Sludge—don't ask me why. He taught classical Latin with as much boredom as we felt studying it. But he started every class with a joke. He was serious about horticulture and farming, however, and decided to make a clearing in the woods along the creek to grow watermelons to sell at the farmers' market. Watermelons, he maintained, developed a much sweeter taste when grown on virgin soil. Some of us immediately volunteered to help clear the land. It sounded so Daniel Boone-ish.

We learned something right away. Clearing even an acre of forest is terribly hard work. To think that humans had cleared thousands upon thousands of acres without chainsaws or piston power of any kind totally astonished me. We piled brush on stumps and burned both, we grubbed out roots, we hoed, we labored in our spare time throughout a whole school year, ultimately clearing enough bare earth for a big patch of melons. Even then there were roots and rocks that we were not able to dislodge, and brush and weeds sprang back up almost as fast as we could cut them down. I now understood why my ancestors kept sheep around while clearing land.

I kept wondering how Indians and the earliest pioneers had cut up logs without saws. The same book that described in detail how log cabin roof shingles were installed had the answer:

> But at the period of which we write [1835], the ground had to be cleared of brush and fallen timber previously deadened every spring before plowing. There being no cross-cut saws, and to save the labor with the ax to cut up the logs, they were burnt into sections by . . . what was called "niggering," putting sticks across logs and setting them on fire. These had to be stirred up often to keep them burning. . . .

These logs were rolled together in log heaps and with the brush were burnt up. Then the field had to be "sprouted," that is the sprouts of green stumps cut off. Generally a patch of new ground would be cleared each winter for a turnip or potato patch and be ready for the spring. (From Welker, *Farm Life in Central Ohio Sixty Years Ago*, vol. 4, tract 86, p. 30.)

It took us a whole year to clear enough land for a watermelon patch, and then only roughly. The melons were indeed very sweet, especially the ones we ate on the sly when we thought Sludge wasn't looking. (I'm sure he knew.) Another lesson learned: *Virgin soil seems to contain nutrients no longer available in farmed-out fields that make watermelons taste sweeter, especially stolen ones.*

The most mysterious textbook in this high-school forest education was a large grove of pine trees among the hardwoods. Pines were not native to this area as far as I could learn. How did they get there? With visions of prehistoric Indians bringing pawpaws from the tropics, I imagined all sorts of possibilities. I think now, using tree books and memory, that these were shortleaf pines. In those days merely calling them pines was good enough for us. The grove covered about ten acres on the highest point of the forest and was known locally as Hicky Hill. No one I asked knew its history. I supposed that it had been cleared for a pasture field at one time and then a few pines were deliberately planted, or perhaps accidentally planted by birds carrying seeds in their droppings. Maybe a forest fire had cleared off the old growth. The pine trees must have reseeded themselves and spread, since some were quite tall and others of varying ages down to Christmas tree height. Evergreens rarely reseeded themselves in my home country, so I was mystified. Even after I had learned the facts of soil pH, climate, and agronomy that try to explain such things, I remained puzzled by this phenomenon.

For a boy from a part of the country where groves of evergreens don't grow naturally, the place was magical. Walking into the pines and being completely surrounded by them was uncannily spooky, but also palpably restful to the spirit. The silence was unearthly. I could see nothing but green pine needles and hear nothing except, on windy days, the sound of the breeze through the trees. Years later, Andrew Wyeth, the famed artist who roamed the pine forests of Maine, told me that he could tell with his eyes closed what kind of evergreen tree he was standing under by the sound the wind made blowing through it. Remembering Hicky Hill, I did not doubt him. And I understood why I liked his paintings and why urbane art critics often did not. They did not know our world.

This pine grove gave me my first notion of what could be called natural or organic Christmas tree farming. The seminary had a long and revered tradition of decorating all the buildings with wreaths and garlands and evergreen boughs at Christmas time, mostly, I presume, because it owned this grove of evergreens that grew without any human labor of planting and pruning and spraying. We would make a grand, joyous trek into our woodland in early December and bring back armloads of pine boughs and bushels of pine cones for making these decorations. It taught me a lesson that would come in handy later on: *A sanctuary of trees can add to one's income and delight by producing holiday decorations.*

Watermelons were not the only horticultural interest of our Latin teacher. He took over the apple orchard that had been languishing on the seminary property. He taught his gang of watermelon workers how to prune trees. When frost threatened in apple blossom time, he would recruit us to tend smudge pots through the night. We were delighted to do that work because we were then excused from chapel exercises in the evenings. I had never heard of smudge pots before, but their smoke and warmth did indeed fend off the frost a little. Just as interesting, at the far end of the orchard, where the trees grew right up next to the adjacent woodland, the apple blossoms survived better than in the rest of the grove, smoke or no smoke. Another possible lesson suggested itself: *Perhaps fruit trees could be grown and managed as a part of the natural forest rather than in artificial blocks of isolated orchard.*

But the best lesson I learned in those days had to do with my old friend, the morel mushroom. Next to the watermelon clearing I found an astonishing patch of them one spring day, at least a bushel basket full. The dying roots of the trees we had cut down probably had something to do with the bountiful growth. A find of this kind would have brought on wild celebration back home. My find rivaled storied stands of morels such as my grandmother told about in the land-clearing days of the late nineteenth century. I proudly took the mushrooms to the cooks, asking them to fix this treat for the student body. The cooks, nuns from Germany, had never seen such strange fungi before. They were leery. I told them to fry them in butter. (You can't go wrong with anything fried in butter.) Later on that day, I was summoned to the rector's office. He wanted to know where I had gotten the idea that these queer-looking things were good to eat. "They are poisonous," he said, quite beside himself with huffiness.

I was astonished. Dumbstruck was more like it. Then outraged. But the seminary was much like the army in that underlings did not argue with their commanding officers. I could only bow silently. Perhaps the rector had good intentions—just thought it best to discourage students from eating wild foods. Perhaps he knew there was such a thing as a false morel, which looks a little like a real morel and is slightly poisonous. He certainly didn't think a mere twerp of a student could know anything about such an esoteric subject because of course he had not been raised in the woods. But whatever good will I tried to ascribe to him, I learned that day another important life lesson: *Priests and teachers and other forms of authority do not necessarily know as much as I do.*

I did protest to our science teacher, who surely knew about morel mushrooms. He appeared nervous, shifty-eyed, distracted. He would not even hear me out. He merely mumbled that the first lesson of the priestly life was to obey orders. Class dismissed. So I learned an even more important lesson: *Those who know the truth will not always have the guts to stand up for it.*

From that day on, I started to doubt my decision to become a priest but, oddly, I continued on for quite a few more years. The main reason I did so was that I was almost always in close contact with the natural environment I loved. After high school, there was a year, mostly awful, spent in northern Indiana, known as the novitiate year, which was for seminarians what Parris Island is for marines. I endured because, again, we could escape in our free time into a nearby woodland that was dotted with lakes. In fact, there was a grove of trees right next to the seminary building that would in a few more years become a parking lot. At that time, it was an abandoned orchard, thick with brush and invading hardwood trees. It provided me a chance to observe what happens when you don't spray fruit trees. About half of the apples were just fine, especially for cider. I could jump the fence that divided the grove from our campus lawn and in that instant vanish from polite society even though there were houses all around.

In fact there was a bar on the other side of our grounds called the Rendezvous. Imagine this. A band of wild seminarians rendezvoused in this old orchard, making cider—putting handfuls of pulverized apple pomace in pieces of cloth and squeezing the juice out by wringing out the rags, all the while listening to the music emanating from the more worldly Rendezvous not far away. Our cider to us was every bit as delicious as the beer was to the customers of the bar. With a dozen of us giggling and squeezing away, we could strain out a gallon or so in an afternoon and let it ferment hidden away there in the thickets. Even then, I thought of writing a magazine article entitled "Making Hard Cider the Hard Way." How could I quit a life so full of so much fun-crazy mischief?

I also stayed on there because I knew that the next year we would be at a seminary college that was not as strict as the novitiate. The college was situated in tree groves along the Grand River in Michigan. The river ran right through the seminary property. Oh boy.

In our new college seminary, I became a river rat as well as a woods rat. I could hear the water of the river tumbling over rocks from my bedroom. By now our gang of hard cider makers had developed a spirit of camaraderie stronger than that between blood brothers. One of our priest-teachers dubbed us "the Sonuvabitchin' Davy Crockett Boys," a title we flaunted. We were ramparts people and proud of it. We roamed the woodland that lined the banks of the Grand River a mile or so upstream and down. We fished for walleye pike, hunted rabbits, and trapped for mink and muskrat. I made myself a pair of mittens out of moleskins. We even had a cabin in the woods, this time courtesy of the wealthy industrialist who had owned the property before the Franciscans turned it into a seminary. We combined studies in Aristotelian philosophy with impromptu courses in wilderness survival tactics. Even under the strict regimen of seminary life, I felt as free as the hawks that I could watch out the classroom windows, hanging high over the river. I guiltily realized that I loved wild nature a whole lot more than I loved the priestly life. But because every day I had ready access to the wildwood, it was difficult to do what I knew I must do: leave the seminary.

The situation was almost amusing, although it did not seem so at the time. Seminary life in the Franciscan order in those days was strongly influenced by monasticism. The ideal was for students to live a monkish life away from the so-called fleshpots of the sinful world. Sequester them out in the country where there were fewer temptations and allurements of worldly life. But that philosophy completely misjudged my kind of temperament and mentality. Temptation for me did not come from the world of men, or even women, but from nature. I did not give a hoot for fast cars, fine clothes, mansions in the sky or anywhere else, travel abroad, fancy restaurants, so-called financial independence, or any other worldly pleasures that money could buy. I wanted only a log cabin in the woods, a rifle, and a dog, as I often said. I was being lured away from priestly life by the temptress of wild nature that religious authorities doggedly kept right on providing me. It was like trying to help a man lead a celibate life by insisting that he live in a women's college dormitory.

I mention all this not so much out of sentimentality for a quaint past nor for the humor inherent in the situation, but because of the theme of this book—the marked way that the trees kept stretching out their arms to embrace and comfort people like me caught in situations of life rife with confusion and at times despair. When poets speak of the sanctuary of the trees, their words are often mere poesy. When I speak of sanctuary, I mean it actually, physically, and literally. I realized that I would have to quit the seminary, not because I disliked the kind of life I was leading there, but because in a few years I was going to have to leave the woodland sanctuaries that went along with it.

Having finally gotten up the courage to disembark, so to speak, I learned that the Franciscans had purchased a farm in Minnesota along the Minnesota River where we would complete our theological training. Damn. I just had to stick around long enough to see what that was like. To me, the totally untraveled and half-cloistered student, Minnesota translated not only into the Land of Ten Thousand Lakes, but ten thousand tree groves. It was right next to Canada, which suggested trackless wilderness at hand. It was also right next to the Dakotas, which meant the Far West to me: cowboys, ranches, maybe Indians, hopefully bears and antelopes. For a young man who did not have enough money to drive to the nearest village and buy an ice cream cone, I thought that Minnesota might be as close to adventure as I was ever going to be able to afford.

And so I stayed on for a few more years, loving the land of ten thousand lakes, millions of trees, and the Minnesota River, where I sometimes sat on a log, naked, and communed with an old hermit beaver. He seemed to me to be as disgruntled with life as I was. Although one might say that I was continuing a huge mistake, it turned out, like all my other mistakes, that going to Minnesota was a fairly smart move. I learned for sure that I not only loved woodlands, lakes, and rivers, but also subsistence farming. I learned what I was meant to do with my life.

And I learned practical things from the woodland wild too. I learned to split fence posts because we were making new fields on our tract of farmland. Knowing about fence posts was hugely important to me because, much later, I would find myself trying to promulgate pasture farming as the salvation of the world, and what pasture farming needed most of all was fence posts. To make one out of white oak, the bark had to be peeled off, especially the end that was going to be in the ground. The bark, said neighboring farmers who were as much my teachers as the theology professors, absorbed and held water sort of like a sponge, hastening decay. A spud, a heavy chisel-like tool about five feet long, was used to scrape off the bark. If the posts were from a tree cut when alive, it should be cut in the spring when the sap was rising (exactly the wrong time for firewood). At that time the bark will separate or "slip" more easily from the wood. Alternatively, if the logs after cutting were allowed to dry a year or two in the open air, the bark also came off rather easily.

This business of removing bark from posts to make them last longer was at odds with the information I had read about logs in log houses. Most books went out of their way to say that the pioneers did not remove the bark from the logs of their houses because leaving it on made the logs last longer. The situation, however, is not the same for both cases. The log in the log home is above ground and so not subjected to the constant moisture of being in the ground. I think the pioneers did not debark their cabin logs because there was no need to. The bark, above ground, would come off in a couple of years anyway.

My tree vocabulary kept increasing. Not that the trees I became newly acquainted with grew only in Minnesota, but for the first time, I was in a position to notice them. American basswood, or linden, was the most interesting to me. It was an extremely soft wood, but strong enough to use for framing farm buildings. Either green or dry, it was easy to drive a spike through. The wood was stringy and fibrous, and the Indians had shredded and woven it into rope and fabric. It was often called bee tree or honey tree, because it blossomed heavily, providing bees with lots of nectar. Its leaves when young made a decent salad. The softness of the wood made it especially favored by woodcarvers. It was a common, cheap tree in Minnesota at that time. Who would have divined that eventually demand for it from woodcarvers would make it a fairly valuable wood? When I finally got my own grove of trees to live in, the first thing I did was plant a basswood. Had I been smart enough to plant a couple of acres of them, today I or my children would be looking at a profitable harvest in about the year 2020.

By now the Davy Crockett Boys were "sophisticated" enough after our days of rendezvousing in an abandoned orchard to know that anything sweet had the possibility of making an intoxicating beverage. What's more, whatever we made was bound to taste tolerably good if for no other reason than that it was forbidden. Forbidden wine, like stolen watermelons, always tastes better. Quaint little wild plum trees (*Prunus americana)* grew on the edges of our woodlands. The fruit was fairly good, better than pawpaws or persimmons to my taste, and, when fermented, packed quite a wallop. We amused ourselves by popping corks on jugs of "aging" plum wine, as if we were opening bottles of champagne. Any resemblance between the two ceased after the popping.

We also investigated the mysteries of elderberry wine, another fruit of woodland edges. We should have learned from the plum stuff not to bottle up the brew too soon. Unfortunately, we were slow learners. We hid the bottles of contraband (making any kind of liquor was forbidden by seminary rules) in the hay mow of the barn, hoping it would age into something a little more delectable than the kerosene-like taste that it first developed. One day the bottles started exploding, just as my father's homemade beer had done back home. We had to give the dairy barn walls a new coat of whitewash to hide our sinfulness.

Something else the Minnesota woodland taught me. Or at least a farmer living there did. He had a large family and was fairly poor. His farm was close to ours. One day when I was visiting him, I happened to notice that one whole side of his barn was covered in squirrel skins and tails. I was taken aback. "Oh, we depend on them for part of our meat supply," he explained. "They are quite delicious, you know, and I have taught the kids how to shoot straight." I had been a squirrel hunter as a child, but it had never dawned on me that in today's world (this was 1953, but we surely thought of ourselves as quite the modern go-getters) a family could provide itself with a significant supply of meat from a tree grove for the cost of a box or two of .22-caliber bullets. Why did he nail the squirrels up like that? "That's my son, bragging," he said with a grin. But then he added: "Sometimes there's a market for them from fur buyers."

Needless to say, I never enjoyed life any more than I did in those years. The Sonuvabitchin' Davy Crockett Boys were possessed of a genius for having fun in the woods in ways that were very unworldly, but not in the sense that the seminary life was supposed to strive for. I can remember several times, around a campfire, asking in all earnestness why we couldn't just stay here like this forever, helping people out who needed help, a merry band of Robin Hoods in our own Sherwood Forest. As full of folly as such words were, I was totally sincere. I really had no other desire in life at that time. One of the theology professors, not altogether jokingly, told me I was a danger to society.

Reality finally brought me to my senses. Because I got good grades, I guess, the order's authorities decided I should go to Rome to finish my theological training. I was supposed to feel honored and thankful to be selected for this move. Or maybe our superiors just wanted to export their biggest problem as far away as they could. But for me it was the end of Robin Hood days. I said goodbye to the seminary. The Franciscans breathed a sigh of relief. The pope would have done so too if he had known what had almost come his way.

The woodland sanctuary had saved me. It had kept me sane (well, sort of) until I found myself, and then it convinced me to leave a life I was not fit for. In a way, it saved both our Latin teacher, Sludge, and my friend Bryan too. They both eventually became missionaries to Africa, living in the bush—the African forest—where they could channel their love of woodland and wildness into helping people, building churches and schools, and occasionally shooting poisonous snakes and rogue elephants that threatened the villagers in their care. They became Robin Hoods in their own way.

Strangely enough, now, after all the years of being separated halfway around the world, Bryan and I are practically neighbors again. We sit at the edge of my tree grove, sipping martinis instead of wild plum wine, remembering those Robin Hood and Huck Finn days of long ago in Indiana and Minnesota. Huck Finn is as appropriate for us as Robin Hood. Mark Twain had long ago become my favorite writer, and he was influenced greatly by the beckoning trees. If you have any doubts about that, read his marvelous description of the tree grove of his boyhood in the new *Autobiography of Mark Twain*, vol. 1 (Berkeley: University of California Press, 2010; pp. 218–20). Nor would Twain, like my favorite artist, Andrew Wyeth, be the last of the famous people who, I would learn, were drawn to sacred groves.

CHAPTER 4

Woodcutting Days

OUT OF THE SEMINARY, totally unprepared for life in the so-called real world, I did what I had always done. I went to the woods. My father allowed me to cut and sell firewood from Snider's Woods as a way to earn a little money. I had no skills that might have qualified me for a good-paying job off the farm, so having this work was a godsend. I didn't know anything about woodcutting either, but somehow I learned how to fell dead trees without killing myself. Mostly I cut up windblown red oaks already on the ground.

The first thing I learned was that the chainsaws then coming on the market to replace hand-operated crosscuts could reduce a man to a raving idiot. They were inferior to the ones today. They did not cut much faster than two men on a crosscut, and they were notoriously hard to start and keep running. Once I lost my temper and threw one against a tree with such force that I bent the saw bar and had to get a new one. So I learned another lesson: *Losing one's temper in the woods only means losing one's money and might mean losing one's life.*

To me a chainsaw was a snarling, sawdust-spitting little monster, and I tried to horse it around with brute strength—precisely the wrong thing to do. I finally learned that a chainsaw should be handled almost as delicately as a violin. And just as you would not try to learn how to play a violin by reading a manual of directions, so you can't learn how to "play" a chainsaw that way either. Even good instructions serve only to persuade beginners that, having read them, they now know how to cut wood. It takes lots of practice and then, like learning to ride a bicycle, the feel of the saw suddenly comes to you. It should do most of the work, not the saw operator. The blade should eat its way into the wood at its own speed. If I tried to force it into the saw kerf faster than it wanted to go, I'd just make it choke. Or in forcing, I would ever so slightly and unknowingly bind the saw bar in the kerf, causing it to growl with disapproval. Just the slightest wrong pressure could cause a bind, and it just took time to learn to feel the bind and avoid it.

Cutting through a large log lying on the ground, I learned to let the saw glide at its own speed forward into the wood and down the opposite side of the log from where I was standing. If I pushed down with my left hand on the handle, it only made me and the saw labor unnecessarily. The left hand should just hold on to the saw firmly, not push down. At the same time, with my right hand on the trigger handle, I learned to lift the back of the saw upward gently so that the tip of the saw blade went forward and down the other side of the log. This is the way the saw works best and fastest. That's what those teeth are for at the back base of the saw bar—to hold the saw against the log while the sawyer tips the front of the blade forward and down, making a vertical cut down the log on the side away from where he is standing. When I sawed as far as I could before the nose of the saw went into the dirt, I could then bring gentle pressure downward on the back of the saw so it would cut through the log on my side. When the saw leveled out in the cut near the bottom of the log, then I would push down a little with my left hand, watching the color of the sawdust. When it turned darker, I knew I was through the log and into the bark on the bottom. It was very important to stop sawing then. Letting the blade plow into the soil under the log even a little dulls the blade in a hurry. Cutting into ice in the fissures of the bark dulls it as fast as cutting into a rock. When there is ice on the wood, I learned to leave the chainsaw in the truck.

I didn't realize how dangerous woodcutting could be until a tree I was cutting down fell directly back toward me, the opposite way I had notched it. What had I done wrong? I had gotten the mistaken notion that if I notched the tree like the books said to do, the tree would automatically fall in the direction of the notch. Not always so. The trick is to insert a wedge in the saw kerf behind the saw as soon as there is room to do so. For this job, a wooden or plastic wedge is necessary, of course, so the blade won't be dulled if it accidentally bumps back against it. Then I needed to keep driving the wedge— sometimes I used two wedges for extra safety—into the kerf as I sawed so that the tree trunk was always tight against the wedge. When there was about three inches of wood left between saw kerf and notch, the tree would not be quite sure which way it wanted to fall, and the slightest puff of a breeze might push the tree back away from the notch if the wedge wasn't there to stop it. With about three inches of trunk yet to saw through, I learned to remove the saw and drive the wedges in as far as I could. If I guessed correctly, the tree would go on over as it was supposed to do without further sawing. Sometimes, though, I had to put the saw back in the kerf and cut a little farther, which might mean backing the wedges out a bit to make room for the saw. Then I'd remove the saw again and bang on the wedges again. Turning off the saw's motor had an extra advantage in that I could hear the first soft creak of the tree rending from the stump and have plenty of time to back away.

A tree is going to fall in the direction of least resistance. So the first thing I learned to do, before doing any cutting, was just to stand under it and study the situation long and hard. Standing and studying was easy work, and in this case it could save hard work, not to mention my life. Which way does the tree lean, even if ever so slightly? I would ask myself. Notch the tree to fall in that direction if there are no other extenuating circumstances. If the tree didn't lean at all, I would study the upper treetop to try to figure out which side had the most and heaviest outgrowth. The tree would be inclined to fall in that direction with a little help from the wedges. If the tree couldn't be felled in the direction of its lean or top-heaviness because of a fence, building, or other tree, or if it leaned pronouncedly toward such objects, it was time to consider calling in an expert. A tree that falls into another standing tree and gets hung up is the woodcutter's worst nightmare. It is cheaper to hire an expert to cut the tree down than to hire someone to drag a tree out of another tree's branches with heavy equipment. In those days, the idea that in the twenty-first century there would be skilled tree trimmers who used pulleys and ropes to swing themselves among the trees and take them down limb by limb was as unimaginable as putting a man on the moon. But now that these professionals do exist, use them when necessary.

There were other dangers. Sometimes when the top of the tree hits the ground, the trunk will bounce up or roll sideways or even spring back, any one of which actions can kill a woodcutter standing too close. Or if the tree did fall the wrong way, I learned to just stand there to make sure of the direction of fall and then calmly walk around to the other side of the stump rather than turning my back and running away in panic. If I ran and the tree fell the way I was running, I might just about make it out to where the highest limbs would hit me as they came crashing down.

Once a tree is on the ground, the danger is not over, especially if the log is a large one, say twenty inches or more in diameter. Sometimes a fallen log would still be propped up on "legs"—large branches that hold the log off the ground. I once cut through a leg-limb and when it popped off, the tree trunk whirled over and a limb-leg on the other side whizzed right by my head. I had not realized that the first limb was holding up the whole weight of the horizontal trunk.

In cutting up a tree on the ground, I learned by trial and mostly error to cut chunks off those parts of the lower trunk, if any, that were free and held above the ground by limbs. They would come off without pinching. Then I'd go to the top end of the fallen tree and cut away all the limbs too small for firewood. I had to think about what I was doing at all times or I would pinch the saw blade. If a limb I was cutting sagged inward on the saw only a fraction of an inch, the saw would be caught in the kerf. Often one must saw upward rather than downward through a branch to prevent pinching.

With the branch twigs all removed, I'd start sawing up stove-length pieces from the smaller branches. I'd leave those branches intact that were holding up the main trunk until I cut off the sections of the trunk that were free above ground level. I'd always be thinking about how the limbs or logs were going to bend or sag when I sawed through them. It was a matter of constantly remembering the effects of gravity, lever, and fulcrum. It turned into sort of a game of skill to see how much of the tree I could cut up without using a cant hook to roll the log over, and knowing when to use wedges in the kerf to keep the log from pinching.

I never learned how to sharpen saw blades really well (to this day), and since it is folly to try to saw with a dull blade I buy a new one every year and take four dulled ones to be sharpened by an expert, hang the cost. In the earliest years I'd have to change blades half a dozen times each winter because I would cut into the ground or ice or old rusted wire embedded in the wood. Now, a new sharp one will last me half the year, and a couple of resharpened ones last the other half. Spending a little more money to keep a really sharp blade in the saw actually saves money because the chainsaw lasts much longer than it does trying to cut with a dull blade.

At first, Dad and I, in one of our more romantic moments, hauled out the two-man crosscut saw to cut up the logs. We would mimic the pioneers, we thought nobly. That turned into a tale of woe. Not even married partners deeply in love should get on opposite ends of a crosscut unless they are very skilled at that work. So there was hardly a chance that a father and son would be comfortable at it, especially when the son, at least, had never done it before. Besides, with chainsaws available, crosscutting was too slow, even though we knew of woodcutters who could cut through a log just as fast with a crosscut saw. But Dad had better things to do. He bought the chainsaw and turned me loose on my own.

One handy trick I did learn from Dad was about trimming branches off a downed log. Most of that kind of work is done today with a light chainsaw, but it is easier and quicker to use a sharp axe. The trick is to chop off branches by cutting through the outside angle of branch and trunk, not the acute inside angle. And to cut from the lower end of the trunk. Your brain says that a limb should lop off easier striking down into the acute angle where the branch grows out of the log. But actually, if you strike at the underside of the branch upward, right next to the log, the axe will sever the branch much more easily.

But while we were still struggling with the crosscut—which I know now was not sharpened correctly—Dad casually mentioned his father's ancient mechanical crosscut saw, which ran off the power takeoff on the tractor. I asked Grandpa about it, and he finally found the derelict old thing gathering rust in his barn. Much to my surprise it still worked, mimicking the action of two men on a crosscut exactly. It turned out to be the most civilized piece of technology that I have ever had the pleasure of using. It seemed slow at first as it worked its way through a large log. But it took me about the same amount of time to split up a big log section as the mechanical crosscut took cutting it off, so there was no time lost at all. The sawing took much less muscle, obviously, and with the tractor barely at idling speed, the work was soothingly quiet compared to running the roaring, sawdust-spitting chainsaw.

Sometimes I was grateful just to stand there and watch that antique saw patiently make its way through a log while I wondered woefully about whatever I was going to do with my life. I knew I must get a job, but it was just so pleasant in the woods that I resisted.

But I still had to deal with customers. For example, I had never before been in the position of selling anything, so I was unprepared for what clerks and salespeople elsewhere must often endure— suspicion and disdain from buyers. I worked hard splitting wood and sold it cheap and thought customers would be grateful to get the wood. But a few of them treated me like I was their servant or slave or an intruder out to cheat them. The really nasty ones would walk around my pickup and stare at the wood as if it were full of disease-carrying maggots. One fellow was particularly loathsome.

"Is that a cord?" he asked in a challenging voice.

"No, sir."

"Well, how much is it?"

"A pickup load, sir."

"And how much of a cord is that?"

"I really don't know, sir. About half I suppose. It is what I am selling you for $15 delivered and stacked."

"Is it dry?" His tone was still rude and suspicious.

"The trees it comes from have been dead for two years anyway."

"Well, is it doughty then?"

I looked at him questioningly. I had never heard of that word, and he could tell.

"Starting to rot," he explained, a satisfied smirk on his face for having shown how much more savvy he was about wood than I.

"No sir, it's not."

"Smells pissy. Must be piss ellum."

"It's red oak, sir, and it does have a slight aroma. Some people like that smell."

He looked at me witheringly, shrugged, and pointed to the place where he wanted the wood stacked. If I knew this wood was red oak, I just might know more about wood than he did, and he didn't want me to find that out. He watched me as I unloaded, and although fully able-bodied, never once offered to help, never once handled even one single stick. If our situations had been reversed, I would have helped unload under any circumstance. But this pointy-nosed little piss ant of the upper-middle class intended to wring every penny he possibly could out of my servitude to him.

One day, reading the local newspaper, I realized why some wood customers treated me like dirt. A series of articles in the paper was supposed to instruct people on the ins and outs of buying firewood. The advice went into pious detail over the definition of a cord of wood: a stack measuring four feet wide, four feet tall, and eight feet long. Firewood sellers were supposed to use the cord as their unit of measurement and the customer was to make sure, by golly, that he got that much wood. Keep your tape measure handy. No one I knew sold wood by the cord because that would be folly. A cord of hickory has twice as much heat value as a cord of pine. The BTU value is different for all wood species. Woodcutters I knew mostly sold wood by the pickup load, and we learned to heap it up or buyers would bitch. We sold mixed hardwoods, and I prepared myself to spout off proudly which pieces were hickory or ash or oak or elm. And how all the wood came from trees that had been dead for several years. But whatever, the buyer could see the amount and kind of wood he was getting for $15 a load and if he didn't think it was enough or he didn't like the looks of it, he didn't have to buy it. The whole tenor of the information being handed out in the paper suggested that firewood sellers were out to cheat firewood buyers. No wonder consumers treated us suspiciously. There may have been some cheaters, but anyone with any experience selling firewood knows that you don't stay in the business long unless you are at least as honest as preachers. Ironically, these articles were written by agricultural extension agents, whose main job it was to help farmers. Since all the wood sellers I knew were small farmers trying to make a little winter money, I wondered why government types who were supposed to be our helpers were undermining our work by questioning our honesty and pontificating on something they evidently knew very little about.

Another experience made a deep impression on me. Dad came home one day very excited. He'd met a traveling businessman and told him about my budding firewood business. The businessman ordered a load of wood. He'd pay $30 for a pickup load if I'd deliver it to his house, which was a bit outside my usual territory. Thirty dollars was big money to me. He wanted it for his fireplace in time for Christmas, which was about ten days away. He gave directions to his house and said he probably would be "on the road" but that his wife would be there to show me where to stack the wood. Okay.

The directions took me out into a rural area outside the town of Bucyrus, our old pickup putt-putting along with its heavy load over back roads and down a long lane to a lovely new home surrounded by woodland. It was just the sort of place I dreamed of having some day. As I pulled up to the house, something shocking revealed itself— shocking to me anyway. Across the backyard stretched a big, fallen, dead elm tree. This man had wood enough for ten Christmases literally at his doorstep but was buying wood.

I knocked on the door, and a woman with two little kids hanging on her opened it timidly. She had known that I was coming, but it was obvious that she was fearful. Here she was with her children far out in a secluded country home with this sorry-looking, scruffy young man staring at her. I tried to be as friendly and polite as I could, and I think she got over her misgivings soon enough. But as she directed me to where she wanted the wood stacked along the side of the garage, I kept glancing out at the big old dead tree in the backyard. She noticed, and she understood.

"Yes, isn't that a shame. We have wood but we're buying wood. My husband would love to be cutting that tree up, too. He loves to do things like that, he loves living out here in the woods,"—she rolled her eyes in a way that clearly told me she did not like being there alone—"but his job, you see, he has to travel all the time." Her voice quavered a bit. "It's a good-paying job, but he has to travel all the time."

Driving back home, I felt contented with my lot in life for the first time since I had come back home. I did not have any money, but I did have all the wood, and food, and love, and a sort of settled stability that this traveling man with all his money could not enjoy. Which, of the two of us, was truly the poorer?

I resolved never to trade peace at home for a high salary on the road. Only for a little while did I break that resolve.

CHAPTER 5

Beginning a Life
in the Woods

My wife and I may not have met in the forest, exactly, but we did do a lot of courting in the woods around her home farm in Kentucky. Mistletoe grew in those trees, a wonder to a northern boy. To see clumps of green up in trees in the dead of winter mystified me no end, especially because at first I didn't know what it was. Needless to say, the first thing I learned about mistletoe was that a person did not have to be standing under a sprig of it over a doorway at Christmastime to get a kiss. Mistletoe grew mostly on black walnut trees on Carol's home farm, and her family always referred to one of them as a Thomas black walnut, the best for ease of cracking out nutmeats, they said. It was years later before I found out that this was not just a bit of family folklore. The Thomas was recognized far and wide among botanists as one of the choice black walnut varieties. Apparently an early member of Carol's family or someone in the neighborhood had planted Thomas walnuts, but no one knows for sure who it was.

The Thomas variety was discovered in Pennsylvania in the 1880s and propagated for sale from then on. As of this writing (2011) it is still offered for sale in Stark Bro's' nursery catalog and I suppose other places. Once again I was struck by local society's penchant for keeping track of the history of its buildings but not of its trees, which often last longer. We assume that the trees we find in our woodlands have been there forever. One would normally assume that a particularly fine nut tree in the woods was a wildling when it might very well be a named variety planted a hundred years ago by a farmer. His fields could be gone, to houses or whatever, but the tree might still be there. And the reason he planted it, if he did, was that harvesting nuts from this tree was at least fifty percent more efficient than from most black walnuts, a detail that could have been important a hundred years ago when people relied more on local tree foods than they do now.

At any rate, this particular tree had low branches and so could be climbed fairly easily to get to the mistletoe. In most trees, the mistletoe grew high up beyond reach. Where mistletoe plants could be harvested, they had to be gently lowered to the ground because the sprigs or boughs were quite fragile. The real masterstroke was to cut off a length of small tree branch with a large bough of mistletoe growing on it rather than just breaking off the sprig. The difference was about $20 in value. Carol's brother, Jimmy, joked about shooting off sprigs with a rifle (he was a crack shot), but even if the bullet severed the stem cleanly, the jolt and the fall would shake off the glistening white berries. The mistletoe, we learned, needed to be lowered gently from the tree with a string or cord.

I was going to college in Louisville as an excuse to be close to Carol. With my usual aimless good fortune, the Franciscans who had educated me in the seminary helped me out with a scholarship to Bellarmine College, now University, where some of them were teaching. The money kept me going until graduation. Then, by the most improbable luck, I received a three-year fellowship in American studies and folklore at Indiana University. With a guaranteed income of something like $3,000 a year for the next three years, Carol and I got married. We knew we could get by on that amount. Without even a shred of common sense, we had a baby nine months later. We wanted a baby. The idea that we could not afford one never crossed our minds. In fact the fellowship paid another $400 per child. We were actually able to put a little money in the bank from that, so the next year we had another child.

The owner of the apartment complex where we lived the first year took a dim view of babies, however, and we had developed a dim view of apartment complexes. We wanted to live in the country, but nothing within our meager price range seemed available. One day I stopped at one last real estate office and poured my heart out to the older man sitting behind the desk. He seemed sympathetic, so I spread it on as thick as I could. I was from a farm. My wife was from a farm. We knew how to work. We knew how to take care of a country place. We were willing to do stuff like pruning and mowing as part of the rent. In fact I liked to do that kind of work. I was older than most collegians. We both knew responsibility. We were starting a family. We had a child and another on the way. He kept shaking his head, saying he didn't have anything to offer, but he still kept asking me questions. I was running off at the mouth rather pathetically about how if I didn't get out where I could see farmland or forest nearby, I was going to go berserk. He kept staring at me. I realized later he was trying to make up his mind. Finally he shifted in his chair.

"Well, as a matter of fact, I own a country property myself which we have been thinking of renting out. We used to spend our free time there, but with advancing age, well, it is getting a bit much to take care of. Do you want to take a look at it?" Then he added, almost apologetically. "It's a log house in the woods."

We loved our log house in the woods so much that I decided, overly romantic as usual, that I would buy the place and we would live there the rest of our lives. It was easy to get part-time jobs at the university—I held three simultaneously for a while—and so I could earn enough money to keep us going until I started raking in the cash as a successful freelance writer—my secret desire. There was even a second log house on the property, which I could use as an office.

That's how naïve I was, but the grove of trees we were living in—about eight acres in size—was paradise enough to encourage any kind of impractical hopefulness. I found out that the property had once been home for Alfred Kinsey, the famous sex researcher and founder of the Kinsey Institute at Indiana University. He too must have been a woodland lover and had spent his spare time turning the eight acres into his own little arboretum. He had planted the woodland with wildflowers collected from all over Indiana. How could we be so lucky! The area along one side of the creek behind the log cabin was a pool of bluebells in the spring and on the other side a glaze of yellow buttercups. With a wildflower guide, I spent hours trying to identify the various species.

In the front of the cabin, there had been a formal hedge and gardens, now beginning to grow over with brush. I set to work restoring some order—work that I loved. I could tell that our landlord could hardly believe his luck. I repaired some of the old split rail fence that bordered the driveway. That's how I learned that the old-timers did not set the interlocking corners of their rail fences on one rock, but two. The lower rock absorbed the moisture from the ground and the upper rock remained comparatively high and dry, protecting the bottom rail from rotting.

What made the tree grove particularly pleasant was the cattle farm next door that surrounded us with pasture fields. The owner was very nice. We could fish in his large farm pond and wander the pastures. If we sometimes felt that our grove was pressing in on us a little too much when the trees were in full leaf in the summer, we had but to walk to the edge of our property and gaze out on a vista of meadows. We had found heaven on earth—we, surely among the poorest families in the county if money alone were the gauge.

I cleared out a little spot in the richer soil along the creek for a garden. I should have cleared out twice as big a plot, just for sunlight, as I had learned from clearing land for Sludge and his watermelons. But it was not my property and the landlord was uneasy about cutting down trees. But I grew a tolerable garden on the shady plot, especially pole beans, which could reach up high on their stakes to get a little more sun. Out in front of the cabin, where I cleared the brush from what had been the formal garden, I planted more vegetables where there was plenty of sun.

The log house was authentic, although the chinking between the logs was mostly concrete and there was a modern basement under it.

When the sun set, you could sometimes see light between the logs, and sometimes in winter a little snow sifted through the cracks, but for the most part it was a snug enough home. Carol complained only that the bare logs of the walls were hard to clean. There was a huge fireplace (in addition to an oil furnace in the basement) with an oven built into the side of it. There was enough furniture, even a television set, so we didn't have to buy anything. Pork chops were 19 cents a pound in those days, sometimes cheaper. We felt we were living fairly high on the hog. Soon child number two arrived. Playing with the children, Jenny and Jerry, in our little paradise under the trees, I was as happy as anyone can hope to be when he has so little money.

To my list of trees, I added gray birch, butternut, sassafras, Osage orange, and yellow poplar. The birches were not native, so Mr. Kinsey must have planted them. I have a hunch he planted the butternut too, because they were not common in the area. I learned that sassafras leaves grow in various conformations, some with multiple lobes, some with one lobe, some with none—all sorts of shapes. And in the fall, all of them turned a blazing orange. We dug up some live roots; washed them; peeled off some of the inner white, rubbery bark; boiled it in water to make sassafras tea; and sweetened it with honey. You can boil a whole chunk of root actually, and in fact boil it several times. Add water to suit your taste. Or you can dry pieces of that inner bark, about the thickness of common cardboard, store them in plastic sacks, and cut off a piece to put in a boiling cup of water just as you would a tea bag, to get a cup of tea.

Sassafras tea is soul food in southern Indiana, and in colonial times tons of it were shipped to Europe under the wishful thinking that it was a key to everlasting life. I think what we made tasted especially good because there was a great hue and cry at that time over the Food and Drug Administration's ban on sassafras. An ingredient in it, safrole, caused cancer in rats when fed in huge amounts. The debate waxed hotly for a decade or so, during which time the people I know who drank their own sassafras tea continued to do so, using unprintable language whenever the FDA's ban came up. The ban on sassafras tea that does not contain safrole or from which safrole has been removed was lifted in 1992. That made me doubt the whole business even more. Did that mean that some sassafras bark does not contain this dreaded ingredient after all? Was the rat experiment flawed, as many claimed, and the FDA just too stubborn to admit it? Or if it did contain safrole, how did one go about removing it from one's own sassafras roots or tea?

The whole business became ludicrous. Go online today and you will usually find a big warning jumping out at you about rats getting cancer from safrole. Then the information goes right on to tell you exactly how to make sassafras tea and where to buy the roots!

I have my own philosophy about such matters. Statistics indicate that a certain percentage of people are going to get cancer, so a certain percentage of the people who drink sassafras tea are going to get cancer too. Did the tea cause it? One thing is for sure. If I do not die from drinking sassafras tea, sooner or later I will die of something else. Sooner or later I will, as Wendell Berry says in one of his humorous verses, "go to one funeral too many."

The big loser in this paranoid event was root beer. It was traditionally flavored with sassafras oil, but now, when safrole is removed from sassafras oil, root beer isn't as tasty to my tongue as it used to be. I remember the homemade root beer that one of my Rall uncles used to make. It wasn't very fizzy, but it had a rich root-beery taste.

At any rate, the sassafras tree is one of the most highly valued traditional medicinal plants in American folklore. Formerly it was a standby in the American diet. The dry leaves were ground into filé powder to thicken and flavor soups, especially gumbo, at the end of cooking or at table. In addition, the leaves, shoots, berries, and bark are eaten by all kinds of wild birds and animals.

Sassafras is a host plant for the gorgeous spicebush swallowtail butterfly; but not all insects, it seems, are comfortable with the wood. Traditionally, farmers used sassafras branches to make roosts for their chickens. It seems strange, but I had to go to graduate school in American studies to learn that. Supposedly sassafras oil, or its odor, discourages lice. Maybe the lice get cancer. A friend has roosts of sassafras in his chicken coop. I asked him why: Did he know about sassafras discouraging lice? No, he didn't. He used sassafras because they were especially straight tree sprouts growing in his woods.

The wood was also used for making bedsteads, presumably because of its ability to repel bugs. Could there have been a siege of bedbugs back then like there is today? Someone should look into this. A fortune might await the first furniture company to turn out sassafras bed frames.

The roots like to send up suckers to form new plants, and left to its own devices, a tree will become a grove over time (see figure 5 in the color insert). It is these suckers that sometimes grow so straight. Transplanting a small sassafras tree is therefore tricky. If you try to dig up what looks like a little seedling, it will generally die because it is really a sprout or sucker growing off the roots of the mother tree. I have successfully moved such a sprout by digging gingerly between it and the mother tree until I located the connecting root. Cut through it and let the little tree grow its own roots for another year. Then move it.

My first run-in with Osage orange trees came at the back edge of the property, where a neglected hedge fence of the trees was growing into a twisted, gnarled jungle. The trees bore fierce thorns, and if the hedge were kept dense, I'm sure it would turn cattle. There was a time, before wire fencing became easily available, that Osage orange was taken from its rather small native area in the South and planted all over the United States as hedge fencing. But it grew too fast to be kept in a controlled hedge by anyone but the most resolute farmer.

Living hedges never took hold in the United States as they did in Europe. In Europe, agriculture did not change much for centuries through the Middle Ages, so there was time and inclination enough to allow hedges to be trained to grow into impenetrable fences and then kept that way with yearly pruning. Hedging was as much a part of medieval life as gassing up the car became in twentieth-century America. Hedges were so effective that in France they stopped even army tanks during World War II. In America we went from Osage orange and hawthorn hedges to fence wire in hardly one human lifetime.

But trying to trim and shape that old Osage hedge, I realized that a return to living hedges as a replacement for metal was not going to happen any time soon. The wood was very tough and impossible, at the stage I found it, to retrain into a hedge. To my amazement, I learned that Osage orange has a tensile strength greater than steel, which is why it was (and is) used to make bows by the Indians and by bow makers today. Osage could probably be used in place of steel and certainly plastic in many other instances. It makes an enduring fence post, but once dry the wood is so hard that even a skilled carpenter can hardly drive a nail into it. The wood is a striking yellow-orange in color. It finishes as smooth and hard as glass and makes beautiful and useful bowls and goblets.

Osage orange, when dry, rates highest of all woods in BTUs. It produces almost as much heat as coal. I had to burn some in the fireplace to see for myself. It burned hot all right. It also popped and crackled like a pan of popcorn without a lid on it. Sparks flew everywhere. But burned in a stove where the sparks would not be a problem, how many cords of that stuff would be needed to heat a home? It would certainly take less woodland acreage than other trees to produce the same number of BTUs, and when harvested by coppicing, the trees would grow back from the roots for regular harvesting about every ten years.

It was fascinating how the strands of my increasing woodland education would connect in unpredictable ways. Osage orange produces green fruit about the size of grapefruit that are often called hedge apples or horse apples. In folklore classes at the university, the subject came up, and I learned that these hedge apples were traditionally thought to be effective as insect repellents and were used all around the pioneer home sort of like mothballs. My woodland knowledge was now connecting to my postgraduate degree work. In this case, unlike so many of the herbal traditions about trees and forest plants that do turn out to be quite effective concoctions after years of being rejected by science, I could find only a little scientific basis for hedge apples' insect repelling properties. I thought about performing my own experiments, but there were no bugs around the cabin bothersome enough to repel except mosquitoes, and we had learned even as children to put pieces of smoldering punk wood in tin cans on the picnic table to keep away this pest. But I was not convinced that hedge apples could not repel insects, and since then some evidence has surfaced that they do. We just don't need to experiment with natural chemicals when we have so many manufactured repellents easily available.

How long did it take, and by what trial and error, for humans to figure out that Osage orange was the best wood in this country for bows, at least as good as English yew was in Europe? How much traditional knowledge of this kind were we losing after the thousands of years it took us to gain it? To my amazement, a little research showed that there were still artisans making bows from *bois d'arc* or bodark, the other name for Osage orange. Turned out the knowledge had not been lost at all, but was just being overlooked by the majority of people who had wandered away from the wood culture and into the metal-plastic culture. There remains a small army of woodworkers out there making everything that has ever been made with wood. What is needed is a large army of consumers to generate more demand for these products—which will happen someday, after the Plastic Age has passed.

The trees were teaching me other lessons as well. When I first tried to grow tomatoes in the sunny front yard where I had cleared away the brush, the plants wilted and died, sending me to the books again. Among the problems that affect tomatoes and other plants is juglone, a chemical compound secreted from black walnut roots. Sure enough, examining the area where the tomatoes wilted, I remembered that I had grubbed up some walnut saplings, and standing close by was a medium-sized walnut tree. I planted tomatoes some fifty feet away from this area, that is, beyond the root zone of the walnuts, and had no more problems. The experience opened up a whole range of speculation. Black walnuts could kill other plants too, including apple trees, the books said. But black raspberries—and currants too—were unaffected. What if a grove of black walnuts and raspberries were grown together? Would the trees keep the raspberries weeded? As strange as that sounds, research showed that I was not the only one who had speculated on the matter, and in Missouri, where black walnuts were being grown commercially, adding the berries under the trees has proved to be practical.

Another thing I learned from Dr. Kinsey had nothing to do with sex. He had either planted, or at least ignored, a growth of Japanese honeysuckle (*Lonicera japonica*), which had gotten started and was in the process of choking a little grove of evergreens to death. Previously I had a special place in my heart for this vicious vine. It had overgrown a fencerow along the lane back to Carol's home in Kentucky and in that first spring when I went to visit her, it was blooming profusely with a heavenly sweet aroma. But this plant, which had seemed so sweetly innocent, was now climbing into Dr. Kinsey's evergreens and shading out the lower limbs, just as it was dragging half of northern Kentucky and southern Indiana into the Ohio River. I attacked. But without herbicides, I gained only a little headway.

There were two lessons here for me to jot into my notebook. Don't let Japanese honeysuckle get started in your woodland. (The various bush honeysuckles, I learned later, can also be a problem.) Lesson two: The neighbor's cows did not allow the honeysuckle to infest the fencerows around our woods. They ate it. Many years later Bob Evans, of sausage fame, but who should be remembered because he was the foremost champion of grass farming—that is, grazing livestock year-round rather than feeding them exclusively on annually cultivated grains—told me how in studies he funded, cattle could survive grazing on honeysuckle in winter when the ground was snow-covered.

We learned another detail about black walnut trees. Don't tie a clothesline to one. The squirrels liked nothing better than to wait until Carol hung out diapers to dry and then they'd climb up overhead and drop bits of walnut husk as they ate the nuts. Fortunately, Clorox solved the problem.

The other end of the clothesline we tied to a huge yellow poplar or tulip tree, a species I had never seen before. In spring, it blossomed with green and orange flowers, like tulips in shape and nearly as large, very attractive but easily unnoticed because the green color blended with the green leaves. I was not used to seeing a forest tree that bloomed so profusely so I studied the yellow poplar more than I might have otherwise. Again, my various strands of education connected. In a class on traditional architecture, I learned that yellow poplar was much favored by pioneers for log cabin construction because the species in its natural setting grew very long, straight logs, perfect for log walls. Also the wood was rather soft and so could be easily worked or notched as in log cabin construction. This softness was unusual for a wood that resisted rotting so well. Sure enough, the logs of our cabin were yellow poplar. When I mentioned this to Carol's father, Vassal, he nodded knowingly. His barn was made almost entirely out of yellow poplar boards. (Yellow poplar is the state tree of Kentucky and Indiana.) Carol's brothers, all skilled at woodworking and carpentering, prized the wood because of its unusual grain. I was amazed when they showed me some poplar they were using to make furniture. The main color of the wood was olive green, but mixed in were areas of white, brown, and a sort of bluish gray. Very striking. About that time, at the university, I somehow got involved in a historic restoration of a house on campus that had mostly yellow poplar wood in its framing. Newly sawn boards of poplar, used in the restoration, were olive green in color, streaked with whitish grain, and soft enough that I could press a fingernail into the boards. The wood was as easy to nail as white pine—another reason early builders of barns preferred it over most other hardwoods.

But the more important point, it seemed to me, was that at thirty years of age, and having lived much of my life around trees, I did not know about this remarkable but common wood. It made me realize how ignorant I was, as were most others in our society, about this wonderful material, wood, which was so ubiquitous around us that we took it for granted.

The yellow poplar in our yard helped me learn something that runs counter to what was accepted forestry practice. Between the two log cabins on the property grew several tremendously old and wide-spreading beech trees. I was immediately reminded of the setting of the first log cabin in my life in the seminary forest years earlier. Sure enough, in two of the four years we lived under these beeches, we harvested good crops of beechnuts. We roasted them in the fireplace, which made them taste even better. The trees reminded me of the instruction I had received when I worked for the Soil Conservation Service, my first job off the farm after I left the seminary. In manuals of forest management, the beech was referred to as a "wolf" tree, undesirable because supposedly, by spreading its dense limbs out far from the trunk, it crowded out other tree species that were more profitable for lumber. The good woodland manager was supposed to cut out the beech trees in favor of oak, ash, cherry, and walnut. But living under these beeches, I started to question that management practice. Beeches are beautiful trees, and their habit of sending out branches remarkably far from the trunk was fine in a yard setting. Their dense shade kept us cool on the hottest days, and because their branches were very strong, they were not likely to break off on the roof in a windstorm or when coated with ice. They were better next to a house than brittle black walnut or, for that matter, the yellow poplar.

But there was more to this business. I often sat on our lawn and watched the children at play under both the beeches and the poplar. If poplars were known for growing tall and straight without generous side branches, why was ours a much more spreading tree, like the beeches? Obviously, there had been clear space around the yellow poplar when it was young and so it grew outwards with spreading low branches. Only in a dense forest did it grow straight, limbless trunks.

Why was that not also true of beech trees? It was, but it took years for me to find that out. When little Jenny, playing at that time under the yellow poplar with her brother, Jerry, grew up, she and her husband built their home in woodland. (I often wonder if her early life could have influenced her.) The woodland they built in had a heavy stand of beech trees. They grew tall and straight and limbless, just like all hardwoods will in a dense stand. A hardwood tree with spreading limbs may seem, in the present time, to be crowding out saplings around it, but in its early years it grew in a clearing or in a savanna-like setting.

As if living in this haven of trees was not fairy tale enough, I started writing during the summer when graduate work lessened a bit and almost immediately sold an article. Carol had insisted that I try to write something funny and so I did. I had no idea I had any talent in this direction. I cleaned up the smaller empty log cabin, installed a chair, table, and typewriter, and went to work seriously, if one can describe humor writing as serious work. I wrote about farming, the only thing I knew well enough to try to be funny about, and sent the essays to *Farm Journal*, the only farm magazine I had ever read continuously. Checks from $150 to $300 started coming in. I think now, overly romantic I suppose, that it was the woodland that I was nestled in that brought me the kind of repose I needed to discover what I was destined to do with my life.

About the same time that my free ride at the university was coming to an end, *Farm Journal* offered me a job in Philadelphia. I took it, even though it meant putting in jeopardy my bid for a PhD. The head of my doctoral committee was not pleased that I was leaving his fiefdom, just as the religious authorities had not been pleased when I turned down higher theological degrees by refusing to go to Rome. There was a terrible obstinacy in me. But now we desperately needed money and the salary I was offered, $10,000 a year to start, was not bad for that time and way beyond anything I had ever dreamed of. Regretfully I said goodbye to my beloved grove of trees and log house. I was convinced that the carefree, wild part of my life was finally at an end. I would now have to put on a suit and tie, take on the manacles of a salaried job in the city, and leave, at least for a while, my true environment.

Was I ever wrong.

CHAPTER 6

Suburban Wildwood

WE ARRIVED in Philadelphia with a very naive innocence about suburban life. Neither Carol nor I had ever lived anywhere for any appreciable time except on farms or schools surrounded by farmland and forest. We suffered from the usual rural impression of the urban landscape: lots of look-alike houses, sidewalks, and streets. We believed those contemporary novels that said life in the suburbs was boring. What we found was neither boring nor citified, but a suburban wilderness populated by all kinds of wildlife, including humans. We had no money except what I could borrow from Carol's parents, and our idea was to buy a house in our price range (that is, real cheap) but that had some acreage with it. My plot was to turn the acreage into a tiny farm from which we could reap all the benefits of living on a larger farm without paying for it. That's when my education in house hunting around a major city began. Wherever I found a place with one or two acres attached to it close enough to Philadelphia for commuting, I was in upper-income territory. Every tree on a property upped the asking price another couple of thousand dollars. Wherever I found houses with five or more acres attached, I was in estate country even rich people could barely afford. Most of the people who lived there, I learned, had the property handed down to them. It was a most ironical discovery. Estates for sale for half a million dollars—and not necessarily with a big old fancy house involved—could have been bought back in rural Ohio for $25,000.

The environment we enjoyed as poorer, lower-middle-class farmers out in rural Ohio was blueblood estate land here.

But we kept looking. We narrowed in on Lower Gwynedd Township in Montgomery County north of Philadelphia because much of it was zoned for two-acre residential sites and I could ride the train handily from there into Center City. Most of the area was not quite urban, not quite suburban, not quite farm country, but a little bit of all three with a range of houses from humble to huge. It actually was an incredibly diverse place with lots of still-open space owned by wealthy families or investors who evidently had no need to sell the land yet for development. There was much woodland, quite a few open fields growing back to woodland, one of which near a crossroads called Bluebell was covered in spring with several acres of grape hyacinths. The meadow was absolutely breathtaking, but no one seemed to notice. Too busy getting their breaths taken away traveling to faraway places, I guess. Nineteenth-century barns and houses still very much in use contrasted with abandoned eighteenth-century farmsteads overgrown with young forest. A few real working farms still existed along with a scattering of recreational horse farms. A factory was hidden in woodland—by design. Zoning regulations specified that any factory had to be screened off by trees. Private and public schools including Gwynedd Mercy Academy contributed many acres of woodland and open fields too. A few conventional subdivisions had been developed, but most of the residential housing was a more or less unplanned sprinkling of old and new homes without sidewalks along single-lane country roads. Wissahickon Creek, bordered by woodland, ran through the township, adding still more of a wilderness touch to the landscape. Driving through the area, we had the feeling that we were going through a rural countryside because so many of the houses were hidden away among the trees.

We had just about given up on finding anything we could afford when we chanced upon a neat little bungalow on the very edge of the township, priced at $22,500 (this was 1964). *Bungalow* was a new word to me. It certainly wasn't a *bunga-high*, but it came with two acres and a hump in the roof. That was dirt cheap for the area even if the roof had not needed fixing. The whole property was adorned with all kinds of ornamentals and trees. I could hardly believe my luck. What was going on here?

Ah-hah. We were looking at a house in what was called in those days a "mixed" neighborhood. This was the area where the servants on the rich estates of Gwynedd Valley had established residences as far back as the Civil War along the road that marked the boundary between Upper Gwynedd and Lower Gwynedd townships. Some of the residents were black. I was warned by those savvy about urban life, to "keep in mind" that an investment in an integrated community would mean that housing values would not rise as they would in pure white neighborhoods. My advisors did not see what I saw: possibly the only two-acre urban farm in the area that I could afford, and it butted right up against a five-acre woodland grove of trees. I didn't care who lived across the street.

For the first time, but not the last, I followed the lesson I had learned in seminary days when the expert authorities had insisted that morel mushrooms were poisonous. I ignored the experts. We bought the house, fixed the roof, and lived happily there for nine years. Our black neighbors were, of course, just as nice as our white neighbors. When we sold, our house had risen in value just like all the other houses in the area had, and it sold quickly. In fact that house was by far the best investment I ever made. It doubled in price.

So began our years in the so-called suburbs. We continued to live our private lives almost exactly as we had before. While others around us went to the Jersey shore or the Poconos for recreation, we stayed home and vacationed in the wildwood around us. We raised much of our food, including our own chickens, eggs, and wheat for grain; cut wood from dead and dying trees to burn in our fireplace; hauled manure for the garden from nearby horse farms; hiked the fields and woodlands around us; gathered hickory nuts and walnuts; gleaned corn from cornfields; did a lot of bird watching; sledded on the hills round about; ice-skated on Wissahickon Creek; found arrowheads in the garden; cut our own wild red cedar Christmas tree from the woods; and picked many baskets of wild raspberries and blackberries from the vacant land nearby. I even found a softball league to play in. Nothing in our neighborhood was what popular culture had led us to expect from suburban life. It was like back home on the farm, only better in some ways. In the back two-thirds of our two acres, bordered by similar two-acre lots on either side, and with the five acres of woodland adjacent to us in the rear, we enjoyed as much privacy as we could have far out in rural countryside where the prying eyes of neighboring farmers leave no leaf unturned. We gardened and farmed and played happily in the sanctuary of what amounted to our own little private arboretum.

My morning walk to the train station was a stroll through woodland and abandoned fields. The terrain was thick with birds and wild animals. Hardly a morning went by that I did not see deer staring out at me through the underbrush. A Canada goose attacked me one morning when I blundered upon her nest along a creek in the woods. I felt like we were living on a new frontier, and perhaps that was true. And when, after a forty-five-minute train ride and a ten-block walk, I arrived at my office overlooking Washington Square Park, another grove of trees!

Unwittingly I became a frontiersman of urban farming. I spent a lot of time in the tree grove behind our gardens, which was almost impenetrable to civilized folk because it was overgrown with thorns and brush. It did not seem to belong to anyone, but had gotten left as an accidental remnant of wasteland between a highway, two-acre-lot zoning, and a church and cemetery property. There was a decrepit For Sale sign out by the highway, but because there was a rumor that the highway was going to be widened, no one was going to build there. The property may have belonged to the state or the county or the township for all I know. I never tried to find out. We used it as our own little park. An old buck deer with a beautiful rack liked this little snag of woodlot even more than I did and was almost always there. But deer are so adept at hiding themselves in small amounts of cover, I am fairly certain that I was the only human who knew of his presence. I would practice my stalking skills on him just to see how close he would allow me to approach. He must have realized after a while that I was no danger. He would tolerate my presence up to about twenty feet of intervening brush. Then he would move a few feet farther away. I would advance. He would move a little. Some days we would circle through the whole woodlot that way.

Some of the trees in this remnant were overgrown with bittersweet. It was American bittersweet, which sports nice clusters of berries, not the oriental bittersweet, which bears fruit in sort of single file up the stem. The latter can become viciously rampant and choke trees, especially seedlings. The American species is rampant enough and needs to be controlled a little too. I had never seen bittersweet climb up into really tall trees like it did here. Some of the vines were as thick as my wrist. It obviously had been growing here a long time. Visiting a greenhouse garden display, we found bunches of bittersweet for sale. We inquired. Yes, of course they would buy as many bittersweet bunches as we cared to sell.

So began our first "crop" from urban farming. Gathering the bittersweet was fairly pleasant work. I'd cut berry-laden vines as far up in the trees as I could reach on a ladder. We'd carry these strands back to our yard and then cut short lengths of vine and berries and tie them in bunches. It was work the kids could help do, and quite profitable for the amount of effort we spent. We sold bunches for fifty cents, and the greenhouse resold them for a dollar. I was surprised at the demand. It was not as if bittersweet were uncommon here in the wildwood like it was becoming back in Ohio, where the fencerows that once proliferated with the vine were being bulldozed away to make big fields out of little ones.

There were many other such possibilities throughout the township. Commercial farming was on its way out, but many woodlots and brushy areas remained or were growing back from when this land had been intensively farmed. Our back acre had an old dead furrow clearly visible running across it. In one new growth of forest between clusters of houses, a great old barn stood abandoned along with a springhouse nearby with cold, clear water still running through it. Judging from the age of the trees, a farmer some forty years earlier must have just walked away from the place, not willing to sell it or use it. I would sit in the springhouse and wonder exceedingly what had happened, as if I were looking at a specter that was invisible to others, which, in a way, it was. I could have gone to the courthouse and found out the story of this place, I suppose, but I never thought to investigate things like that then, as I would today. There was an old mill house hardly a half mile down our road, lending to the area a sense of a ghostly, nineteenth-century past.

Old fields were being overrun not only with new-growth woodland, but blackberries, raspberries, elderberries, and something new to me, wineberries (*Rubus phoenicolasius*), which were similar to raspberries but "escapes" from domestic gardens. The idea that horticulture had prevailed here long enough for garden plants to run off into the woods was most intriguing. Immigrants from Europe had been gardening here since the late 1600s, which meant that woodland and dale would reflect nearly two more centuries of "civilization" compared to the part of Ohio I had come from. Some imaginative nursery company probably advertised the wineberry vigorously at one time and everyone had to try it, same as now with other exotic plants. I never found anybody still growing wineberries, which were not very tasty to me, but once again, without knowing the history of this remnant woodland, one might easily conclude that these berries were wild natives.

Blackberries and black raspberries proliferated in the woodland pockets, along roadsides, railroad tracks, and waterways, not to mention on the estates and horse farms. We would knock on the doors of estates unannounced and ask if we could hike along their horse trails and pick wild berries and nuts. Invariably we would receive permission to do so. There was a marvelous acceptance of the public in the area, or at least of our family, which would not have been true in more traditional farm country back in Ohio. Maybe it was because we knew some of the property owners by riding on the commuter train, or maybe it was because we seemed to be about the only ones taking advantage of their hospitality. In one of our woodland picnic spots through which a lively little spring-fed creek ran, we were accosted once by a landowner on a horse. He seemed a bit provoked at first. I was making the kids a little waterwheel in the creek like my father had made for me. The landowner was intrigued. I told him we came to this spot often and that we were there not to harm or disturb anything. In fact, I could act as a sort of free caretaker and report to him if I saw anything questionable going on. He never challenged us again.

We found another horticultural "escape" in the tree grove behind our place. Cherry trees were growing there that I could not identify. When ripe, the fruits resembled black sweet cherries but were somewhat smaller and less fleshy than the sweet cherries growing on our property. After much research (the cherry family is very large and has been cultivated for many centuries), it appeared that these trees were escapes of *Prunus avium*. Birds eat cherries in a garden or orchard, then excrete the seeds everywhere. But seedling trees like this do not usually come true to the parent. Since sweet cherries and sour cherries and crosses between them are widely grown, it was very difficult to know exactly the parentage of our particular escape. But the fruit was quite good, even though of smaller size than named varieties of sweet cherries, and we would have harvested more of them if we did not have our own domestic trees growing on our two-acre "estate."

Carol was reminded of a scene from her childhood. There were wild cherry trees growing on her farm in Kentucky too, and she and her cousin would spend hours sitting up in the branches gorging on the fruits. She was sure the fruits were not wild black cherries or chokecherries because, believe me, you would not gorge on either of these two brackish-tasting fruits. But what variety those trees were, she was not sure. Maybe they weren't wild escapes at all, but planted by the same mystery person who planted the Thomas walnuts. To me the real significance was how much food there was growing wild or semi-wild, and no one cared about it.

We were always running into a new tree species everywhere we walked in the township. Temple University had a branch out our way devoted mainly to horticultural research, which meant another tract of woodland adorning the township. When I pulled into the parking lot the first time I saw a towering tree with leaves unfamiliar to me. Also, there was a stench in the air that smelled like too many dogs were running loose on the property. The smell was emanating from what looked like fruit that littered the ground under the tree, and the fruit was obviously emanating from the tree. When I asked about the identity of the tree from one of the people working there, I was transfixed by his answer. I was looking at a ginkgo tree, a species that, according to fossil records, dates back 270 million years! The man smiled at what I am sure was a look of utter disbelief on my face. But that was only the beginning of my surprise. Ginkgo trees know something about survival. They survived the bombing of Hiroshima in 1945! And that awful smell was not really fruit in the usual sense but a sort of fleshy covering over the seeds. The nutlike meats inside the seeds are an esteemed food throughout Asia. In fact, the ginkgo could provide debate material for just about anything botanical one wanted to argue. Good to eat maybe, but eat more than about fifty seeds at a time and you could be poisoned. Beautiful yellow leaves in the fall, but they can cause a rash like poison ivy on those allergic to them. It is regarded as a possible cure for attention deficit disorder, or maybe not, depending upon which scientific opinion one wants to believe.

For days my mind kept going back to those ginkgo seeds. How could humans have decided to eat something that came wrapped in a gooey mucous that smelled like feces, that would blister skin allergic to it, to get at a seed that had to be washed and cracked to get a nutmeat that, eaten in excess, was poisonous? Why had human civilization developed such an intricate, intensive kind of knowledge? I finally figured it out, I think—another of those very obvious answers that are so hard to discover. In my work environment as a farm-magazine editor, I tended to think of everything from an agricultural point of view. Therein lay the answer. People would go to such fantastically far-out trouble to get food because they had no choice. Unlike modern times, when we take modern farming for granted, for thousands upon thousands of years there was no way to till the soil in large amounts, but all too easy to increase population beyond carrying capacity. When that happened, human society had to explore every food possibility that nature offered, or die. Civilizations had risen (and fallen) on the expertise of hunting and gathering food.

But no one was much impressed with what was for me a sensational discovery. With all the tremendous advances in science, we could as a society survive just fine on naturally growing plants, especially trees, if and when it was obvious that tillage farming would just mean more erosion, more lost cities in the desert. I wanted to write about this, but you can imagine how that went over with a farm magazine. When I would tell acquaintances about my "new" tree that was 270 million years old, they mostly just shrugged. So I merely stored away my knowledge. At least I knew that if I were starving to death in a land destroyed by nuclear warfare, I could hope to find ginkgo trees, wash away the stinky stuff on the seeds and eat them. As strange as a thought like that might seem, there is some comfort in it. The ginkgo can outlast all things human and nuclear and be patiently growing when the next round of evolutionary man should arrive on the scene starving hungry.

In another grove hardly a thousand feet from our house on the other side of the road I first met what I think is the most unusual tree in the American forest. I was walking along, minding my own business, as they say, a little solemn and forlorn because it was November and I was thinking winter. Suddenly, I was face to face with a shrubby little tree that was shimmering with bright yellow blossoms! At first I wasn't sure they were flowers. How could they be, this time of year? Looked more like little fluffs of narrow yellow ribbon hanging on the branches. I raced home to study my tree books. I was sure this quaint plant had to be some exotic escape from a long-ago English immigrant's garden.

It was a witch hazel, an appropriately bewitching name for such a strange little tree. But it was not a stranger and in fact was quite common in cut-over woodland in the eastern United States. More to the point, it was another example of legitimate folk medicine that Native Americans had taught the early settlers to use. In this case, witch hazel oil helps soothe and heal skin rashes, cuts, and bruises. In fact witch hazel is commonly sold in drugstores all over. Where had I been?

Over the next year we visited our new acquaintance frequently. The yellow blossoms of November turned to calyxes that looked like tiny urns—in folklore, these receptacles for the nuts or seeds were said to be the wood elves' drinking cups. The calyxes or husks stayed fairly greenish for a whole year, turning brown in the frosts of the following fall. Then an almost alarming event took place. The husks cracked open with such force that the seeds, brownish black with a white dot on them, shot out with a loud popping noise. The seeds can travel up to forty feet and cause pain if they strike a person in the head or face. I stood around awhile, hoping to get wounded so I could write about it, but no luck.

Water dowsers, at least in times past, preferred a witch hazel branch for finding water, so the books said. The word *witch* as applied to this tree had nothing to do with the usual meaning of "witch" but was a corruption of the Old English word *wych*, which means "flexible." Witch hazel branches are indeed very flexible, and I have my own contrary explanation for why it became the choice for dowsing rods. In earlier years, I had gone through a period of being extremely interested in divining rods (another cultural use of wood) and had learned a thing or two that dowsers do not appreciate hearing. I studied the folklore involved too, at the university. I watched dowsers at work, I listened to stories of how the power was so strong in some dowsers that when they held their forked sticks over a good water source, the attraction was great enough to almost wrench the dowsing stick out of their hands if they tried to stop it from pointing down to the underground water. So I experimented. I discovered there was a bit of a leverage trick involved. Grasp the ends of the two forks of the Y-shaped branch in one's fists with the stem pointing out ahead. With just the right amount of pressure on the very flexible branches, I could make it look for sure like the stick was tipping over toward the earth while I was trying with all my strength to hold it back. The way I was bending the branches forced the pointer downward. That would explain why witch hazel was called witch hazel. The wood was, indeed, very *wych*—very flexible.

I was also enchanted by how the evergreen trees that grew all over this area of abandoned farmland reseeded themselves. I think these were Virginia pines. In my home country, if you wanted evergreens you had to buy plants and set them out. Here I could have all the evergreens I desired for free, just by transplanting the proliferating seedlings or planting the pine cones.

My knowledge of trees grew considerably in our suburban wildwood also because the former owner of our property had planted some exotic species there. One was a beauty called a golden chain tree or laburnum. In spring it fairly dripped with long pendulous clusters of bright yellow flowers—very attractive. For several years I admired it greatly, growing near the house next to a little wading pool that the former owners had also installed. It was hard to keep the kids out of the water, and we didn't try. Then, one year, I decided to find out more about the tree. To my dismay, all parts of laburnum are poisonous. I was facing another example of what I now called "sassafras syndrome."

The "authorities" had moved heaven and earth to ban sassafras tea from human society even though people had been drinking it for unnumbered generations. But I could find little hint in nursery catalogs about the possible toxicity of laburnum. Sometimes there was a brief, passing mention, between the glowing adjectives about the tree's beauty, that, ahem, well, yes, this plant is toxic in all its parts, but nowhere was anything close to a red flag raised. Will some wise savant far up there on a mountaintop contemplating the mysteries of life please explain this dichotomy to me? We felt we had to cut the tree down because of the kids playing around it. We had enough dangers to deal with on our suburban frontier. At least there were no sassafras trees around to rain cancer down upon our hapless heads.

The former owners of our poor man's estate had planted other trees and ornamentals new to me: a weeping cherry, boxwoods, dogwoods, flowering crabs, all kinds of fruit trees. The white birches may have been a mistake since they do not live long and died while we were in residence. But they were so beautiful that the lack of longevity could be excused. Not so for the Lombardy poplars planted along the back border of the property next to the woods. They were not, to my way of thinking, very beautiful—tall and skinny and rarely living to be twenty years old. When I cut them down (not very good firewood either) I carelessly made the same mistake I had made when cutting firewood back home years earlier. The trees were only about eight inches in diameter, so I figured they would fall easily whichever way I notched them. Once again, one of them fell away from the notch. I'm not sure why; it just did. What made this a memorable mistake was that it fell exactly on my ancient walking wheel cultivator standing all alone in a garden plot nearby. There are 360 degrees in a circle, but the tree fell in that one degree where it landed squarely on the cultivator, smashing it beyond repair. Things could have been worse. It missed the chicken coop.

It would have been difficult if not impossible to use wedges on an eight-inch-diameter tree to make sure the tree fell toward the notch. There was not enough room to insert the wedge behind the chainsaw bar. Since then I have learned a little trick from a timber cutter friend. In a case like this (he used it on bigger trees too) he would leave a little bit of uncut wood intact at the beginning of the cut opposite the notch, sawing in behind it and then across the diameter of the trunk. Then, when the kerf was getting close to the notch and the tree ready to go over, he drove wedges in on either side of the little section of intact trunk that he had left uncut. With the wedges firmly in place, he then removed the uncut section by plunge-cutting with the tip of the blade, allowing the tree to fall the right way. Looks really clever when done correctly, but it requires experience.

The Lombardy joke, as we referred to the tree destroying the cultivator, taught me a lesson I would learn over and over again. Trees advertised as "fast growing" should be avoided in landscaping. In the world of plants, there is a law of diminishing returns. If a tree species grows faster than average, it will generally be less valuable as wood and invariably will not live long.

Most oak species grow slowly, and the wood contains at least twice as many BTUs as poplar, has twice the strength, has four to five times the longevity, and so forth. What's more, the seemingly slower-growing trees aren't all that slow. Once rooted down well and in good sun, an oak grows plenty fast enough, as anyone knows who has to worry about trees crowding each other in a yard or shading out a garden plot, or growing over a roof. If one is willing to be a little patient while a tree is growing its first ten to fifteen feet up, from then on slow-growing trees are much more desirable in a yard.

At *Farm Journal* magazine, my responsibility was covering the news in fruit and vegetable production, which was, typical of my life experiences, the area of farming I knew least about. But it worked perfectly with my secret schemes for turning our two acres into an urban farm. Being fruits and vegetables editor was like taking college courses in horticulture, only I was getting paid to do it. Reporting the news in these areas provided me with all kinds of ideas about growing high-value crops on small acreages. I began to entertain fanciful schemes. Blueberries grew wonderfully well in this soil, another great curiosity since I had never seen them before. I would start a little blueberry farm. Maybe. I dug a hole back behind the chicken coop and buried a cattle watering trough. I would funnel the water off the chicken coop roof and raise fish in the tank. Maybe. We had four huge oak trees in the yard. I learned on visits to orchards in California that the Native Americans had perfected ways to soak the tannin out of acorns and make delicious meal for bread. I could do that too. Maybe. The crabapple trees bore tremendous crops of fruit without spraying. We could make delicious exotic jelly and sell it. Maybe. I would open a roadside market for woodland products. Maybe.

I began to hatch a plan. I would rent the back acre of the properties on either side of me. After I got to know my neighbors well, I was fairly certain they would agree to do that because they were tired of mowing all that lawn. One of them had a very nice planting of blueberries already on his back acre and he might even be willing to partner with me. I would rent or buy the remnant tree grove right behind us. That would give us about ten acres altogether to play with.

One reason this dream was so enticing was what I had learned from the neighbor right across the street from us. He was a professional gardener, now retired, but still tending a large, exquisite planting of iris in a glade between his big old brick Victorian house and his grove of pine trees. He was actually hybridizing his own varieties. He wanted to develop a bright red iris, which he said did not exist, and make a fortune selling it. He was even more a dreamer than I was, but he opened up a whole new world to me. Flowers could be a cash crop too, and a very lucrative one. He also had chickens and scrupulously saved every scrap of manure and bedding for compost.

What was just as amazing as the iris idea to me was that I could stand there between the flowers, the chicken coop, the grove of pine trees, and the house and be as hidden from the world as if I were standing in the middle of the Jersey Pine Barrens not so far away, where he had lived previously and an area I became very interested in by and by. The way privacy and woodland solitude could be achieved in a small place just with landscaping was most intriguing. He had a tiny urban farm going here, with its own possible commercial crop— iris sold either as bulbs (rhizomes) for planting or as cut flowers.

This possibility of finding woodland sanctuary even in areas of quite dense human population manifested itself even in the city. Not far from the offices of *Farm Journal* (it was headquartered in a big city because it was originally published for farmers "within a day's ride on horseback from Philadelphia"), there were many historical monuments and houses and little walled gardens, much in the fashion of the walled gardens of England. These were open to the public, more or less, but hardly anyone frequented them. I did. At noon, I would walk the several blocks to these walled gardens and tree groves to soak up the tranquility to be found there. The life of a magazine reporter can be very hectic, and these interludes helped me just like woodland in the countryside did. Sitting in one of these walled gardens, the first thing noticeable was the quiet. Though I was in the heart of a city, silence lingered among the boxwoods, dogwoods, Bradford pears, and rhododendrons. It got me to thinking. Why should such lovely places belong to the wealthy only? The poorest person can grow trees and flowers. The poorest person could, in fact, make bricks and pile them up into walls. All it takes is mud and sunshine, which is sort of true of trees too. And if bricks were out of the question, the poorest person could make wooden stockades from the trees and provide privacy and beauty too. Did we really need so much money in the world?

Just as trees kept intruding into my human environment in seminary, college, and graduate school, so now they stalked, literally, into my downtown *Farm Journal* office. An elderly man, a farmer as he turned out to be, came in, bearing wood. When he asked the receptionist downstairs if he could see the editor in charge of that subject, she sent him to me. She always sent visitors with offbeat interests to me since I was generally thought to be the magazine's token offbeat person. None of us were accustomed to farmers with enough aplomb to come sauntering into downtown Philadelphia without warning, so I was very curious. He drew two blocks of wood out of his satchel, set them on my desk, and commenced to talk about what he called the fastest-growing tree in the world. That moment marks the true beginning of this book, although I did not know that until much later.

The farmer's name was Miles Fry, and he was quite the character, surely one of the most amazing people I ever met. He milked cows out in the middle of Pennsylvania, near the town of Ephrata, and since I also was, or had been, a milker of cows, we had instant rapport. (Two milkers of cows will find each other, even in a stadium full of non-milkers of cows. I think it is the aura of suffering and patience that lingers over anyone who has spent a lot of time with the back end, or the front end, of a bovine.)

Anyway, he finally got down to the reason for his visit. He had been experimenting with hybrid poplar trees and had a notion that he could save the world with them. I was a sucker for saving-the-world notions, so we got along fine. All you had to do, he said, was shove a live twig from a hybrid poplar tree into the soil of a spoil bank or any other land wasted by the hand of mankind, and it would sprout, grow, and attain a height of twenty-five feet in five years. Not only did it turn wasteland into productive soil, but as I could see, the wood made fairly decent lumber too.

So began a truly amazing episode in my life. I went out to visit Miles's hybrid poplar plantations even though *Farm Journal* was almost totally focused on corn, hogs, soybeans, cotton, and cattle. The way his trees grew on spoil banks was truly impressive. On good land, well, you almost needed to stick the cutting in the ground and jump back fast to keep the tree from knocking your hat off. So I wrote a little article, I'm sure in that vein, and eventually it ran in the magazine. To the utter surprise of everyone, except maybe Miles himself, replies came pouring in, and even more filled Miles's country mailbox. In a few months he had a file cabinet with some twelve thousand letters in it from all over the world. Nothing like that had ever happened at the magazine, even when we ran articles on the first three-hundred-bushel-an-acre corn yield. For the first time, I realized that my keen interest in trees was shared by quite an army of people out there.

The response launched Miles and his son Mort into a new business, growing and selling hybrid poplar cuttings and trees. Eventually the family expanded into the greenhouse industry, and today the company is one of the largest producers of flowers in the country. They still sell hybrid poplars (check out Frysville Hybrid Poplars online), but it is only a minor part of the business now. The trees have been mostly marketed over the years for residential screening since they do grow fast enough to screen off a house quickly from, say, a street. But since it is so easy to start a new tree with a cutting, and so hard to get rid of one after it has rooted (cut one off at ground level and another pops up, making them excellent for coppicing), the market has dropped off. Most of the poplars the company sells today are for landfill and wasteland bioremediation. On some sites where the soil has been almost totally sterilized by industrial pollution, engineers have found that they could dig a hole down as much as ten or twelve feet to groundwater, stick a hybrid poplar down that far, and it will root and grow and over the years absorb the poisons out of the soil into the tree fibers.

Mort Fry took over the business after his father's death in 1982. One of the most novel ways he tried to use his fast-growing trees for energy production was as a fuel for methane gasifiers. I remember well when he wrote me enthusiastically of a gasifier that he and his engineers had built and installed in his pickup truck bed, running the truck on hybrid poplar wood. He once, just to prove a point, made a trip up through New England and used scrap wood and branches he picked up along the road to fuel the truck. This was in the early days of "green" energy, and of course we were very excited. His gasifier really did work, but as all of us learned who have been involved for a long time in green energy ideas, this was yet another alternative that was more costly than oil and gasoline. Eventually Mort parked his truck and started building greenhouses and growing flowers. This project is worth a story in itself because he still lives on the farm where he grew up milking cows, and in fact the whole family lives nearby, with a grandchild now coming into the business. Nine generations of the Frys have lived and worked on that farm, always adapting to the changing times, but always, to this day, remaining farmers and keepers of their land.

A most fortunate acquaintanceship that came my way in the suburban wildwood was a fellow editor at the magazine, Dick Davids. He was a self-taught naturalist who had grown up in the north woods of Minnesota and would go back there to die. He had come to our cabin in the woods in Indiana and talked all night, then called a few days later from Philadelphia and offered me a job. We shared enough love of woodland and farmland to have instant rapport. He was also a master at journalistic writing and taught me enough to keep me from being fired. We developed a close friendship.

Dick came for a visit soon after we had gotten situated in our new home. As I was showing him my suburban wilderness one day in early May, he stopped suddenly under the two big pin oak trees in our yard and said: "Did you hear that?"

I looked at him stupidly. I heard nothing unusual. "I think you've got warblers moving through." He had grown quite excited. I still looked at him stupidly. Warbler was a word in the dictionary to me, meaning a singer of human song. The raspy noise that I did finally hear was totally unfamiliar. He divined my ignorance.

"You got binoculars?" he asked. I shook my head.

"You gotta get binoculars." He trotted back to his car in the driveway and came back with a pair. Peering up through the tree branches, he grunted and pulled me toward him with a free hand.

"Look up there." He shoved the binoculars in my hand.

At first I saw nothing. I swept through the branches with the lenses and then, suddenly, there was a little bit of feathered jewel flitting about while making a high-pitched, buzzy sound: bright orange throat, black above, black-and-white striped below.

"It's a Blackburnian warbler," he said. He was trying to get the binoculars away from me, but now I caught movement farther up in the tree. To my astonishment, another little bird was flitting about, a bright yellow bird with orange stripes on its breast. Dick identified it as a yellow warbler. I was totally carried away. Before the afternoon was over, we had sighted three other tiny, brightly colored birds, which Dick identified as a parula warbler, a magnolia warbler, and a black-and-white warbler. In less than an hour I had become a committed bird watcher, swept away by the awesome realization that these birds had been part of my woodland life all along, and I had not known it. Every spring they migrated through at least the whole eastern half of the nation, even on the homelands back in Ohio, and I had not known that they even existed. It took binoculars to see the color. Otherwise the tiny birds looked like just large insects buzzing in the trees. I did not know it at the time, but Dick Davids was also a respected authority on birds and would eventually write a book about ornithology. He could identify all the birds in America even though he was color-blind. I have him to thank for introducing me to one of the most charming aspects of living among the trees.

Then something else quite striking happened to keep my inner mind focused on the forest. I discovered the Pine Barrens. Or rather Dick kept insisting that I do some exploring there, emphasizing over and over again that just a few miles from either Philadelphia or New York was one of the wildest places in the nation with an assortment of wildlife—including some human inhabitants—equal to any wilderness. Among other startling facts, there were over twenty varieties of wild orchids there.

I learned that there was something totally enchanting about the Pine Barrens, about a thousand square miles of unbroken forest that was (in a much larger sense than Lower Gwynedd township where we lived) a suburban wilderness to the cities that surrounded it. I had always thought of New Jersey in terms of Camden, Trenton, and Jersey City, and considered it, unfairly, as the tailbone of creation. That these cities existed right beside the Pine Barrens was awesome. Once Carol and I and the kids almost got lost in the Barrens, since it is extremely easy to lose track of your place in the sameness, or seeming sameness, of these pine and oak woodlands. Fortunately, I had noticed the direction of the current in the stream of pure but tea-colored water where we stopped and entered the trees. The forest floor was white sand, the plants different from what I was used to seeing. As we frolicked along in this strange Land of Oz, I suddenly realized that I had lost my sense of direction. But luckily we found the creek again, surely the same creek, and I knew enough to follow it upstream to get back to the road.

My main interest in the Pine Barrens was the fact that blueberries flourished there, and I was thinking of a suburban blueberry farm. But I had so little time to explore this huge suburban forest that my knowledge of what was going on there was scant indeed. Just at this time (again, with the uncanny happenstance that always seemed to occur just when I needed it), John McPhee, my favorite writer back then, published his book, *The Pine Barrens* (1967), first in the *New Yorker* and then in book form the following year. (I quote from the 1981 edition below.) That was precisely the time I started traveling into the Pine Barrens. But without McPhee, I would not have had nearly enough knowledge to realize that there was a larger connection to my slowly forming enchantment with woodland than merely whimsical attraction. McPhee acquainted me with the forest dwellers in the Pine Barrens themselves, and his words gave me that little tingling sensation in the back of my neck that made me suspect that I might be on to something that my brain could not yet discern. Here's McPhee, quoting the piney woods dwellers:

> "I'm just a woods boy," a fellow named Jim Leek told me one day. "There ain't nobody bothers you here. You can be alone." . . . [H]e was sounding two primary themes of the pines. Bill Wasovwich said one day, "The woods just look nice and it's more quieter. It's quieter anywhere in the pines.". . . Another man . . . said . . . "A sense of security is high among us. We were from pioneers. We know how to survive in the woods.". . . "I love it here. I can do as I damn please. I love the woods. I could live in a sixty-five-thousand-dollar home [remember this is the 1960s] on Telegraph Road but I love the woods."

I understood that kind of talk. McPhee's description of life in the Pine Barrens revealed a remarkable example of how a woodland culture could take care of itself. The economy of the Barrens at that time was based on production and sales of sphagnum moss, blueberries, cranberries, Christmas decorations (including lots of pine cones for New York City markets), and wood products, including charcoal. People who looked poor and lived in unpainted houses could in fact, as McPhee pointed out with ever-growing reverence for his subjects, have all the money they needed or wanted. They didn't paint their houses because that would make their property taxes go up. People chose to live in the Barrens because they liked independence more than money or acclaim. It has been nearly forty years since I've been in the Pine Barrens, and I suppose by now the march of "development" has penetrated even its fastnesses. But I like to think not. I like to think that there are woodland culture people still living there and showing us the road to survival.

In about 1970 Dick Davids resigned and went back to the north woods of Minnesota where he had grown up. I was angry a little, not because he went back to his roots, but because I wanted to do the same and was afraid to. Afraid I did not have enough money. I envied him so much. Then he wrote a book, *The Man Who Moved a Mountain* (Philadelphia: Fortress Press, 1970), in which he examined in marvelous detail life in a backwoods community in the Blue Ridge Mountains, making the same points that McPhee had done with a Pine Barrens community. Here again there were people who were willing to endure hardships that modern life promises escape from, simply because they loved the woods. Unwittingly, he also provided me with significant information for this book, which I did not even know I was going to write someday. He described how important the American chestnut was to the economy of the backwoods and suggested that the tree's demise (due to a chestnut blight introduced from Asia early in the twentieth century) might explain more of the poverty in Appalachia than the Great Depression, which had occurred about the same time. The American chestnut had provided a major source of food for humans and hogs, plus direct cash income from selling chestnuts to urban markets. The wood was ideal for building, fencing, and fuel. The tree also provided medicine. Davids quotes a mountain mother: "A grove of chestnuts is a better provider than any man—easier to have around too."

Someday, perhaps, the new blight-resistant strains of chestnuts that have been developed could once again cover the Appalachian hillsides, could spawn a new woodland culture that would not have to live on welfare. There are plenty of people who want to live that way, but they have been taught that it is impossible.

Where the pharmaceutical factory stood in Lower Gwynedd Township, hidden by woodland, I had another out-of-world experience. The factory owners did not discourage hikers in their woodland, and so we often walked back into the trees, which also included quite a stand of rhododendron. I think, but could never document, that this flowering shrub was native to the place, not planted by humans. Then I discovered a very dense grove of hemlock trees. I felt just as I had felt years ago on Hicky Hill in that pine grove of southern Indiana, only more intensely. The hemlock foliage was much thicker, and the further I penetrated it, the darker the surroundings became although it was midday, becoming finally almost like night. And utterly quiet. I might have been in a boreal forest of northern Canada for all I could tell. The trees were large, blocking out all sign of the sky, and the resulting light, or lack of light, was uncannily spooky. I wondered who had planted these trees because I doubt they would have grown that thickly in a natural stand. But I could not know for sure. If they were well over a hundred years old, could it be a natural stand? To go into a place like that with vexing journalistic endeavors crowding my mind was like entering a cloister. In a little while, peace ruled in my mind. It was at this time that I discovered and was getting to know Andrew Wyeth, certainly one of the world's greatest living painters. I often thought that if I could get him into this grove of hemlocks, he could and would reveal the secrets of his creative process to me. But it took me thirty more years to get an audience with him.

There had to be natives of the area who knew the natural history of this hemlock grove as well as I knew the history of our oak groves in Ohio. Hemlock bark was used commercially for tanning leather, so perhaps the stand had been purposefully planted about 1800 for that reason. But I did not know how to go about finding the people who might retain that kind of memory. I was a stranger in a strange land. I always felt that I was merely visiting, waiting to go home.

But if I did not know the past, I surely could see the future. This idyllic suburban wildwood was changing. More and more subdivisions pressed in, more and more zoning fights kept local authorities busy. The pressure of population would have its way. If people were going to work here, they must have a place to live, so the inevitable had to happen. It came to me shortly after the wooded and shrubby area I walked through every day to the train station became a busy scene of surveying. The houses were coming. This part-field, part-shrubby woodland lay directly across from the William Penn Inn, one of the area's finest restaurants. The owners, not to mention many of the patrons, became very incensed over this development, and when they couldn't stop it, they purchased land in front of it along the highway and across from the restaurant, and put up an earthen bank that obscured the new development from view. One could sit in the restaurant and look out on a scene that had not changed for maybe a century: trees, brush, open field, and, most of all, no houses. That bank was as perfect a statement of what was happening as an artist could paint or a novelist could write.

The new highway construction that threatened to take the little woods behind our property went from rumor stage to public hearing stage. Citizens got up to rant and rave against it, against anything that would threaten, in their minds, the harmony of their place. The whole area for a radius of thirty miles beyond Philadelphia's limits became a scene of feverish dispute. The developers almost always won, because, of course, population was rising fast, people had to have a place to live, and even the protestors kept right on having babies. Few people seemed to see the causal connection and the mathematical certainty that uncontrolled birthrates and suburban wildwood cannot forever coexist. I realized then that we had come to this place at that precise moment in its history when it contained an almost idyllic environment of city, suburb, and countryside. Society was not willing, probably was not able, to keep it that way.

Another turning event in my life happened at this time. A little book of poetry happened across my desk called *Farming: A Handbook*. I read hardly five poems in it and was so moved that I walked right down to my boss's office (Lane Palmer) and told him that I was going to Kentucky to write a story about a man named Wendell Berry who wrote much better poetry than Whittier or Longfellow or any of those other so-called fathers of American literature. Since I seldom volunteered to travel, I think Lane was taken aback. He allowed the trip even if this Wendell Berry guy did not raise record-breaking crops of corn or soybeans, our usual hero types in the magazine.

So it came to be that along the Kentucky River, in his cabin in the woods, I met the man most influential to me as a writer and woodsman. He would become my close friend and remains so to this day. One of the things I remember from that first visit was walking in his woods. He picked up a persimmon, gouged out a seed, cut it open with his pocketknife and showed me how the face of the inner seed so cut looked exactly like a tiny tree. Later he wrote in the poem "The Wild Geese":

> . . . We open
> a persimmon seed to find the tree
> that stands in promise,
> pale, in the seed's marrow. . . .

(From *The Selected Poems of Wendell Berry* [San Francisco: Counterpoint, 1998])

I came back from that first visit knowing for sure that I wanted to live like Wendell Berry and know the woods as he did.

A salesman came to our door not long after that, wanting to sell us cemetery plots. Death was not something that I had thought about much. I realized immediately that I did not want to be buried in a strange land, even though this strange land had been a delight. I couldn't explain that feeling even in the depth of the hemlock grove, and fortunately Carol did not demand that I try. Snider's Woods, and Kerr's Woods and Adrian's Woods were calling me, and they were promising me, or so I divined, that population pressures would never destroy my Wyandot County with "development." Carol and I talked far into the night. She was kind enough to go along with moving to Ohio rather than back to her homeland in Kentucky, where "development" had already turned her home farm into a subdivision. At least Ohio was closer to her family than eastern Pennsylvania. Or as Wendell would say, from his home in Kentucky, moving to Ohio was almost like becoming neighbors.

CHAPTER 7

Our Own Sanctuary at Last

As we looked for a homesite in Ohio, I had but one absolute requirement. The land had to have a more or less mature woodlot on it. It had taken me forty-three years to figure out that I did not want to freeze to death some day just because some power beyond my control turned the electricity off. But everyone else looking for a place to build a house in my home county must have felt the same way, because available land with a grove of trees was scarce but very much in demand. Our county might justifiably be referred to as the birthplace of the forest-destroying bulldozer, *Bulldozonius destructans*, and those who still owned wooded land didn't want to sell it. In the end, family came to the rescue. My great-aunt, who had been very fond of my mother, walked into my brother-in-law's real estate office and said she had heard that "Gene was looking for a woods." She owned one, part of a farm she had inherited. Nor was it just any old woods. I had walked in it since childhood. It was hardly two miles from Snider's, Adrian's, and Kerr's woodlots. It was connected to Albert's Woods, which was almost connected to Vent's Woods, which was almost connected to Raymond's Woods, which was almost connected to Adrian's Woods. I had come back home, not just in vacuous general terms, but literally. My great-aunt said she wanted to keep Rall land "in the family." Another family member thought he had been promised first chance to buy the woods, but his interest was mainly hunting. When I told him he could shoot squirrels there for the rest of his life, he relinquished his claim.

It is hard to put into words what buying this woodlot meant to me. Half a lifetime it had taken me to realize where I belonged and to earn enough money to go there. In the city, I had been told that I "was throwing my life away" by coming back to live among the cornstalks, thought to be far removed from intellectual life. I was especially doing the wrong thing if I wanted to succeed as a writer, in which case it was necessary to stay close to the suckling breast of New York City from which the wellsprings of literary accomplishment were thought to flow. I might have been a slow learner, but at least by now I knew *for sure* that such was the great literary lie of American culture—knew it beyond all the blandishments of a civilization that did not seem to realize it was in decline.

We built our house at the edge of the woodlot and the barns back among the trees on the east side of it. Since then we have planted more trees between house and road so that, for all practical purposes, we are surrounded by about six acres of woods. The barns are well protected from the prevailing westerly winds, so it is almost always comfortable working around the farm animals on cold winter days. Even the house is now protected from most winds, and we are often surprised to walk out to the road on the north side, or the pasture on the south side, and find that, yes, the air is colder than we thought it was. The windbreak benefits of woodland are never emphasized enough.

Another three acres of woodland border the creek at the very south end of our property. It was only partially wooded when we arrived but is now all trees. The situation in this grove is quite different from that of the main woodlot, an interesting detail in itself. Two woodlots hardly a thousand feet apart can represent somewhat different tree communities.

Then, after we had been living here for about ten years, another unforeseen event occurred. The Kerr farm, ninety acres including the thirty acres of Kerr's Woods, owned all those years by the fabled "two old ladies in Columbus," but farmed and managed for over a century by Ralls, came up for sale. The owners were asking $2,000 an acre, which was high for farmland at that time and outrageous for woodland. A farmer who seemed willing to buy it made no secret that he would bulldoze the woods as the only way he could justify that price. Our family was at wit's end. We considered Kerr's Woods part of our home. To see it destroyed was unthinkable. None of us thought we could afford to pay $2,000 an acre for the farm, but decided that if we divided the property into various parts and each of us bought a part, we could swing it. Two of my sisters and their husbands and Carol and I divided the woods into three parcels, and each couple bought ten acres. Our brother bought the farmland. The other prospective buyer, who said he would bulldoze the woodlot, decided to back out of the picture. I suppose he didn't want to face our wrath for the rest of his life. So all of us, together, saved Kerr's Woods.

I was now keeper of some seventeen acres of trees, in three different parcels. In common, all three had at one time or another been pastured by sheep. All of them contained hardwood trees of mixed ages, ranging from at least 150 years old to mere saplings. I was also a constant student of other woodlots close by. I could say that I attended about ten different woodland classrooms with hundreds of trees for my teachers: four kinds of hickory, five kinds of oak, black walnut, wild cherry, sugar and red maples, white ash, white and red elm, box elder, black willow, cottonwood, buckeye, a couple of ironwoods, hawthorn, hackberry, honey locust, and mulberry. To these I added basswood, butternut, sycamore, sassafras, weeping willow, catalpa, serviceberry, red pine, white pine, blue spruce, dogwood, redbud, persimmon, pawpaw, red cedar, English walnut, pecan, and the usual array of domestic fruit trees.

Each of my three woodlots has a different story to tell over the last thirty-seven years that we have lived with them—actually over half a century if I count my growing-up years in them. The most important lesson of all those years was that much of the instruction in forest management manuals is unnecessarily strict and demanding of labor. Sometimes management can shorten the time it takes to bring timber to harvest, but only by a few years, which in the long run is hardly worth the extra labor. You might improve the stand a little by laborious pruning, but nature will do it for you most of the time. It just takes nature a little longer, and when humans butt in, they are almost always assuming a future they are not sure of. Where I tried to follow standard management advice, the trees today look about the same as where I did not try to follow any advice. Trees have been growing together for many millions of years, and they know how to get along just fine without much help from humans. The architect and manager of the forests is the sun, not humans, and learning that truth was the beginning of my woodland knowledge.

The woodlot next to the house I have of course watched more closely than the others. I watch it every morning as I dawdle over coffee at the breakfast table. In walking through it several times a day on the way to the barn and back, I figure I have walked the equivalent of all the way across the United States and back again.

The first and most profound lesson the trees have tried to teach me is patience. Trees measure time not in minutes, hours, days, weeks, or years like we do but in decades and centuries. Patience? For example, right out the kitchen window on an ancient bur oak tree, there is a low limb that died in 1975. It still has not fallen off the tree.

This woodlot thirty-seven years ago was somewhat open and had fewer trees in it. Sheep had been pastured in it off and on up until about ten years before our arrival, so there was hardly any stand of young trees, just old ones and the brush and seedlings that had grown up after the sheep were taken away. The old trees that were left were mostly white oak, red oak, black oak, pin oak, white ash, shagbark hickory, shellbark hickory, and pignut hickory. There were two old sugar maples and two old red maples. Sugar maples are not common in woodlots in this area, so I was surprised to see them and to this day can't account for why they were there. There were none in our other two woodlots. Yet these trees became by far the most influential ones in the woodlot.

Because the management manuals said that in this area oak and hickory are the "climax" trees, that is, the two species that remain dominant in a woodlot when it "matures," I was surprised that seedlings of these varieties were not growing in the shade of the other trees, while maple seedlings flourished. I decided to try to clear up the brush, much of it multiflora rose, that contributed to the shade and made walking through the woodlot very difficult. Fortunately, at that time I could not afford a tractor-powered brush cutter big enough for this purpose, and, without one, clearing the space between the big trees was a slow and arduous task. I say fortunately because, if I had mowed the forest floor, I would have clipped off the seedlings, mostly maple, just getting started in the underbrush. When a neighboring farmer told me that these seedlings would grow up and shade out the brush without my help, I wisely chose to listen to him.

He was right, but realizing that took what I did not have enough of: patience. All around me the trees were preaching patience and I would not listen. I wanted to thrash and crash around, exerting my own kind of order on the woods, hoping to make the tree species I favored grow a little faster. But now I desisted. In about four years I noticed—it seemed suddenly and surprisingly—that there were places among the trees where I could walk without getting clawed by multiflora rose or blackberry canes. In another four years the forest floor was almost clear of thorn bushes but now becoming overgrown, to my way of thinking, with seedling maple trees. Still not understanding the patience of the woods, I spent a winter month or so laboriously thinning out these seedlings in one part of the grove so there was only one about every ten square feet to grow straight and tall if I kept pruning them like the books instructed. What a waste of time. First of all, rabbits were girdling many of these little seedlings, eating at the bark because there had been no acorns or hickory nuts the preceding fall and the bunnies were starving. Their chewing got rid of some of the trees without any effort on my part at all. But like the ones I clipped off, lots of the seedlings injured by the rabbits sent up another stem in the spring. Secondly, as they grew and as the others not harmed by me or the rabbits grew, gradually some rose up a little taller than the others. As soon as that happened, the taller ones grabbed the sunlight and grew faster while the lesser ones shaded out lower branches of the taller ones and were themselves eventually shaded out by the faster-growing taller ones. Nature was thinning out the stand just fine, leaving nice, straight, properly spaced saplings without any effort on my part. Had I done all that work myself, by hand, I might have gained a year or two of growth faster than nature would achieve, but at enormous cost of time and labor.

What I thought was another calamity seemed to confront me. Close examination showed that almost all the surviving seedlings were sugar and red maple. That was okay, since the idea of owning a sugar bush someday was delightful. But I wanted oaks and hickories too, so I spent a lot of time fruitlessly trying to get them started in the shade of the maples. No way. I should have been pleased and satisfied just to watch a fine stand of sugar maple take shape right before my eyes without any work on my part. Sugar maple has so many good points: good fuel wood, good furniture wood, glorious color in fall and spring (its gorgeous yellow blossoms in the spring go largely unnoticed by humans). And of course there's the syrup and sugar made from the sap.

Then I noticed that, around the edges of the woodlot and in a few places where enough sunlight sifted down through the old oaks and hickories, indeed there were a few oak and hickory saplings growing up, along with a sprinkling of ashes and elms. Sometimes I didn't notice them until they were taller than I was. In fact, there was a hickory at the back edge of the woods that I didn't see until it started bearing nuts. The nuts were of excellent size and easy to crack to extract the nutmeats. Another lesson in forest patience penetrated my dull head. A white oak or a hickory will live a century or maybe two in the best of circumstances. If deer, squirrels, birds, late frost, disease, insects, maple shade, and sheep got every nut or acorn ninety-nine years in a row, in the hundredth year, just one acorn and hickory nut escaping all dangers and sprouting two new trees would mean that the species had a chance to live perhaps another two hundred years. Obviously, the odds of acorns and hickory nuts sprouting trees were better than that.

We had lived with our trees a whole year before I made another delightful discovery. Along the west side of the woods was a wild apple tree. To my surprise, the apples on it were of nice size, quite tasty, and without disease or insect blemishes. My old idea of growing fruit trees in a mixed stand with other trees came back to me. The tree was growing in partial shade, but that may have been the reason that it has never needed pruning. Or it may be, as Masanobu Fukuoka says in his classic book *The One-Straw Revolution*, that a fruit tree, never pruned, never needs pruning. At any rate, this wild apple tree has continued to grow but produces less fruit every year as the oak trees around it gain ascendancy and shade it more. I have resisted cutting down the nearest oak to give the apple more light (I have plenty of apple trees elsewhere). I just want to see what happens. What happens, I've concluded, is that fruit trees will only survive in the wild if other taller trees are not allowed to overshadow them. The peach trees in the woods only survive because they are in a glade next to the chicken coop beyond the reach of other trees' shade.

How did this apple tree get here? In our part of the country all wild apple trees are attributed to Johnny Appleseed, but this one is not old enough even were that a possibility. Maybe it came from an older tree he planted? More than likely it came from a pioneer orchard. The government made planting orchards on homesteads obligatory in the early settlement days, and the old plat map I have shows one such orchard directly across the road from our place. This tree's isolation from other apple trees probably explains its relative lack of insect and disease attacks.

Realizing that forest management meant I had to start thinking in decades and centuries, not years, I began to adopt a radically different woodland philosophy. It was sort of a passive approach like the wisdom of Buddhism preaches. Don't try to dominate everything. The climax of oak and hickory in my woodlot was only temporary and was now becoming a maple climax, with a few oaks and hickories lingering around its edges. Accept it. A hundred years from now, a disease or perhaps windstorm or fire might kill off enough of the maples so that the few oaks and hickories now gaining a foothold at the edge of the woodlot would again march into the places where the maples had ruled, and another generation of forest managers could teach students about oak-hickory climaxes. Climaxes were, relative to the eons of natural woodland growth, short in duration, much like the sexual kind.

This new philosophy persuaded me to stop stewing so much about the seeming contrariety of nature. For example, grazing livestock in the woods is considered bad practice. But sheep had been grazing in my woodlots for years. The sheep of long ago no doubt harmed my woodlot by eating the seedlings for a decade or two or three. But even thirty years is a mere blip on the tree calendar. I could say that, without the sheep, I might have had a sugar bush twenty years sooner. But who can know for sure? In the meantime, former owners had cut out oaks and black walnuts for lumber that might not have grown so well if the maples were there. Nor did the sheep, as forestry manuals contend, keep existing white oaks from attaining veneer quality by trampling around the roots too much. A large herd of cattle might do that, or a bigger flock of sheep, as the manuals say, but I still have one veneer-quality white oak in this woodlot I haven't sold despite the sheep. I missed an opportunity to sell a few more because I waited too long. (It is very difficult for me to cut down a big tree in the glory of its maturity.)

I worried awhile about the deer, which are now so numerous that they are harming forest land in many areas. A whole herd of them gather right outside our bedroom window all winter to eat the white oak acorns under our yard tree that the squirrels miss. And they eat seedling trees too. But they are certainly not yet as pervasive as sheep were for so many years. The deer threat will dwindle too, I am sure, and squirrel populations also will vacillate. It is fruitless to worry about trees that outlive many generations of the animals who live on them. This past winter, when the deer and squirrels seemed to eat every last acorn that the insects didn't eat from the yard oak, I was amazed to find, in March, that there were still dozens of acorns rooting down. The real work of humans is to make sure that the woodlands are not turned into more concrete or corn. Nature can handle the rest.

After years of my lazy nonmanagement, the young maples measure from twelve inches in diameter on down to mere saplings. The trunks go straight up, the tallest about thirty feet to the first branches, and the trees are spaced as if by design every ten to fifteen feet or so from each other. Their bright orange-yellow foliage in the fall outside our window is breathtaking. The floor of the woodlot is clear. When the leaves fall in November the golden woodlot floor is more beautiful than any lawn. In summer an occasional wildflower or wild bush might find a shaft of sunlight to grow in. One year a few Indian pipes, that strange wildflower that has no chlorophyll in its ghostly gray herbage, appeared, but never again (see figure 16). Folklore says the plant grows where a human died and rotted away in some time long ago. I like to believe that.

The red maples, which love the shade of the old trees as much as the sugar maples, are more numerous toward the back of the woods where their mother tree grew but has since died. I probably should worry about them because red maple foliage is considered poisonous to livestock, but I've never lost an animal yet. These maples bloom red very early in spring and come alive with buzzing bees and chirping red-winged blackbirds. They can be used to make syrup but are not as efficient at that as sugar maples. As I write this, the red flower clusters are falling right on the paths the sheep take to the fields. The sheep don't eat them . . . so far. But I found a dead squirrel among the fallen blossoms. Could it have been poisoned by eating the flowers?

The sugar maples are almost big enough to start supplying us with syrup, as their mothers did before they died. In summer, the maple-shaded darkness is cooler and far more comfortable to me (my wife disagrees) than the air-conditioned house. Here is a model for a suburban woodlot that requires no work at all and no mowing and is just as pretty as and far more energy efficient than a lawn.

In the meantime, nearly every year, one or two of the big old oak and ash trees die and I harvest them for firewood, gates, fence posts, trellises, and other uses. I have never had to cut down a live tree in this grove for fuel. Forestry management manuals talk about thinning out crooked trees or "wolf" trees or trees of lesser timber value, but by the time I cut out the dead ones, there's no more time for thinning, and I see no real reason to do it anyway. The trees have, over the years, more or less thinned themselves. Now, older and wiser (I hope), I rarely cut down even dead trees. The wind will blow them down in due time. Patience. Cutting down trees is dangerous work, no matter how much experience one has. Both of the professional timber cutters I employ, even with their many long years of experience, have been seriously injured by falling trees or chainsaws.

One way to avoid having to fell a big tree is to sell the log out of it. Then the timber guy cuts the tree down and I have easier access to all the branches for firewood. My timber buyer has been very good to me. If I put on a really pitiful look, he will fell a dead firewood tree for me while he is here harvesting other trees that he has bought.

Sometimes, when I wait for the wind to blow down a dead tree that has no marketable value beyond what the wood is worth as firewood, the lowest part of the trunk near the ground will rot (that's why the tree blows over), but compared to risking my life, I don't mind losing a little wood. If you have a dead tree that is already rotten at the bottom before you notice it, remind yourself of how dangerous such a tree is to fell. When you start cutting through it, you can't be sure which way it will crumble and fall. Let the wind do it.

Straight out the breakfast window, past the ancient bur oak with its thirty-seven-year-old dead limb, past the old hickories at the former edge of the woodlot, past the patch of ash seedlings under the hickories, and in front of the young maples, stands an American elm. I have kept an eye on it for thirty years. It too challenges the experts. I can use the window frame like a plumb line to show that the trunk is almost perfectly straight (see figure 13). It is a sermon to the efficacy and efficiency of the sun, the architect of the trees. It is about eight inches in trunk diameter now and at least thirty feet to the first limb. How it grows so straight and clean-limbed is a wonder to me, since we are taught that there are no straight lines in nature.

Forest management also dictates that I must prune off lower limbs as a tree grows to make sure it has a nice clean log up fifteen feet or so. But I did not have to do so here. When a tree is shaded on all sides equally and must reach straight up to get to the sun, pruning is not necessary. The tree books universally sing the praises of how the American elm has a spreading shape—some people even call it the spreading elm. It does grow that way when planted in the open, as along a city street. But in a natural woodland setting, it grows straight up like almost all the other trees do and only spreads out if it gains ascendancy over all the trees around it.

The other reason this tree so pleases my morning coffee time is that it is not supposed to be there. Thirty years ago, tree experts predicted dourly that the elm would be extinct by now because of Dutch elm disease. Nobody thought to inform the trees. What actually happened, and continues to happen, is that the elms bear seed at an early age, before the disease kills them. Even a sapling of only three inches in trunk diameter can put out seeds. So while the old trees die, new ones sprout. Now the trees are gaining on the disease because there is no longer a huge population of big elms for the bug that spreads the disease to feed on, so the bug population is dwindling. Young elms are living longer and spreading more seed. We have at least ten now growing vigorously in our grove, whereas when we came here, most of the standing elms were dead.

Scientists are reporting the possibility that certain American elms have been developing some immunity to Dutch elm disease. American elms are usually tetraploid but some diploids have been discovered (having two sets of chromosomes per cell nucleus versus four for tetraploids, if you were paying attention in high school biology class), and they are apparently less susceptible to the disease. Maybe that is what is happening here. All I know is that there are new elms in my woods and they are living longer than they did ten years ago.

A similar kind of turnover is already evident with white ash trees that are dying all over the place from the emerald ash borer. I have enough dead ashes in my woodland to supply all the firewood I will need for the rest of my life. But when foresters and landscapers tell me to kiss the white ash goodbye, I lead them by the nose into my woods. Right along the path to the barn, there are two patches of ash seedlings—scores of them. I exchange greetings with them several times a day. They are my good friends. The tallest is about five feet now, growing slowly in the partial shade, the top sprig nipped off last winter by the deer, but none the worse for it. It is three years old and still only the diameter of my finger. Obviously it is not yet old enough to interest a borer. It will take six to eight years anyway for these seedlings to reach borer-food size, during which time the borers, running out of bigger ashes, will start to starve. I hope.

There are, in fact, little ash seedlings coming up all around the edges of the woodlot where the heavy shade of the maples doesn't reach. They bear seeds when the trunks are hardly as big as my wrist and so continue to seed new trees faster than the borers can kill them. These trees may not live long enough to make big logs, but smaller ones will still be coming up when the emerald ash borer has become a third-rate also-ran. Or so I argue. Like the Dutch elm beetle, the borer will decline in population. All we humans have to do is make sure the woodlands stay woodlands, and nature will do the rest. Suburban residents who bemoan the loss of their beautiful elms and ashes could ensure new trees simply by not mowing parts of the lawn near the old trees. But, horrors, that would not look neat.

All that money that the government spent killing millions of white ash trees in an attempt to stop the spread of the borer was totally wasted, unless you were one of the people who got paid for doing the killing. The government experts who fumed at me because I would not let them cut down my ashes now usually admit they were wrong. Others blandly state, as if they had been saying it all along, that cutting down ashes won't stop the disease, but they "had to do something."

Not all trees succeed in my home grove. I tried to introduce a silverberry, a more southern tree, but it died. For some reason beech trees will not last in the grove. They grow awhile, then die in summer drought. My two pecans from seed that came from an island in the

Mississippi near Dubuque, Iowa, were touted as able to bear nuts in northern climates. They continue to grow but have not produced any nuts. I think in that Mississippi River location the water protected them from late spring frosts, the way Lake Erie does the peach orchards in northern Ohio. My sylvan peach trees produce fruit about every other year because they are protected from late frosts a little by the surrounding forest trees. I did get a sassafras from another nearby woodlot transplanted successfully, so we can go on risking our lives drinking sassafras tea if we wish. Shingle oaks have become a rarity, but one volunteered—I presume it came from the one shingle oak in the contiguous grove belonging to our neighbor. Ours will, I hope, eventually bear acorns and start other trees. Who knows? Someday a new owner might need some shingles.

One of the most enjoyable pastimes in the grove has been reintroducing wildflowers. Some, like wild geraniums, Quaker-ladies, mayapple, jewelweed, rue anemone, wood anemone or thimbleweed, and crowfoot violet, which is quite rare, were already present or soon came in on their own. Regular purple, white, and yellow violets also are burgeoning. I found some of the tiny, sweet-smelling purple violets growing in the road ditch nearby and transplanted them. I brought in big-flowered trillium, sessile trillium (toadshade), hepatica, Dutchman's britches, wild blue phlox, yellow dogtooth violet, bluebells (*Mertensia*), Virginia waterleaf, and Jacob's ladder. All these wildflowers grow in woodlots nearby that were never grazed. The seeds can evidently remain dormant in the soil for great periods of time, until conditions are right for them to grow again, or not. They might have returned on their own, but maybe not in my lifetime, so I wasn't going to wait. Three species I tried to introduce, rue anemone, bloodroot, and fire pink, died out in a few years. Since they flourish in other woodlots in the area, I don't know why they didn't last.

Sometimes a new variety appears inexplicably and then never again, like the Indian pipe already mentioned, and a Canada tiger lily. From nurseries we bought and planted in the lawn next to the grove winter aconite and snowdrops, which bloom very early in

March, sometimes in February, plus windflowers, grape hyacinths, and Siberian squill. None of these require much care. The wood anemones began to diminish once when a maple sapling grew up enough to shade the patch, so I cut down the sapling. All these flowers spread on their own if conditions are right and greatly increase the enjoyment of living in the woods.

CHAPTER 8

The Creekside Grove

THE SECOND WOODLOT, along the creek at the rear of our property, has turned into a decidedly different kind of tree grove. It had been grazed by sheep up until we bought the property, and I would initiate grazing there again about six years later. It was mostly pasture with a grove of young ash trees in part of it. These ashes were there because one big old mother tree had been allowed to remain from timber cuttings in the early 1900s.

The first thing I did was plant black walnuts in the rich black soil next to the creek, the kind of place where this valuable tree likes to grow. One walnut already grew there. Although black walnuts like full sun, these grew well enough with ash nearby because ashes do not cast heavy shade and are slow to leaf out in spring and among the first to lose their leaves in the fall. I planted only about a dozen walnuts that first time, but every one sprouted and grew. They now have trunks about twelve inches in diameter and have been producing nuts for about ten years.

Carol and I planted more walnuts on the open areas of the grove. Sometimes we did this by opening a slit in the soil with a shovel and dropping in a nut, or sometimes I would keep my throwing arm limber for the next ballgame by hurling walnuts, hull and all, in the general direction of areas we wanted to plant. Nuts can sprout and grow even if partially on the soil surface. I suppose squirrels helped too, although I think they ate more than they planted. The whole three-acre plot is thick now with additional walnut trees from about six inches in diameter on down in size. It is such a pleasure to watch money grow this way with little effort on my part. I suppose there are a hundred trees that, barring some catastrophe, could grow into high-priced logs, maybe even of veneer quality worth at least a thousand dollars each. A really good veneer black walnut could be much more valuable than that if demand remains as high as it is now. I will be long gone before these trees attain that size, but I wonder if I don't get more enjoyment out of watching them grow and multiplying board feet by hopeful dollars in my head than the person who will eventually sell them.

When it comes to "managing" my growing walnut trees, I faced what was to me a puzzling situation for a while. The trees do not seem to need as much pruning as the manuals assume. I attended several demonstration events at commercial black walnut plantations to learn what that was all about. Walnut tree farmers were demonstrating how to cut off low side branches as soon as top growth developed vigorously, and if the tree grew a fork on top, to prune off one of the forks so that the other developed into a central leader. I did a little of that on my trees, but there were so many of them I just didn't have the time to do like the professionals were doing. But I kept reminding myself that those big old walnut trees that were selling for thousands of dollars for veneer grew up in days before chainsaws and limb loppers were invented.

What has happened to these trees in the last ten years is rather remarkable. My natural plantation of walnuts is much thicker than the ones I visited to learn how to prune. There's a tree now about every four to six feet apart. The trunks are about three inches thick and about fifteen to twenty feet tall. The side branches have all died at about an inch in diameter. I can break them off easily. But even that is unnecessary because, as the trunks expand, they squeeze the dead branches off. These trees are pruning themselves, while those I had planted in a fencerow along an open field grew side branches almost as thick as the leader, turning them into a spreading tree hardly fit for future logs.

The lesson that I slowly and clumsily started to learn in our log cabin days now became clear. The sun rules. Where there was a canopy of old trees around but not too close, or a thick stand of young trees, the sun can't penetrate to the growing saplings except when it is high in the sky, from about ten o'clock in the morning to two in the afternoon. The little trees have to grow more or less straight up to get sunlight, and their side or lower branches, unable to get sufficient sun, dwindle and die as twigs. The sun almost literally pulls these little trees straight toward the sky and short-changes the side branches. On the contrary, the side branches on the trees growing out in the open can get all the sunlight they need from early morning until late evening. So in the case of a commercial walnut plantation, where trees were being planted in open fields and not too thickly, the side branches compete with the leader and grow outward almost as fast as the main trunk grows upward, thus ruining the trunk for good log production. So in this case it is necessary to do some pruning of side branches, at least until a clear trunk up to about fifteen feet is established.

It's all about available sunlight. A peach tree growing next to our chicken coop grew upward just fine until the elm tree nearby started crowding in over it. The peach tree bent away to get to the sunlight and is now growing almost horizontally, instead of upright, to get out of the shade of the elm. Sunlight seems like such a soft, passive, gentle kind of force, but it is strong enough to bend tree trunks.

Now that my grove of walnuts is pruning itself, I suppose I should thin the trees because the stand is too thick for all of them to grow to maturity. Perhaps, but I am thinking that they will thin themselves in nature's good time. If I do it, maybe the one I thin is the one natural conditions would favor to keep on growing, while the one I choose to save is the one that nature would eliminate.

I learned one illuminating fact from the professional growers. If a black walnut comes up crooked or without a good central leader, you can cut it off at ground level after a year's growth, and it will, almost every time, pop up a nice straight new little trunk the next year.

One of the biggest lessons I have learned from all this is that most trees will spread readily if the conditions are right. Much is made in the news of volunteers setting out big tree plantings in new forest-reclamation projects, which is fine, but if there are already trees or woodlots in an area, they will spread themselves. Just make the land available for them. I have watched at least five hundred black walnuts sprout and grow now in my three woodlots over the last ten years, all from nuts. A black walnut seedling, like most hardwoods, is difficult to transplant because of the long taproot, but it takes me, or a squirrel, only a couple of seconds to plant a nut.

Much is made in proper management manuals about controlling weeds in new tree plantings. If you enter one of those government programs that pay for planting trees, you must control weeds to get your money. While it is necessary to control weeds in evergreen plantings—at least here where evergreens do not grow naturally— it is not usually necessary in hardwoods. I think the reason for the weeding prescription is entirely cosmetic—it just looks nice and neat for the trees to grow in a lawnlike landscape. Perhaps hardwood seedlings won't grow up quite as fast with weeds cluttering up their air space, but on the other hand, they will be encouraged to grow a straighter leader. Hardwood trees from seed will come up through the weeds and eventually shade out the weeds in most cases. In fact, you can't stop them. You just have to have the patience to endure the unsightliness until the trees gain ascendancy. Once when I worked for the Soil Conservation Service, I asked why we were advocating multiflora rose as a living hedge fence when it was proving to be a pernicious weed. One fellow worker, with training in wildlife management, smiled almost devilishly and replied: "Because there will be places where it will not be controlled and it will then protect new hardwood trees coming up through it from livestock."

In the case of black walnut, the juglone that the roots exude is poisonous to tomatoes, apples, asparagus, and some other plants and discourages the growth of some brushy weeds like blackberry canes around the trees (but not multiflora rose, unfortunately). In only a few years, I could detect the juglone effect: the brush and weeds growing up around my little trees started to thin out, while bluegrass, which likes to grow under black walnut trees, increased. After cutting off a few upstart multiflora plants, I can now walk between the trees in most places fairly easily. I am getting a sort of rough lawnlike landscape after all.

Because of the juglone, most foresters do not recommend growing black walnuts in a solid stand, but with other species interspersed. The juglone seems to affect walnut trees themselves adversely. It is better to encourage a mixed stand anyway, because no one can predict what is going to happen to a grove over the next century, and it is better to let nature (maybe with a little human help) work out a variety of trees to cover all situations. Since ash trees were already growing in the creekside woodlot, and since their leaves do not cast heavy shade, I thought my walnuts were in good shape growing with the ashes. But the ash borer is killing the ashes now, and whether or not new little seedling ashes will come up in time to help the walnuts, I don't know yet. The future is, well, unknown, especially when one is thinking in terms of decades and centuries, not years. I am reminded of a lament that a tree farmer related to me. About two decades ago, he was advised to let his white ash grow and cut out the green ash in his grove because at that time there was some bug or disease threatening green ash. So he did. But that threat went away, and now he has only white ash trees, which are succumbing to the ash borer.

There is as much controversy about the toxicity of black walnut's juglone as there is about the toxicity of whiskey. Here are two passages discussing the subject that demonstrate the confusion very well. The first is from the book *Black Walnut* by Bob Chenowith (Champaign, IL: Sagamore Publishing, 1995): "In Kentucky, black walnut trees are often planted along the fences of thoroughbred horse paddocks to provide shade for the valuable horses, to encourage bluegrass growth, and to provide eventual income" (p. 39).

Now, here is a quote from a recent issue of the *Draft Horse Journal* (Spring, 2011). At the end of a short article warning horse owners not to use walnut sawdust or shavings as bedding, which is a fairly agreed-upon precaution, comes this sentence: "Black walnut is such a problem of horses that you don't even want the trees in your pastures or paddocks. They can cause respiratory problems if your horse eats the leaves."

Veterinarians I've asked seem to agree with the second point of view, at least in general. Black walnut and horses don't mix, they say. I can't agree at all. My brother-in-law allows his draft horse free run in Adrian's Woods (which he now owns), and it is full of black walnut trees, many of them with limbs low enough for a horse to reach. My sheep have had access to my little black walnuts in the creekside grove for several years now and seem to suffer no ill effects. I've often heard, in fact, that a good horse and livestock wormer can be made from soaking black walnut hulls in water.

The creekside woodlot has several honey locust trees, sometimes called yellow locust, growing on it. This tree has good qualities and bad. The long beans on it are good livestock feed, as the classic book *Tree Crops* points out with ample evidence. My sheep eat them readily in late fall and winter. As children, we amused ourselves by scraping the sweet gum out of the pods and eating it. The seeds, when still green, we once cooked like peas. They were not as tasty as peas but were edible enough. Honey locust has better than average BTU output for fuel wood, but it pops and crackles and so is not suitable for an open fireplace. The wood itself has an unusual whitish and pale pink grain. I still have some slabs of it curing above the garage. I feel guilt and remorse whenever I look at them. Back when I thought that I would be making part of my income from selling unusual woods from my groves to woodworkers, I cut down and hauled a honey locust log to a neighbor who still had a big stationary sawmill. When he cut the wood into boards, he ran into some nails in the log. I was so embarrassed. It took him a day at considerable expense to sharpen the big saw blade again. I had nailed a bluebird house to that tree and then forgotten after the house rotted away and fell off. The lesson here: Don't pound nails into trees. You will forget them sure enough, and someone will ruin a saw blade sometime in the future.

The problem with honey locust is its terrible thorns and the fact that when livestock eat the pods, they spread the seeds and therefore the trees in their manure. The thorns bristle out from the trunks of the trees, sometimes several inches long. They not only poke but burn, the pain lingering like a bee sting. It is almost impossible to work around honey locust with a tractor and not end up with a flat tire. At first, I thought I could use the thorny tree to make a living-hedge fence, an idea that has always intrigued me. I tried to trim and prune and train the trees along a length of fence line, but it was awesomely hard work, and pruning seemed to make the limbs grow even faster out of control. I could tell after two years of trying that a locust fence to turn cattle would take twenty years to develop, after which the hedge's lower limbs would slowly die off from shading, leaving gaps close to the ground just big enough for contrary sheep and calves to get through. The mistake I had made, according to an old book I found later, was that at the end of the very first year, I should have cut the trees back to the ground to encourage bushiness and then, in the second year, cut them back to just two feet high. But even done correctly, honey locust hedges are too difficult to control, and the idea was abandoned when wire fencing came along. Like the Osage orange hedge I had tried to train, the work is too much with no guarantee of results.

The good news is that there is now a thornless honey locust, which has been propagated for landscaping but also championed as a pasture tree, although of course not for hedging. The locust is a legume and can pump nitrogen into the soil from the air like all leguminous plants, thus encouraging the grass to grow better. Because the leaves of locusts are rather fine and delicate, the tree does not cast heavy shade, which again helps the grass in a pasture situation. Because bluegrass is a cool-season grass and can't stand drought, the light shade would be especially beneficial in preserving moisture along with the nitrogen the honey locust puts in the soil.

Hawthorn, or what we call white thorn, was another tree that started to grow in the creekside grove about the time we acquired the land. I did not know it then, but sheep had kept this thorny little tree somewhat controlled before that. I was still imbued with the idea of making a living-hedge fence, and hawthorn was traditionally used for this purpose in England. When I saw these little white thorns coming up, I thought I was in luck and planted them in a row along the western boundary of the farm, with visions of an English hedge fence in my mind. A good friend of mine who is a veteran farmer came to visit, and when he saw what I had done, I thought maybe he was going to pass out in agitation. He took me out to his farm and showed me how one of his old pastures, too hilly to cultivate, had gone completely to white thorn, the seeds spread by birds eating the little applelike fruit. He and his father had spent the better part of two lifetimes trying to eliminate the trees with hoe, shovel, cattle, and regular mowing, all to no avail. I went home and pulled out my little white thorn transplants.

However, I still didn't completely give up on the idea of a living-hedge fence. I wanted a tree-lined fence for sure, or thought I did. I also liked the idea of having a wildlife cover connection between the two woodlots, which a wooded fence line could provide. And third, I needed shade for the livestock in all the pastures. I had first planted black walnuts in a couple of the fence lines because I was overly influenced about their value. I alternated black walnuts with apple trees, thinking that the apples would provide fruit not only for us but for the livestock, and of course we could gather the black walnuts for table use too. I had read that the juglone in black walnuts could kill apple trees but did not really believe it until some of the apple trees died. But the main reason black walnuts are a poor choice for a fence line tree is that the wood, while beautiful for furniture, tends to break easily under heavy weight or in heavy winds. Limbs tend to blow off in storms, the bigger ones smashing down the fence.

By accident, I found that red cedar was the best tree for fencerows, in my situation, although I hasten to add that any tree growing in fences is going to cause problems. You have to want trees there badly enough to put up with the extra work that's sure to be involved. I wanted something on our farm to remind my wife of her home farm in Kentucky. Red cedar trees grew all over her home grounds, so I pulled up a bunch of seedlings there and planted them along the west side of our farm between the two woodlots. When that worked out fairly well, I planted another line of them down the middle of the pasture area between the two woodlots. Almost all of them grew, despite some rough handling. The first advantage of these trees was that the livestock would not eat them as long as they had enough grass to graze, so I didn't have to protect the trees from browsing.

Within ten years, the cedars made a nice hedge, although not thick enough to keep livestock enclosed. In twenty-five years, they had grown tall enough and entwined enough above the woven wire fence (I had planted them about fifteen feet apart) so that there was no open airspace above the fence. This had the startling effect of making it a deer-proof hedge. The deer could easily jump a livestock fence but would not jump into the prickly cedar branches above the fence, or haven't yet.

The sheep love to huddle under the cedars for summer shade (see figure 7). Winter winds are never as severe on the lee side of the thick cedars, and the sheep will often yard up on winter nights next to the trees out of the wind rather than go into the barn. Many birds eat the blue cedar berries, and this is one reason bluebirds don't fly south any more. But the excreted seeds cause the trees to spread fast and furiously. Fortunately little cedars will not grow back if mowed off, so they are fairly easy to control in pasture. In woodland they tend to come up wherever sunlight is sufficient.

We use the heavily berried boughs for Christmas decorations, and now we have plenty of little trees from which to choose a Christmas tree, just as Carol's family always used to do in Kentucky. People are very picky about their Christmas tree and have made a fetish of trying to get the perfect shape of the perfect species. But our free cedars have their own homely beauty and a heavenly smell. I think of the millions of wild cedars growing throughout the Appalachian Mid-South that could be used for Christmas decorations without all the expenditure of labor and money that commercial Christmas tree farms must spend. If tree farmers could grow and sell red cedars, they might start making some real money, since much less labor would be involved. The tree does not have to be pruned, and the deer won't eat it if there is anything else available.

Red cedar wood is streaked with deep maroon-colored grain and is very beautiful. Carol's brother makes jewelry boxes out of the wood (see figure 4). Recently friends asked for some cedar wood because they were having problems with clothes moths. I cut a thick branch, and they sliced it into disks to put in their closets and clothes drawers. That did the trick.

I would be remiss if I did not mention that red cedars carry cedar-apple rust disease, which can affect apples, particularly yellow varieties. But so far, our apple trees have been unaffected. "So far" in this case is about thirty years.

Even the black willows that grow right at the edge of the creek in the creekside grove have a lesson to teach. Willow wood is light and soft, but very tough. You rarely have to worry about it splitting when you drive a nail into it. It was often used to make artificial limbs in the past. It is just another example that reminds us that we are not bound to a Plastic Culture. We can even replace some body parts with wood.

CHAPTER 9

The Flowering of Our Woodlands

WHEN WE DIVIDED Kerr's Woods into three ten-acre parcels so that we could afford to buy all of it, our family had no idea that, by doing so, we would be setting up a demonstration of three different ways to manage a tree grove. It just turned out that way. Otto and Rosy wanted to keep their ten acres the way the sheep had left them, a more or less open, parklike, grassy grove. They used a tractor and rotary mower in place of sheep, allowing a new tree to grow here and there under the old canopy. Jim and Jenny sold the marketable trees in their grove, opening the grove to more light. Carol and I did nothing at all for about ten years except cut firewood from dead trees. On three occasions over the course of thirty years, we sold a few trees. Our son also brought in a band-saw mill to make lumber for the house he was building and other uses. We let the brush grow under the old canopy except for driving lanes through the trees that we keep mowed. Off these paths, the brush was almost impenetrable for awhile. Slowly, it began to disappear in favor of sapling trees. The same is true of Jim and Jenny's grove, except that with the old canopy more or less removed, there are more new trees coming in faster and, at first, more brush than in our grove. From a purely economical viewpoint, the heavier-logged grove has produced more rapid regrowth of forest.

Eighty years ago, Kerr's Woods did not extend down to the creek at the back of the grove the way it does now. Always there were about three acres along the creek that was pasture, kept shorn of trees by sheep. There was even an ancient rail fence along one stretch of the creek to keep the sheep out of an adjoining cultivated field. The sheep kept the creek banks clean of all brush and weeds in quite a dramatic way, as could be seen by how brushy and tree-covered the creek banks were in the adjoining property that was not grazed. As children, we first ventured along these "outer banks" beyond our home property to trap muskrats and to fish in the shallow water, which was then full of small catfish, chubs, grass pike, rock bass, and minnows. Dad also set lines to catch turtles, a delicacy tastier than fried chicken to us. Venturing forth "behind Kerr's" to check our trap lines in the middle of the night was the ultimate adventure for my oldest sister and me. We felt that we were journeying far from the haunts of dull human society, into a wilderness fraught with the "evil that lurketh in the night," as Mom, with a little smile, liked to quote from the Bible. In fact all aspects of our lives playing along the creek and in the woods were full of exquisite excitement. When I first heard urban people talk, or authors write, about the dullness of rural life, I could only shake my head in profound pity at such ignorance.

Today, thirty years later, that bit of pasture has turned into young forest and brush. Up above the creek, under the old trees, all three groves blossom abundantly with wildflowers in the spring. Kerr's had always been a haven for spring wildflowers that bloom and mature before the trees fully leaf out. Also Adrian and Raymond did not usually put their sheep into the woods until June, after the early flowers had matured. Grazing not only didn't hurt them but kept the woodland floor clear of brush that might have shaded them out.

To walk in this woodland in early May is nearly heaven on earth for the wildflower lover, especially in Otto and Rosy's part, which is clear of all thorny brush. I have not yet found my very earliest favorite, hepatica, which I did get started in our home grove. But all the others spread out over the forest floor in a riot of color. Bloodroot, still sought today by herbalists for medical reasons, is an early standout.

Then comes a flood of violets (yellow and blue), dogtooth violets, Dutchman's britches, squirrel corn, purple cress (sometimes only for a day or two), Quaker-ladies (bluets), trillium, anemone, wild phlox (especially glorious carpets of them), Greek valerian, Jacob's ladder, spring beauty, jack-in-the-pulpit, wild geranium, and some I still can't properly identify.

Meanwhile, another sister and her husband, Brad and Berny, bought Adrian's Woods, the one we played in most as children. Adrian's provided an added wildflower delight. My younger sisters had always gathered there in the spring to enjoy a splendid patch of wild blue irises. Later, wild hyacinths started growing there too. Today, the irises are gone, but in the same general area there is a rampant growth of wild hyacinth (see figure 9), which seems to have strengthened now that Brad and Berny have cleared out underbrush and gotten a nice stand of young black walnuts started. A few wild hyacinths appeared for a while in the creekside grove here on home grounds after I had cleared away underbrush but then disappeared when I allowed the brush to come back. Wild hyacinth has a showy, pale lavender-blue flower. Its bulbs were used by Native Americans and pioneers for food. One has to marvel at the resiliency of this wildflower. Hyacinth seeds evidently can wait beneath the soil indefinitely until conditions are right for them to germinate and establish themselves.

Just in the last few years, about forty years A.S. (after sheep), patches of fall-blooming great lobelia appeared along the creek in both Rosy and Otto's grove and mine. This deep bluish-purple flower can be seen some distance away against the brown landscape of late fall. That's why it is not likely that we just missed seeing it in earlier years. It is not a rare flower in this part of the Midwest. I presume the sheep grazed it to near extirpation. So what has triggered its reappearance now?

There have been similar appearances of rarer wildflowers in other parts of Ohio. I was fortunate enough once to be assigned to do a magazine story about the mysterious occurrence of prairie white-fringed orchids in Killibuck Wildlife Area in eastern Ohio. This wildflower had been considered long gone from the state until, in 1980, it was rediscovered in northern Ohio. The second occurrence, which I wrote about, came in 1988. In both cases, the flowers appeared not in pristine undisturbed land, as might be expected, but in what had been cornfields just ten years previously. Guy Denny, retired now from the Ohio Department of Natural Resources, and a foremost expert on wildflowers, helped me on that story. As he put it, "Wildflower seeds can lie in the ground for years and years and then grow again when conditions are right. There's a lot we don't know about wildflowers."

One of the joys of a tree grove is that such new appearances can happen at any time. We found in Otto and Rosy's grove last year a sort of rare flower called green dragon (*Arisaema dracontium*), which is related to jack-in-the-pulpit. A few years ago, I spied in Kerr's a little patch of goldenseal, and we have found a few plants of ginseng growing again in the old Snider's Woods, which my sister Jenny now owns.

Sometimes a "new" discovery is easily explained. The whole family was excited when a dogwood tree was found blooming in Kerr's because there had never been dogwoods there to our knowledge. Then I remembered. I had planted a bunch of dogwood seeds there about twenty years ago! (It has since died. Too shady.)

I have learned that one should keep a notebook of any additions one makes to a woodlot. I've never done that because I've always thought, until I got old, that I could remember everything. Just this year, walking along one of our lanes in Kerr's I found butternuts. I was totally astounded. There had never been a butternut tree in Kerr's. Where in the world had this one come from? The tree was young, about twenty years old, with a five-inch diameter, tall and skinny, reaching for the light. For days I was puzzled. Finally it came back to me. I had planted it myself, right along the lane where I hoped it would get enough sunlight, and indeed it had. I had forgotten completely about it, as with the dogwood.

Kerr's Woods is interesting to a woodsman because as far as we know—and we know rather far—it was never logged in any systematic commercial way. The Kerr owners had a strict rule. The Ralls who farmed for them could harvest a tree only when or if it blew down. No tree could be cut down, not even a dead one. That meant that there were plenty of nesting sites for birds and squirrels in the hollows of dead trees.

I know of only one exception to the Kerr rule. One huge old black walnut was harvested in the early fifties. It must have been a very valuable tree to persuade the Kerrs to go against their rule. I remember it because Cousin Raymond said the buyer also dug out the main roots right below the trunk. An unusual, very decorative veneer can be made from the wood where roots and trunk meet.

If the woodlot had ever been logged, it would surely have been more than 150 years ago because that is the age of the giants that still stand. A few of them die every year, and it is my sad/glad responsibility to harvest them in my grove. My timber buyer scolds me for waiting too long, but I can hardly bear to see these behemoths crash to the earth. The first couple of times I sold such a tree, I made sure my grandchildren witnessed the felling because they will not see the likes of it again in their lifetime. There is a point at which the tree shudders before it begins its descent. Then slowly it tips, picks up speed, often with a kind of wailing death cry from rending wood fibers, and hits the ground with a *whump* that literally shakes the earth underfoot. The air, in the aftermath, seems to shimmy and shiver, as if saturated with static electricity. Then follows an eerie silence, the absolute end to a very long life. I look at the outstretched log and I see the Wyandots, who very well could have nurtured the tree into existence, weeping as they were forced to leave these woods and remove to Kansas in one of the most notorious examples of injustice in our history.

The giants are oak trees, white, red, black, even one huge pin oak. A few giant ash trees are dying now, more from old age than from the emerald ash borer. The elms are returning here as in the home grove. The white oaks, however, are the overarching monarchs. The ones still standing have thirty feet of saleable log in them and at least three cords of firewood in branches. I have lost money by not harvesting them in their prime. My excuse is that the birds and wild animals need them for food and nesting sites.

But I finally did see the logic of selling a few trees before they got old and lost their value for veneer. The first buyer was a young chap who thought he knew all about oak trees, and most everything else. He seemed to consider me an ignorant landowner who couldn't tell a maple tree from an umbrella. He was buying for a Japanese outfit—this was back when the Japanese lost a lot of money trusting American veneer suppliers. He told me how extremely considerate he was to be able to offer me $700 each for maybe a dozen of my trees. He had no idea that I had practically named all the big oaks that might possibly make veneer grade and had gone through the grove with a government forester to calculate their worth. When I declined, he became insulting. Only a dumb farmer would refuse such a generous offer. After about his third visit, I said that if he could find five trees worth a thousand dollars each, I'd sell them. I thought he would go away then because I doubted heartily that I had five trees worth that much at that time. He pretended to be having a stroke. Then, to my surprise, he agreed. I said I would have to make sure his check cleared at the bank before he even started up his chainsaw. Again, he seemed to die a thousand deaths at such callowness.

His check cleared, and he picked out his five trees. One of them did not have even a good saw log in it and he just left it lying there. So I sold four trees for a little over $1,200 each, which was a fairly good price at the time. A few years later the white oak market to Japan sort of dwindled. I think I know why.

The timber buyer I sell to now lives right down the road from me. He's always been fair, and in fact has done me many favors, like felling a tree next to the barn that I was afraid to cut down. I've learned a lot from him too. I am lucky that his place of business is nearby because he can afford to come this short distance to harvest just a few logs at a time. Buyers from farther away want to cut at least a good truckload or two at a time in order to make it worth their while to travel any appreciable distance.

In my experience, most landowners have an exalted idea of how

FIGURE 1. There is a wide variation in hickory nuts. All of these come from the same four-acre woodlot. The variation is in size, ease of cracking, quality of taste, and thickness of shell and husk.

FIGURE 2. My peach trees grow well in a forest glade around the chicken coop. Surrounding trees protect somewhat from late frosts. Chickens control peach tree borers, and virgin forest soil means good healthy growth.

FIGURE 3. Boughs of red cedar make attractive Christmas wreaths. Bluebirds come right up to our door to eat the berries.

FIGURE 4. A cedar jewelry box made by Keith Downs from a red cedar that grew in the woods not far from the cabin where he was born.

FIGURE 5. Sassafras is a woodland tree that also makes a beautiful lawn ornamental, as can be seen here. I dug up a sprout in the woods (see text for how to do this successfully) and planted it in my sister's lawn. Note how it has grown more sprouts up around the main trunk to make a picturesque clump of trees. The foliage is obviously beautiful, and the tree has many food and herbal uses while attracting unusual birds and insects. In colonial times, tons of sassafras was shipped to Europe because it was thought to be very beneficial as an herb and tea, and it was often used in bed frames and chicken roosts because it supposedly repelled insects like lice and bedbugs. PHOTO BY DENNIS BARNES

FIGURE 6. Mixed-growth woodland like this site next to our house will yield a cord of firewood and an eight-foot log for lumber per acre every year without diminishing itself.

FIGURE 7. The author with his sheep in front of a cedar fencerow. The cedar trees shade the sheep in summer, protect them from harsh winter winds, and extend branches thickly above the fence so that deer won't jump over. PHOTO BY EVAN LOGSDON

FIGURE 8. The view out our kitchen window in late October. The maple trees are in their full golden glory.

FIGURE 9. Almost miraculously, this lovely ground cover of wild hyacinths appeared in Adrian's Woods a few years ago. None had grown there for decades. Native Americans and early white settlers ate the bulbs of this flower like we eat potatoes today. The trees here are young black walnuts, which my sister and brother-in-law, Berny and Brad Billock, the present owners of the woodlot, encouraged for future timber sales. Sheep graze this woodlot but obviously don't eat the flowers. PHOTO BY DENNIS BARNES

FIGURE 10. This is what happens when you don't mow your lawn for twenty years. It grows up in trees, much like those in this photo of an abandoned farmhouse.

FIGURE 11. The bees on this hickory firewood may be hard to see in the photo, but as I split and stacked the wood on the first warm day of early spring, they came flying in from all over to suck up the sweet sap still in the fresh-cut wood. I could close my eyes and almost think it was May, not March.

FIGURE 12. Sycamore trees often become hollow in old age. Pioneers used them for living quarters while building their first log houses. Some imaginative farmer removed the top off this tree, put a roof over what remained, and cut a door in the side to make a smokehouse. PHOTO FROM THE HISTORICAL COLLECTION OF OTTO VENT; COURTESY OF DENNIS BARNES

FIGURE 13. In a proper setting, you don't have to prune side branches from trees to get good, clean logs. These trees are growing straight, tall, and limbless up to thirty feet without any pruning because available sunlight draws the trees upward, not outward, and naturally shades and prunes off the side branches. The tree in the center here is an American elm, which is usually seen as a spreading tree because it is normally planted in lawns or along streets where there is ample sunlight to grow lateral limbs. In a natural forest, almost all trees grow up, not out.

FIGURE 14. A prime example of "fast wood" products direct from the forest. This butcher block is a section cut from a sycamore log with legs on it. Jason Frey built it for his mother-in-law, and it has stood for many years now in her kitchen. Sycamore is a good wood to use for this purpose because it does not absorb odors from foods as much as most woods.
PHOTO BY DENNIS BARNES

FIGURE 15. These spoons were hand-carved by Rich Roth from wood harvested in his seven-acre woodlot. He and his wife say they have saved $88,000 in twenty-five years heating their home with their own wood and have a growing business selling Rich's practical art. PHOTO BY MAX ROTH

FIGURE 16. Indian pipe, often referred to as the ghost-flower, because, lacking green chlorophyll, the plant is a haunting silver-gray. In folklore it was thought to grow where a human body was buried or otherwise returned to organic matter in the woods. If so, many many human bodies must have been interred in Kerr's Woods, because in the wet summer of 2011 scores of these plants grew up spontaneously where we had never seen Indian pipes before. PHOTO BY DENNIS BARNES

FIGURE 17. A chainsaw wood carving. Chainsaw sculpturing has become a high art—an example of the flowering of a new woodland culture. PHOTO COURTESY OF JOHN FICHTNER

FIGURE 18. These wood flutes were made by John Fichtner and his high school students using wood directly from the forest. Mr. Fichtner composes music for the forest flute and plays the flute himself. PHOTO COURTESY OF JOHN FICHTNER

FIGURE 19. When we think of the architecture of a tree, we tend to look at its height more than its spread. This photo hardly does justice to this gigantic black oak with a trunk diameter of over six feet but does show that it has grown as wide as it is tall—note especially the branch on the right. Obviously in its early stage of life, some two hundred years ago, the tree grew in a clearing. PHOTO BY DENNIS BARNES

FIGURE 20. The author as a teenage seminarian beside the log cabin he and his friends used as a rendezvous and clubhouse in the woods. PHOTO BY BRYAN HOBEN

much their wood is worth because of wild stories they hear, especially the one about the walnut that supposedly sold for $30,000 or so. And they believe that all timber buyers are dishonest. I don't agree at all. As in any business, cheats don't last long. Anyone who can multiply numbers can look up the formula for how to measure board feet in a log and then measure the log and check the current market prices. Or call in a second or third buyer if they're not satisfied with the first. The best way to make sure you aren't cheated is to check with farmers who have sold a lot of logs and ask them for references. And it is not usually a good idea to sell to anyone who offers you one price for everything in your woodlot. Better to cut selectively, marking and pricing each tree to be sold.

Limited clear-cutting is not a bad thing if done in patches or grids within a grove; that is, if you have, say, a twenty-acre woodlot, you can actually help it by clear-cutting an acre here and an acre there to bring in more sun. But leave other acres around the clear-cuts so the old trees there can hasten reseeding. Clear-cutting is bad when it is practiced on a very large scale, like clearing a whole woodlot. Faced with the prospect of no income from the clear-cut woodlot for another seventy years or so, a landowner will invariably bulldoze the stumps and plant corn.

I've made two more very selective timber sales over the years in my grove, consisting of three veneer white oaks for $700 each (the price has gone down considerably today), and a few black walnut, red oak, and white oak saw logs. Altogether over thirty years we've sold about $10,000 worth of trees. My son used lumber from the woods for his house. We hired a man to bring in his band saw to cut the logs into lumber and figure we got about $3,000 worth of oak and cherry from that. I cut a couple of cords of firewood every year too. The way I figure it, the woods has nearly paid back the $20,000 we paid for it, and it is in better shape now than it was then. Nor does that count the recreational value we have enjoyed. If I had cleared it and grown corn on it for thirty years, I might have had a net profit of $50 an acre average, so at the end of thirty years I would have made $15,000 and not have any woodlot at all. Of course, I should figure the value of harvested wood over the whole period of time those trees were growing, but by the same token, the corn farmer should figure the cost of a thousand years of soil fertility that the preceding forest provided.

Managing my grove, I did do a little pruning in one area of the woods where there were no large trees shading the ground with a thick canopy. Here I found, to my delight, young white oaks about six feet tall. I did not have to prune them but just cut away brush and other seedling trees that were threatening to grow above them. White oaks, if given a little headway above the surrounding competition, will soon shade it out. All it required was a bit of snipping of the competition with a limb lopper and hand pruners so that it was below the white oaks' top growth.

In the back of the grove along the creek, the old pasture there was rapidly growing a new stand of black walnuts, just as had happened in the creekside grove on home grounds. I planted some walnuts in the bit of land away from the old-growth woods, but this time not so thickly as I had done in the creekside grove. I doubt, now, that I would have had to do any planting, because there were two bearing black walnuts already there along the creek and, with help from the squirrels, walnut trees soon came up on their own all over. Also a few oaks, hickories, and ashes have come up, so the eventual stand of new trees will be mixed. Having learned from the creekside grove that a stand of walnuts with other trees around did not have to be pruned much, I saved myself a lot of sweat here. In the open, sunniest area, I did prune side branches from a few of the walnuts, but not much. Near the old-growth trees, I did no pruning and watched in amazement as some of the walnuts grew straight up; they are thirty feet tall now with nice clean trunks devoid of side branches.

Another experiment I tried did not turn out so well. I tried to establish a little grove of evergreen trees within the larger grove of hardwoods. I was remembering Hicky Hill, of course, and the grove of hemlocks that had delighted me in the suburban wildwood. I also thought it would be nice to grow a few Christmas trees. (This was before I understood the potential of red cedars for this purpose.) So

I picked out a plot in the middle of our grove that was already sort of open except for an infestation of multiflora rose and cleared it. I planted mainly blue spruce and green spruce, plus a few pines. I learned quickly enough that, unlike starting hardwoods, I had to mow around the little evergreens or they would have been swamped by weeds like burdock. The evergreens did not grow vigorously. Burdock so loves to come clomping into any clearing in the woods, and little evergreens have no chance against their leaves, which are as big as rhubarb leaves. Moreover, even though the plot was about one hundred feet square, it did not provide nearly enough sunlight for the evergreens. Massive oaks and ashes and hickories even five hundred feet away kept the sun from shining on the plot except for a few hours around midday. The little evergreens sulked while the weeds and hardwood seedlings seemed to enjoy my fruitless mowings. The only good result of this experiment was that a few nice oak and hickory saplings eventually got started in the clearing.

Only after I had become a grove keeper for a few years did I realize the importance of keeping driving lanes open to get logs and firewood and maple syrup out of the woods. Such trails also make hiking through the trees easier and more enjoyable where the canopy has not yet shaded out the underbrush. Lanes arranged so that you can get within 150 feet of any tree seems to be about right—they can be farther apart if you have log lifting or dragging equipment or log with horses, which allows you to wiggle up closer to trees off the lanes. I try to stack firewood along the lanes, but even when I can't, there's always a way to sneak a pickup in through the trees to get close enough to the ricks of wood. If you log with horses, lanes wide enough for a pickup or tractor are not necessary but are still nice. Of course driving lanes will tempt the uninitiated to try to use them in thaw time and get stuck, possibly injuring trees near the lane. I think every one of us who enjoy Kerr's Woods have managed early in our association with it to bury a tractor or pickup in its spring mud.

The three groves form a mighty compelling attraction for wildlife. Rosy and Otto live right in their grove and maintain a beautiful farm pond next to it. The water attracts almost as much wildlife as the trees do. They have had snapping turtles lay eggs between their pea rows, squirrels chew the sparkplug wires on their tractor, minks kill their chickens, deer and raccoons ravage their gardens. We can match their every story except for the egg-laying turtles. We get brown snakes and spotted salamanders in our gardens. But Otto can top that too. He once came face to face with a red eft in his woods. It is the juvenile form of the red-spotted newt, which is not quite as startling red. Even though it is supposed to be common, none of us had any idea such a creature lived here in central Ohio. And about that red coloring: the red eft carries toxins in its skin, although evidently not ones particularly dangerous to humans. But it's another example of how often nature uses, as we use, the color red as a caution light.

Nor did we know that baby great-horned owls are pure white and a million times cuter than their mothers. Because of the big, old, often hollow trees in all three groves, great horned owls have been common there until West Nile virus got them. They are coming back now. One old tree in our grove broke off in a windstorm, and mother owl decided to rear her young in the trunk hollow that remained, even though it was exposed to the weather. We could see a baby owl from the ground easily because it was as white as snow. I love great horned owls because they are about the only wild animal left that will prey on cats. There are so many feral cats around that they are killing too many songbirds. And no, I am not a cat hater. We have three of our own.

I also like coyotes, even if they sometimes kill one of my lambs, because right now there is nothing much around here that can take down a full-grown raccoon. Anyone who lives in a tree grove where there are big hollow trees must learn to live with this "cute" creature that is possibly the most destructive wild animal in America. But coyotes can handle little raccoons—as well as young groundhogs.

Probably the nicest thing about Kerr's Woods today is that if I start with Great Uncle Dave, five going on six generations of our family now have used it as a playground. One nephew has even built a house in it, and his children play under some of the same trees that we oldsters did so many years ago.

CHAPTER 10

Naming the Trees

I HAVE AN EMBARRASSING CONFESSION to make. Years ago I was one of the editors of a book titled *Trees for the Yard, Orchard, and Woodlot* (Emmaus, PA: Rodale Press, 1976) that has a dreadful mistake in it. I want so badly to exempt myself from blame by saying it happened in a chapter I didn't work on directly, but I have a notion I would have overlooked the error anyway. There were people working on the book much more knowledgeable about trees than I, and they didn't catch it either. On page 258, there is a description of chinquapin oak that is pure malarkey: "Because of its small size, the wood of this species is only of moderate importance, even though similar to white oak in quality. What wood that is lumbered goes into construction work. The acorns are reputed to be sweeter than any other oak."

The first sentence of that description is dead wrong. Chinquapin oak grows to a huge size. I've been frequenting a grove of them for over thirty years now. Some of these trees tower just as tall and wide as any of our white oaks. The second sentence of the description is a dead giveaway that it was copied out of some old publication or was copied from a book that copied it from an old publication. Eighty years ago it was customary to attach to the description of almost any species of tree some reference as to its importance or lack thereof in construction because in earlier days there was a possibility that almost any wood might find its way into a building. But chinquapin oak is scarce, and if you can find a board of it in any house or barn built in the last thirty years, I'll buy you a steak dinner at the restaurant of your choice.

The third sentence of the description is true but only by accident.

The description actually belongs to the chinquapin, not the chinquapin oak, although it is not very helpful for that tree either. We editors just got our paragraphs misplaced. The real fault or confusion in this matter lies in the haphazard way we humans name trees. The chinquapin tree is a member of the chestnut family, and someone many long years ago decided it was appropriate to hang the name on an oak species because it has an acorn sweeter than any other acorn and almost as sweet as a chinquapin chestnut. The chinquapin is a small tree, and it would indeed have limited construction use. The erroneous description did get the Latin name right for chinquapin oak: *Quercus muehlenbergii*. But while Latin names are touted as a way to avoid the confusion of ever-changing colloquial names, obviously it didn't help in this case.

The situation just gets messier because there is another tree called the golden chinquapin that grows only along the Pacific Coast. It is not exactly a chestnut but a relative, *Castanopsis chrysophylla*. Aren't you so glad you asked? The chinquapin of the middle United States is *Castanea pumila*.

Before Google, I used the 1947 *Yearbook of Agriculture* volume *Trees* to identify the various species, but it is somewhat outdated today. By some strange quirk, this authoritative source does not even list the chinquapin, only chinquapin oak and golden chinquapin—and has little to say about either. My other reference book, worn out from my constant thumbing, is an old edition of the usually reliable *Taylor's Encyclopedia of Gardening*. It has chinquapin described correctly, but there is no listing at all for chinquapin oak! It lists thirty different kinds of oak and even includes a few old Latin names that have been superseded by new Latin names—another reason that using the Latin labels can be just as confusing as using colloquial ones. To make the whole affair look even more like some conspiracy, *Tree Crops*, J. Russell Smith's classic book on trees that champions the use of acorns for food, gives only one sentence in the whole book to chinquapin oak, the oak with the most promising acorn for this purpose.

I get a little overwrought by this because the chinquapin oak really does produce the sweetest acorns of all American oaks, including the California white oak, which was once a major food source for Native Americans on the West Coast. Chinquapin oak acorns do not need to be soaked and strained in water to get rid of the bitter tannin, or at least not soaked nearly as much as other acorns. Chinquapin oak acorns are not as tasty as hickory nuts or walnuts but, even raw, are tannin-free enough that they surely would be much more economical for flour or meal for humans or livestock than other acorns. It would seem to me, although I haven't tried cooking with any acorns, that here we have a possible replacement for American chestnut, which was so important in Appalachian diets before the chestnut blight came along. Why does it seem to have been ignored?

At first I thought maybe chinquapin oaks did not bear heavily enough to be practical as a staple food source, but watching ours, they bear a crop quite like white oaks do, which is to say about every other, or every third year, and then they bear heavily. The only drawback, which only proves the acorn's worth, is that the wild animals go after it with great devotion. They know a good thing when they taste it, and if you don't get there early in the season you won't get any at all.

We need to give the chinquapin oak a new colloquial name. Call it sweet oak maybe.

When we writers start levitating in awe about trees, we often tend to do it on the basis of bookish research rather than actual field experience. We can't know as much about all of them as we would like, so it is easy for us to make mistakes. After several generations of copying each other's book knowledge, the errors feed on themselves and multiply. Had I not wandered accidentally under an oak tree whose leaves looked different from other oak trees in our neighborhood, and then tasted one of its acorns, I would never have realized the error in the book mentioned above. Even then, that first time, I learnedly pronounced the tree to be a chestnut oak, which it slightly resembles. Fortunately again, I already had planted a chestnut oak in my own grove, and when I compared the acorns and leaves, they were not alike at all. Even finely wrought book drawings of the two species can be confusing if not compared to the real thing. Chestnut oak acorns are larger and lighter colored. Sweet (chinquapin) oak acorns are medium-sized and a deep and attractive maroon brown.

Another mystery of the sweet oak grove, which is on property my son and his wife and other members of her family own, is that these trees are not at all common in our county. How did these get here?

I can make up a story that I am almost certain is true, based on studying the archaeology of Native American culture and agriculture. As I pointed out earlier, before Europeans came here, the Indians managed the forests much more than historians used to think. Some of my son's sweet oaks are 150 to 180 years old, surely, comparing their size to white oaks I have felled and ring-counted. It is highly likely that the people living here back then, and earlier, cleared a space in the forest with fire, because oaks won't grow in primeval forest shade, and planted sweet oak trees that they knew bore acorns that could be roasted right off the tree into a delicious meal. If these trees were not deliberately planted, how can a grove of them here and nowhere else in the neighborhood be explained? Lending credence to this supposition, sweet oak, that is, chinquapin oak, has been found outside its natural range, a fact that has mystified foresters. I theorize that prehistoric communities carried the acorns away and deliberately planted them in new places.

Some younger sweet oaks are growing up around the old ones, and that is very fortunate because deer and squirrel populations are growing by leaps and bounds (literally), and there's not much chance of a sweet acorn escaping them right now. I have gotten one tree started here in our home grove, so I am hopeful that I have continued sweet oak trees in this area for at least another two hundred years. The only reason I have not planted more is that it has taken me so long to work my way through my case of mistaken identity and understand the food value of this tree.

Today it is a bit easier to name trees because of search engines like Google. They leave no leaf unturned in their lists, descriptions, and pictures of trees. What really enhances this way of identifying trees is that you can take your cell phone or iPad into the woods with you and compare pictures and descriptions with the real leaf, bark, blooms, and seeds at hand. I have been spending a considerable amount of time lately trying to tell the difference between white (American) elm and red or slippery elm in my groves. Even though I am quite familiar with both, distinguishing them is not easy. Here is a description of white elm from Wikipedia: "Elm leaves are alternate, with simple, single- or most commonly, doubly serrate margins, usually asymmetric at the base and acuminate at the apex. The genus is hermaphroditic, having apetalous perfect flowers which are wind-pollinated, although bees do visit them. The fruit is a round wind-dispersed samara flushed with chlorophyll, facilitating photosynthesis before the leaves emerge." Unless a person has gone to graduate school for forty years or so to learn the language of botany, such a description might as well be written in Greek for all the help it can give in identifying white elm. Fortunately, that kind of Rosetta stone prose is accompanied by photographs and drawings. Even then, finding an illustration that exactly matches the trees in my woods is not easy. I've learned that I must examine leaf, or bud, or bark in minute detail, then compare those tiny details carefully with the pictures, always bearing in mind that some of the pictures might be mistakenly labeled.

Sometimes the name of the tree gives clues to its identity, but only in certain situations. A white (American) elm is so named because the wood is light colored and also to distinguish it from red elm, which has dark reddish wood. But the only way you can discern wood coloring is to saw into the wood. That doesn't help if you are looking at live, growing trees you don't want to injure.

Red elm is often called slippery elm because the bark on the inside is coated with a glutinous sap. But again, you can only see the slipperiness by cutting up a log.

If you study the seeds (called fruit if you are a botanist), the white elm seed is about the size of a little fingernail and slightly oblong, while the red elm seed is a little larger and rounder. But when you are in the woods, examining an elm seed, it is very hard to determine which one you are looking at unless you have samples of both at hand.

Verbal descriptions of bark are almost useless in identification, unless the bark configuration really is unique. A shagbark hickory has very shaggy strips of bark dangling off the trunk so you can hardly mistake it. But for most of the hardwoods, trying to use words to describe the bark is not helpful. Here's some from the book *Trees*, cited above.

> "Bark gray with deep, diamond-shaped fissures and narrow, forked ridges."
>
> "Bark gray, scaly or fissured."
>
> "Bark gray, separated into thin scales."
>
> "Bark gray, irregularly furrowed into flat ridges."

Those bark descriptions above are for white ash, black ash, yellow buckeye, and mockernut hickory, respectively, but are of no help at all in identifying an actual tree in the forest. Even when the color, fissures, forks, plates, and ridges are more or less described accurately, the tree scout has no way of knowing when deep fissures become shallow fissures, or when narrow forked ridges turn into irregularly furrowed flat ridges. And a lot will depend upon whether the tree trunk is from an old tree or a young tree of the same species. Also, bark of the same tree differs slightly in different climates. Red oak bark in northern Ohio looks somewhat different from red oak bark in Kentucky. And if you can distinguish northern red oak from scarlet oak from Shumard oak by looking at the bark only, you are a master tree watcher indeed.

I have only in the last year been able to distinguish accurately between mature white oak and black oak because, under certain conditions, the bark sometimes looks about the same, depending on the age of the tree and how the light hits the tree. The shade of gray and the checkering can look almost the same, especially when I'm hoping that the tree is a white oak, which sells for much more money. So my judgment is biased from the start. I will point out what I want to believe is a big, veneer-quality white oak, not a black oak, and my timber buyer will stare at me almost pathetically and correct me, as he has done many times. Of course, once the trunk is cut into, the difference is obvious because black oak wood has a deep maroon color and white oak a light color.

The only tree easy to identify by the bark is the black walnut. If you suspect that you are looking at this species, shave off a thin slice of the bark with a pocket knife. The bared surface under the outer skin of bark will be very dark brown if the tree is a black walnut. In all other hardwoods that I know, the shaved surface will be lighter colored than the bark.

Leaves are by and large the best way to identify a tree. For example, the leaf lobes of the white oak family are rounded, but in the black oak family they are pointed. This is always true in my experience. However, if the time is winter, or the tree limbs are only high in the sky as is the case with a big tree, there may be no leaves around to make the proper identification.

In the long run, success in naming trees requires living in the woods or walking through them often, in company with someone who has learned the names of the trees from long experience. A timber buyer can be the best teacher. After about the twentieth time you have seen a white ash, you assimilate all the white ash details in your mind and you know what you are looking at almost by instinct.

You may have to learn several colloquial names for the same tree, with the probability that untutored but knowledgeable tree experts may use the same colloquial name for more than one tree. "Piss ellum" is a favorite name for slippery elm in the Rall family, because the copious sap under the bark has a slight odor of urine about it. But I have also heard white elm referred to that way, even though it isn't as odoriferous.

What really makes tree identification difficult is the natural hybridization always going on in the woods and the amount of crossbreeding that tree scientists are doing. In the natural world of my woodland it is difficult to find two shagbark hickory trees that have exactly the same kind of nut. They vary in size, in shape, in thickness of shell, in the color of the shell, in the thickness and tightness of hull, in ease of extraction, in nutmeat size related to shell size, in taste, in how soon the tree comes into bearing, in earliness or lateness of maturity, and in whether the nuts fall readily in the fall or hang on into winter. That same variability holds true of shellbark hickory. To complicate matters even more, the two species may hybridize. Since the hickory and pecan are closely related, crosses between them, called "hicans," must be taken in account also.

While all this natural crossing is going on in the hickory for example, humans have also been busy making crosses and developing improved varieties that they name, propagate, and sell. Then one must go through similar exercises in identification with the other, less palatable hickories: mockernut hickory, water hickory, red hickory, pignut hickory, nutmeg hickory, and bitternut hickory. We recently found a tree growing in the wild grove behind our daughter's home that mystified us for a while. It turned out to be a bitternut hickory with foliage not much different from other hickories and even sort of like white ash, but with more of a smooth, tan bark than most other hickories. But it has one telltale detail uncharacteristic of other hickories. The leaf buds in late winter and early spring develop a distinctly yellow color.

All the hickories have colloquial names, and the same name often applies to more than one kind. Resorting to Latin names is not much help either, since scientists are constantly changing, dropping, or updating the names as they make new discoveries or develop new strains. My sisters' way of identifying the hickories in Kerr's Woods is perhaps the best solution. They give the individual trees that bear really choice nuts their own proper names. If they mention Long White, we all know exactly which tree is under discussion.

Tree watching can become just as enjoyable as bird watching and is easier to do, since the trees are not going to fly away before you get them in focus. Since there are about a hundred species that you could come across in almost any part of the country that is forested, you are not likely to run out of new ones to get excited about any time soon.

CHAPTER 11

How Big a Woodlot for
Fuel Independence?

THIS QUESTION IS PROBABLY IMPOSSIBLE to answer with any great accuracy because there are so many variables involved. But that's why it's so much fun to discuss. The general rule of thumb says an acre of woodland can produce one-half to one cord of wood a year without diminishing itself. That would depend of course on annual rainfall, length of growing season, and richness of soil. It would also depend on how many trees are growing on that acre presently, and of what age, and especially of what kind of wood. A cord of oak can produce twice the BTUs as a cord of pine, so again, simply measuring by the cord doesn't tell you much about relative heating value.

But cords per acre or BTUs per acre are not as important in determining adequate woodlot size for fuel independence as the amount of heat required to keep the house comfortable. This presents a whole computer full of other variables. What indoor temperatures do the humans involved desire for comfort? How big is the house? How efficient is the stove or furnace or fireplace? How well insulated is the house? Is the house designed to take advantage of passive solar heat? What is the average winter temperature where the house is located? Do the occupants want to rely on wood exclusively for heat or only for backup? How much backup? Do they just want a good pile of sticks around to throw at loose running dogs?

Four cords of good seasoned oak per year might be a safe average for all situations, but averages aren't very helpful. Old Tom Smith, who years ago lived in the house next door to us, said he nearly drowned during a rainy spell in our creek, which has an average depth of about four inches. I asked our market-garden friends Andy Reinhart and Jan Dawson how much money they calculate they have saved by burning wood almost exclusively for the past fifteen years or so. They don't know and point out that the amount of wood burned is not the best way to calculate money savings. "What we save comes mostly because our house is modest in size and we built it into an embankment on three sides so it would be easy to keep warm," Jan points out. "The side open to the south is mostly glass to take advantage of solar heat. We burn much less wood than a typical suburban house with the same amount of space in it."

Before an inquiry into the amount of woodland a homestead needs for fuel independence can even begin, there is an overarching fact of life that must be addressed. The first time I saw this "fact of life" was in a Clemson University Cooperative Extension bulletin in 1974 when it was first being suggested that using renewable wood for electric power generation might not be as impractical as most environmentalists believed. A tree in its lifetime "produces oxygen and consumes as much carbon dioxide as it will release when it is burned. Fossil fuel such as coal or oil releases carbon dioxide and thermal energy withdrawn from circulation million of years ago." In other words, burning renewable wood maintains the balance of oxygen/carbon dioxide necessary for life as we know it. Burning fossil fuel upsets that balance because the oxygen released by the ancient trees that made coal and oil has long since dissipated. No matter how handy or cheap fossil fuel is, or even if the supply is infinite, which it isn't, what is the use of burning it if the result is a steadily diminishing oxygen level? Nor does burning wood create the potential hazards and troublesome by-products that come from nuclear energy facilities. It may well be that for those of us living in less congested areas, there will be no choice but to use wood once we resign ourselves to living in modest homes rather than castles.

I suppose the first step toward ascertaining how much woodland one needs to keep the house warm in winter would be to rank the species of trees by the amount of heat each produces per cord, since we seem bound for all eternity to measure firewood in cords. But if you already have an established woodlot, the trees in it are what you will be using, whatever they are. Even if they are not of the highest BTU value, they will generally do the job. Pine has by volume only half the value of oak in BTUs but will burn just as hot—actually hotter. You just need more of it. By weight, a pound of pine will provide as much heat as a pound of oak; the pound of pine will just take up more space.

But BTU value on paper is not a good way to assess the fuel value of wood. More important is how dry and well seasoned the wood is. I can't emphasize this factor enough. A really dry piece of, say wild black cherry, which has only average BTU value, will burn more satisfactorily than a piece of high BTU oak that has not been dried completely. Moreover, starting a fire is much easier if you have well-seasoned wood. Ease of starting a wood fire is very important when you are doing it every winter day or maybe more than once a day (see chapter 18). Often homeowners get discouraged and decide to go to some more automatic heat source simply because, without truly dry wood, getting a fire to start quickly and keep on burning hot is too much of a chore.

By truly dry wood, I mean wood that has been split into three- to five-inch thicknesses (round wood rarely does dry enough in some species), then seasoned *for at least two years.* The manuals almost always say that four to six months or over a summer are adequate. Don't believe it. Rack the split wood up at least for two summers out where it gets sunlight and air and then get it into a woodshed or garage or some such sheltered arrangement in the fall before you burn it so that you don't have to sweep snow off it when you bring it in the house. A University of Maine Cooperative Extension information sheet on forest conservation (December 1973) says it well: "Even though wood has been cut and stored under cover for six to ten months, moisture content will still be 15 to 25 percent.

This moisture must be driven off in the burning process before the wood can be consumed. . . . Green wood will not burn until the water has been driven out and evaporated." John McPhee in *The Pine Barrens* (cited earlier) has one of his piney woods characters saying the hottest fire comes from green pine laid on a bed of hot oak coals. That contradicts basic physics and chemistry. The fire may *feel* hotter if the pine being burned is full of volatile oils, but the real secret here is the bed of hot oak coals. On the other hand, a little rain or snow on wood that has been seasoned for two years doesn't hurt its heat output. It is just too much botheration to get it burning in the stove unless you have hot coals already present.

So the very first consideration in determining the size of the woodlot you need for fuel independence has little to do with the number of trees, or the denseness of the wood, but the quality of its seasoning. The first line of business is to get two or three years ahead on your wood supply. Many people are too busy or too procrastinating to do that and so never enjoy wood heat to the fullest. And that's what having your own woodlot is really about: joy and peace of mind.

Ranking wood by BTU value should also not take precedence over some other considerations. Unless there are other reasons that you want to grow Osage orange, like for making bows or other specialized woodworking projects, you might not want to plant it or encourage it if already present. Although it is very high in heat value, perhaps highest of all, it is a hard and thorny tree and once established is not easy to get rid of. Cutting it dulls your chainsaw blade fast, and a stump will sprout right back up. This is also true of black locust, but I will later on contradict myself about this tree a little because of its other advantages in specialized situations. Mulberry wood is a high heat producer too, but as I have said elsewhere, it spreads fast and its seedlings can become a nuisance around gardens.

Also, ease of splitting is more important than BTU value if you split by hand with a maul. Red oak splits much easier than white oak or hickory in most situations, so even if it has less BTU value, you may find it more convenient to split two cords of it than one cord of white oak or hickory. Any wood from a log more or less free of knots is much easier to split than knotty wood, so a woodlot with a dense stand of straight, knot-free logs is much more desirable for splitting, hang the BTU value. This is especially true of evergreens. If grown out in the open, they have lots of side branches and the log is almost impossible to split without a mechanical splitter, which means more expense. Some woods are hard to split even when the log is free of knots. White elm is the worst.

If you are selecting trees to grow in your woodlot beyond the ones already there, or are thinning out unwanted trees, you might value multiple use of your grove more than simply the highest possible yield of BTUs. You want your trees to provide you with intangible products like fall color and the mellifluous song of the wood thrush in the evening as well as tangible goods like forest food, shade, and windbreak. That means you will want a variety of trees, some of which may not have high BTU value. Those plans and schemes that endeavor to produce the very highest yield of firewood per acre turn the woodlot into a commercial operation not all that different from growing corn commercially. I don't mean to be critical of such endeavors at all, but most lovers of tree groves are looking for more than just fuel.

Another consideration about forest productivity that needs to be put into the equation is a point of geometry. A tree that is six inches in diameter puts on an annual growth ring that may be about the same as the annual growth ring on a tree with a diameter of 30 inches. But the amount of wood actually being added to the bigger tree is quite a bit more. But this is tricky addition. You must then try to figure out if the one bigger tree is actually taking up the space that several smaller ones would be occupying, and if those several smaller ones together are adding on as much wood to their growth rings as the one large tree. Good luck.

Having said all that, I am loath to place importance on listing trees according to their heat output per cord, but some well-meaning editor will surely insist that I do it anyway. Okay. Rankings are readily available in many books and manuals and from search engines, comparing the BTUs in a cord of wood to its equivalent in No. 2

fuel oil or gas or electric heat. Don't take the numbers too precisely. A billet of wood split out of the center of a three-hundred-year-old white oak log is going to produce more BTUs than one from a sixty-year-old log because the wood in virgin timber is significantly denser. Also, I find among the various texts on this subject that the numbers can vary considerably. White oak may be given a BTU output per cord anywhere from 24.6 million to 28.2 million BTUs, with equivalency ratings of 135 to 200 gallons of heating oil. Some of these numbers are probably outright mistakes: Some authors (like me) are famous for carelessness with numbers, and of course the price of fossil fuels varies from year to year. The only number that doesn't change, and I'm not sure of that either, is the BTU value of heating oil or gas.

Shagbark hickory, black locust, ironwood, and Osage orange are all about equal in BTU value, between 25 and 30 million BTUs per cord. Dogwood is very dense wood and probably belongs in this top category too, although I have not seen it listed because not much of it ever ends up as firewood.

In the next category down are the oaks, especially the white oak and red oak families; apple, and probably most other fruit trees, especially mulberry; hickory species other than shagbark; honey locust; beech; sugar maple (rock maple); white ash; red elm; and yellow birch. These are all in the 20 to 25 million BTU range. Red elm is not always in this category, probably because it gets confused with white elm. Red elm burns nice and hot; white elm does not. The old refrain says elm "burns cold." The same old saying says that, "Ash wood wet or ash wood dry, a king shall warm his slippers by." That is sort of true, but ash wood dry is a whole lot better than ash wood wet. What I like about ash is that it not only burns well and lights quickly if it's dry, but it doesn't seem to leave as many ashes, despite its name. When I am burning white ash, I have to carry out only about half as many ashes as when burning hickory or oak.

In the next lower category are black cherry, black walnut, tamarack, white birch, red maple, and green ash, with BTU ratings per cord of around 19 million. Solid, dry black cherry is one of my favorite fuel woods, again because, like ash, it seems to burn more completely with fewer ashes to carry out. Since cherry is a highly prized furniture wood, it seems wasteful to burn it, but the market is down right now, and if a log isn't nearly perfect, it is worth more as firewood than as furniture wood.

Most of the other common trees, like sycamore, silver maple, willows of all kinds, aspen, and basswood, plus all the evergreens, are lighter, and softer and average about 17 million BTUs per cord.

So can you save money cutting and burning your own wood? Again the floodgates of speculation open as various experts get very precious about adding in every real or imagined cost they can think of, like wear and tear on your chainsaw per cord, cost of a pickup truck for hauling per cord, how long a pair of boots lasts, or cost of a mechanical splitter per cord (I never have used one). I suppose one must figure in the cost of keeping the horses if you use a team to drag out logs. Or if you use a four-wheeler to haul your wood, it costs only about a fourth of what a pickup sells for. And don't forget the wear on your splitting wedges, which must amount to at least a penny per century.

But to play the game to the hilt, one must wax eloquent on the plus side too, not just about the amount of fossil fuel your wood replaces but considerations like the value of the ashes for fertilizer and the value of the exercise you get splitting the wood. Wood ashes contain considerable potash. If you buy muriate of potash in small amounts at garden supply stores, it can cost over a dollar a pound. Over every winter I collect about four hundred pounds of ashes that I spread on garden or pasture. Pound for pound, wood ashes don't contain as much potash as chemical muriate of potash, but the ashes are considered organic and the nutrients in them are more quickly available to plants. Also, ashes contain lots of calcium and serve as a substitute for agricultural lime to sweeten the soil. The way I figure it, they are worth just as much as the muriate of potash.

It so amuses me to listen to proponents of fossil fuel of one kind or another question in minute and negative detail the cost and efficiency of a wood-burning stove, applying a scrutiny that they never use in examining their gas, oil, or electric heaters. I would like to see the efficiency numbers involved in fracking gas out of shale, or pumping oil up from two miles below the sea, or removing mountaintops to get coal, or mining uranium and making nuclear power plants "safe." The proponents of these "high-efficiency" heating units should also prorate the cost of the oil spill or the cost of ruined groundwater supplies while fracking for shale gas as preciously as they like to prorate the wear and tear on my maul as I split wood. Then calculate, if possible, how much cost is involved in getting all that fossil fuel refined and transported to every home and business that uses it and paying an army of workers to refine and deliver the fuel and account for every speck of it until consumers pay their bills. Defenders of fossil fuel primly remind us woodcutters that what we consider profit from our trees we must spread over the hundred years or so that it takes for the tree to grow. Do they spread the cost of their coal, oil, gas, and uranium over a span of the millions or billions of years it took for these fuels to collect in the earth?

Compare all that fossil fuel effort to the family at home in the woods, whose source of heat is growing nearby at no expense to mankind—actually providing atmospheric and environmental benefits as nature produces it. When the tree is cut down, the woodcutter hauls it maybe one thousand feet at the most to his house, often less; maybe even carries it by hand or wheelbarrow or uses horses to move it. He or she makes sure there is another tree already growing to take the harvested one's place. If you add in *all* the costs and benefits of home heating, I daresay, your own wood from your own grove is far and away the cheapest and most beneficial fuel available.

Using a price of $3.50 a gallon, which is about what heating oil costs as I write, and a BTU value of 139,000 BTUs per gallon, a cord of hickory rated at 28 million BTUs has a value roughly of $700 a cord—about five times what it sells for. I don't care how imaginative or poetic the experts want to wax in calculating every single imaginative cost involved in getting that wood from your grove to your stove, I am sure you can't squeeze more than $300 per cord of cost out of that gross profit, leaving you $400 a cord net profit over burning fuel oil. In my own way of accounting, where cutting wood is as much recreation as labor, and where I put an intangible but priceless value on the security I feel when the electricity goes off in the middle of the winter (the electric generator and hookup stuff I'd need instead would cost a couple of thousand dollars anyway), I reckon my firewood to be a very profitable spare-time activity using only dead wood not marketable for other purposes. Those trees when growing meanwhile are preventing erosion, protecting and recharging groundwater, producing oxygen, contributing to clean air and carbon sequestration, and providing food and shelter for humans and wildlife. My experience is that I could get all the wood I actually use for heating from five acres, even after selling the bottom, high-grade eight-foot log for lumber or using it for purposes other than heat.

Just for fun, I roped off a 50-foot-square area in my woods behind the house here—about an eighth of an acre. Within that square there are 3 very large trees, 1 white oak and 2 black oaks, each with a diameter of about 32 inches. The rest of the space is taken up by 44 trees with trunk diameters from 10 inches down to sapling size. Multiplying by eight, that means roughly 24 large trees and 352 smaller trees per acre. Whenever I have tried counting trees in other old-growth sections of my woodlots, I get between 300 and 350 trees of all sizes, so my roped-off area is fairly representative. Because of the many trees I have cut down, I know that these trees represent two ages: the big old trees are over one hundred years old, the young ones from forty years old down to year-old saplings. What are missing are trees between about forty and one hundred years old. That sixty years was roughly the time this woodlot was pastured. The sheep kept about half a generation of trees from growing. However, it is my experience from studying non-pastured groves that if sheep had not been present, there would be, along with the 3 old trees, about 10 that would be forty to one hundred years old but fewer of the younger trees because those intermediate ones would have taken up space and sunlight for some of the younger ones now growing there. The sheep did not lessen the overall production of wood, only delayed it. Without a calculator and an expert to help figure out the total number of board feet present, five acres of this kind of tree stand can keep me supplied with wood, even with the lack of trees from that intermediate sixty-year interval.

I'm not sure my way of reaching this conclusion is legitimate. You be the judge. Let us say I am going to live forever, or that someone is going to replace me who lives like I do. Using the 50-square-foot model, I have 24 big trees per acre or 120 per five acres. Two of these giants can provide me with my annual supply of firewood (three to four cords). So it would take me 60 years to use them up, probably a little longer than that because the ones not harvested would mostly be growing larger during those 60 years. In 60 years the oldest of the younger trees, let's say 80 of the 352, will be nearing 100 years of age. I would need 3 of them to produce my annual supply of firewood for the next 10 years. The remaining 50 would then be 110 years old and I would need only 2 of them per year for firewood. In 10 more years there would still be 40 trees left that were 120 years old. They would easily last until the next aged trees were nearly that old, so there would be a continuing supply of wood forever, barring tornado or bulldozer.

With 17 acres, I have much more than I need for fuel, but the surplus allows me to let trees grow longer before harvest if I am so inclined. That means a few big old dead and hollow trees for wild animals and birds. Another reason I think it is important to have older trees growing in the woods, other than the sheer delight of it, is the point of geometry mentioned above. A tree of 30-inch diameter and a tree of 12-inch diameter might add the same width in annual growth rings, but obviously the larger tree's circumference means considerably more increase in wood than is the case with the smaller one. This can be very important when trying to grow veneer-quality logs, since the larger logs are increasing in value much more than the smaller ones. The downside of that is the risk that lightning might ruin the log for veneer.

Could wood supply a significant and self-sustaining source of home heat and energy for society at large? Could Ohio, the state I live in and am most knowledgeable about, get, let us say, half of its energy requirements from trees? Not if humankind cannot manage to bring population in line with fuel supply. But if people ever evolve enough to understand the absolute necessity of population control, then the question is not an idle one at all. Even electric power companies have been among those asking the question. To put it another way, just how many BTUs could the forestland of Ohio produce without depleting itself, if we really put our minds to it? Putting our minds to it would mean that we managed the trees of our cities and suburbs and farmland at least as assiduously as the way we manage our commercial forestland and applied the best forest management practices to many more acres that now grow volunteer trees and brush haphazardly.

There are about 500 million acres of commercial forest land in the United States, varying all over the place in the amount of wood actually growing there. That figure is not very helpful for purposes here since it ignores all the acres and half acres and quarter acres outside the commercial forests that could potentially be used for forest food and fiber production. Ohio, which is a fairly average state in its proportion of woodland to farmland, has about 7.8 million acres in commercial forests and who knows how many in noncommercial groves. My county, Wyandot, is so intensively farmed that it is often not credited in the statistical tables as having any noncommercial forestland at all—a shockingly false notion, since I live on such land. The surprising fact about the number of acres in forest statewide is that the number has been going up, not down, as we are often led to think. That is true of almost every state where there's enough rainfall to support trees. (Pennsylvania is down slightly at the moment.) The forested hill country of southern and eastern Ohio has increased significantly. Even in the northern and western regions where society seems to prefer corn to trees, the decline in forests has leveled off, and woodlands have even increased a bit, mostly because, in intensively farmed areas, the hillier areas along rivers and creeks that were in permanent pasture in the middle of the twentieth century are reverting to forest again, as I have pointed out earlier. If you examine these vagrant areas of unmanaged woodland along creeks, rivers, and steep hills, you will be struck by the awesome amount of dead wood that is rotting away unused. You can say that the rotting wood is adding to the organic matter in that soil, which is true, but most of this kind of land is already chock-full of organic matter because of years of wood wasting away.

These tree groves in areas of more intensive farming, as well as the trees in urban and suburban areas, are the most interesting to contemplate in terms of new sources of fuel and energy because their extent and capabilities are largely unknown. These little, and sometimes not so little, out-of-the-way groves generally have fertile, even virgin soil because they have always been in pasture (or backyards), and they could support a good, dense stand of trees. If all of them were managed at least as intensively as the best commercial forests, how much additional energy could they supply? And this could happen under totally delightful circumstances if families would occupy such groves and love them.

As early as the 1970s, scientists and foresters, seeing a future in which nuclear energy might become the new norm as coal, oil, and gas became more and more expensive to get out of the ground, began wondering whether part of our energy consumption might come more practically from trees. That was the inspiration for the Clemson report referred to above, which went on to say that it takes about 350 square miles of forestland—let's say an area 10 miles by 35 miles—to fuel a 400-megawatt electric generating plant. Nuclear reactors seemed to offer much better efficiency in the 1970s than burning wood, so the idea did not gain much support in science, nor among environmentalists.

But now we know a whole lot more about the costs and risks of nuclear power and realize that the amount of available uranium or other elements needed for nuclear reaction is limited too. When the environmental advantages of forestland are figured into the equation, wood energy begins to look very exciting if we do not burn more wood than the forest can naturally replenish. Could that be done?

Scientists and foresters pursuing this idea have done lots of experimenting on growing trees more like a farm row crop than as a forest. In the 1970s they tended to concentrate on fast-growing trees, especially hybrid poplars, which were pioneered by my friends, the Miles Fry family (see chapter 6). Since hybrid poplars react well to coppicing—that is, they grow back quickly when the tree trunk is cut off close to the ground—foresters at Penn State experimented by planting trees one foot apart with two feet between rows and harvesting the wood every five years thereafter. Hybrid poplars were especially suitable for this purpose because they would readily grow from cuttings, not seed or transplants, and so on proper terrain could be planted mechanically. In five years, a plantation like this would produce about thirty thousand pounds of main stem-wood fiber per acre, or over forty thousand pounds if the whole tree were fed into the chipper. That amounted to some seventy-eight cords of pulpwood per acre in thirty years (thirteen cords every five years)—quite a bit more than the forty-five cords from red pine, twenty-seven from aspen, or twenty from oaks that was being obtained from more traditional forest harvests.

Today pulpwood production for fuel energy is coming mostly from plantations of pine in the South. The pulp is pelleted and sold to homeowners as a home heating fuel or used in chipboard or flakeboard by the construction industry, but also much of it is being used to fuel bio-energy power plants, especially in Europe. All this is, of course, controversial from an environmental point of view. No one is sure just what would happen in the long run if we relied on such plantations managed like an agricultural monocropping system. If it worked well, would humans harvest more of the wood than the forests could replace sustainably? And shipping wood to power plants in Europe doesn't sound very energy efficient to me.

Information on pulpwood production and use is easily available and hardly the focus of this book. It has its dark side and its bright side. I confess to being extremely leery of any large-scale operation extracting wood from forests since history has shown it invariably leads to excess. But the idea of using trees for energy is intriguing and needs to be investigated more. One application of the idea I found in quite an unlikely and very old place, *The Economist Library*, published quarterly in Springfield, Ohio, in a volume entitled *Success in Farming* written by Waldo Brown in 1886. In chapter 20 (pp. 223–28), he describes his experiences in growing small acreages of trees for firewood, fence posts, and other uses. Considering that, at his time, timber was still something most farmers were trying to get rid of as quickly as possible, Brown shows extraordinary vision, insisting that more money could be made from timber than from cultivated crops and urging his readers to put out tree plantations immediately. I will quote just one part of what he says where he surely seems, 125 years ago, to be writing specifically for this book.

> If firewood or a quick-growing windbreak is the object sought, I would advise Soft Maple. I cut a half-cord of wood last spring from eighteen trees of Soft Maple occupying a single row fifty feet long, which had been growing nine years. This would be at the rate of over twenty cords to the acre with the rows one rod [16.5 feet] apart. I have trees of this timber eighteen years old which measure from three and a half feet to four feet in circumference and I estimated they will make over a half cord each. Near my farm is a plantation of two acres of Black Locust which was started in 1850 [from seed]. . . . In 1879, eleven years after it was cut off clean, the owner began cutting the second crop of posts and I visited it and made a careful examination of it. When planted in 1850, the trees were four feet apart each way; but they were thinned out and sold for bean poles and stakes, so that at the time it was cut off the trees stood eight feet apart. When I visited it eleven years later, I found that each stump had thrown out from three to seven sprouts and the largest of these were now large enough for posts and cutting them out was a positive advantage to the remainder, and as the stumps averaged over four of these sprouts I found that over two thousand posts could be cut and still leave the original number

of trees—680. . . . In twenty years from the first
cutting, if the straightest and best trees were allowed
to stand, one to each stump, there would be 680 trees
that would make several posts each. . . .

There is much more know-how and sheer genius being displayed
here than the words tell us. First of all, black locust is one of the
densest woods with very high BTU value, and so excellent for firewood
as well as fence posts. Unlike most dense woods, black locust grows
comparatively fast. Most opportune of all, it splits easily. Black locust
was the wood favored for splitting out fence rails in pioneer time.
It responds very well to coppicing, obviously, but what Mr. Brown
doesn't seem to appreciate since he gives detailed instructions on how
to soften the seed so it sprouts readily, black locust will grow well
from cuttings. Just stick a twig in the ground and stand back, says a
friend of mine who considers the tree something of a pest on his farm.
Last but not least, black locust does not rot in contact with the soil.
It used to be used not only for fence posts but ship hulls and other
places where wood comes into contact with water. The wood's only
drawback is that its hardness will dull saw blades quicker than most
woods, but it takes a beautiful finish that woodworkers rave about.

Nor does the genius end there. In a later sentence, Brown notes
that on his own farm, in his locust grove "there was growing there a
heavy crop of blue grass. . . ." But of course. Black locust is a legume.
It puts nitrogen in the soil to make the grass grow better. Because the
leaves of the tree are fine, not heavy, enough sunlight gets through
to encourage the nitrogen-fed grass to grow better in summer when
bluegrass often stops growing because of dry weather; the light shade
of the trees is still enough to keep the ground slightly moist. The only
dark side to black locust is that it is slightly toxic, and horses have
been known to sicken from chewing on black locust fence posts. If I
had a horse eating fence posts, I'd deduce that they were probably not
getting fed properly. I've checked with several farmers who pasture
animals where black locust trees are growing and they have not had
any problems in this regard.

So what Mr. Brown has here is an almost perfect example of sustainable forest farming. Although he was more interested in fence posts (a topic I will turn to in the next chapter), it is obvious that the wood, coppiced the way he describes, would also produce a bountiful supply of fuel wood. Though he seems to prefer the faster-growing "soft maple" (I think he means red maple rather than silver maple, but I'm not sure) for fuel, I would argue that since black locust has twice the heat power, it would actually produce more fuel per acre even if it grew more slowly. But why quibble over such a detail? What we need today is more Waldo Browns.

But I think a more fruitful kind of endeavor is to look at acreages that are already growing trees and figure out how to use them, even when they are not managed in such an intensive way. For example, I was driving through Shaker Heights and Cleveland Heights in Cleveland, Ohio, recently and was struck by how much of these beautiful, old, well-heeled residential areas are really old-growth forest with houses in them. And I mean real old-growth forest—lots of huge trees towering over the castlelike residences so densely that the houses are almost hidden from view.

My first thought was how much people love trees, because there is considerable risk involved when these trees inevitably die or age enough so that storms drop them on their houses. My next thought was to try to calculate how much wood was growing here in this urban forest, which will probably end up in a landfill.

Let us take, just for discussion purposes, five square miles of this kind of urban forest. A square mile is 640 acres, so five miles square would be 3,200 acres. An acre of established woodland can produce a cord of wood a year without diminishing itself, so the experts more or less agree. With good forestry practices it can do better than that, but let's assume that every acre in this old-growth urban forest would produce half a cord a year because the houses and lawns take up some of the room. So this tract in Cleveland could be producing 1,600 cords of wood a year. At, let's say, $200 a cord, that's $320,000 a year.

Now try to imagine how many wooded urban acres there are in this country. We're talking millions and millions and millions of dollars in wood mostly going to waste due to a lack of planning and management. The main problem is that we don't think in tree time. Humans are lucky to live 80 to 90 years. The life cycle of trees is twice that at least, but it is, nevertheless, a cycle. But because it extends beyond a human lifetime, we don't really know how to plan for it. We tend to think of our beloved trees as monuments, but they are living things. We should be planting them and harvesting them on a schedule of about eighty to a hundred years to take advantage of their value as lumber or fuel while avoiding most of the possibility of storm damage. The issue is increasingly pertinent because as more and more suburbs age, so do their trees. Every storm now means a much greater threat of property damage and power outages.

The management plan should first involve the choice of trees. Maples and oaks, for example, are just as pretty as smaller ornamental trees but contain more BTUs for fuel and better wood for lumber. But even small trees can make good firewood, and some of them (dogwood, for example) are high in BTUs or useful for making specific wooden products. Persimmon wood used to be used for sidewalk and road pavers that were almost as durable as brick.

The supply of this kind of wood is only going to increase tremendously. Newer subdivisions and their trees are in the process of becoming the mature urban forests of tomorrow. Older village and town residential areas are already facing lots of problems because of storm damage and power outages as their trees grow bigger and older. Starting now for a planned, orderly cycle of harvesting old trees and growing new ones, of varieties known for good lumber or fuelwood products, will at the very least alleviate the cost of removal and could eventually become a profitable enterprise. It will also generate jobs. Already there is a big increase in the number of tree-removal businesses, increasing use of bucket hoists and tree-handling equipment. You may have noticed, if you live in an urban forest, the appearance of a new job skill. A new brand of tree trimmer has come along who swings from tree to tree on ropes, able to remove huge tree limbs over houses with a chainsaw, piece by piece, in places where no other removal method is feasible.

Since residential homeowners almost always prune their trees as they grow, they can start doing it to produce clean-limbed, valuable logs for lumber sales. This kind of urban forest farming is a totally win-win situation because, although the rewards of selling the wood may be years and years away, the reward of enjoying the trees as they grow is ongoing, and the environmental benefits of those trees taking in carbon dioxide and releasing oxygen are lifesaving. Used to be, timber buyers shunned yard trees because of nails and other hardware so often embedded in them. But enlightened homeowners can avoid this problem, and new magnet gadgets can detect metal in logs quite handily now. City planners have often proposed the idea of managing urban forests for wood, and there are entrepreneurial minds already doing it. What are we waiting for?

CHAPTER 12

The Dark Side
of the Woods

ENDURING LOVE ACCEPTS A PARTNER, warts and all, and that is true also of the relationship between humans and the forest. Rousseau waxed eloquent in his philosophical conviction that virtue and innocence were to be found in unspoiled nature, but he did not live in the woods. The forest is not as tranquil as we romantics like to think of it. For one thing, trees are in constant conflict with each other, fighting for sunlight.

As I wrote earlier, my mother forbade us, as children, to play in the woods when the wind was high. I never understood that until I had lived in the woods for several years. There is always a tree growing old and about to blow over or fall of its own weight. Even on perfectly still days, a big dead limb might suddenly let loose and come crashing down. It is not safe to walk just outside the tree stand either. A tall tree might fall out into the open on the edge of the woods since it will be leaning that way anyway trying to find sunlight. Recently, a dead elm fell out on the lawn where I walk every day. It reminded me of a fanged snake lashing out from the cover of the woods.

Perfectly healthy, stout trees that produce crops of nuts or fruit can be a menace. Even an acorn packs quite a wallop, falling from fifty feet above you. And a black walnut, almost the size of a baseball with its heavy green husk, could knock a woods stroller out.

Legend has it that Johnny Appleseed was in the habit of wandering through the woods with a kettle over his head. That is supposed to be an indication that he was a bit addled. But maybe he was simply protecting himself from nuts and fruits. Or if not that, he may have been trying to keep flies and mosquitoes from buzzing and biting him around the ears and neck. I myself pin a piece of cloth sprayed with insecticide around the lower edge of the ball cap that I wear to keep away the infernal deer flies when I am in the woods in summer. If I had nothing else, I'd use a kettle too. Biting insects are the most irritating part of the summer woods. But I have noticed that deerflies, our most pestiferous bug, are only very active at woodland edges. Deep in the dark woods on a summer day, they are not so bad. The darkness stops them, I think, because they do not like to go into a dark barn either.

You can get lost in the woods much easier than you might think. It has happened to me several times, and it can be profoundly frightening. Wandering aimlessly in the woods, the hiker tends to walk in a circle without realizing it. Once in Maine, on a rainy day when I could not see the sun even if the canopy of trees had not blocked it, I only realized that I was lost when I encountered the same blazing red maple tree a third time. It took me that long to realize I was walking in circles. At that point, the lovely woodland around me looked as forbidding as the gates of hell. I was scared badly and knew it. I tried very deliberately then to walk in a straight line, although I did not know which direction would take me out to open air again. I stumbled upon an ancient, deteriorating wire fence. Farm boys know that fence wire always goes in a straight line. Sure enough, I finally came to the edge of the woods and a road. Following the road, I eventually found my car. I remember feeling much more exhausted than the walking should have warranted. I knew the weariness of fear followed by deep relief.

When unnerved by feeling lost, even familiar objects take on strangeness. Once in what we call the Big Woods, which I could almost see out our kitchen window if our own woods did not block the view, I was hunting morels, my head down, going from tree to tree without any sense of direction. The Big Woods is only big to us, being about sixty acres in size, which is not so big except in this Corn Belt country where woodlots hardly average five acres in size. I had entered the woods on the west side, my plan being to walk straight through it to the east side, where we usually find morels. Eventually I came to what I thought was the east edge of the woods, when, in fact, I had swerved in the deepest part of the woods only to emerge on the north side. The barns and houses on the horizon, which I had observed all my life, did not look at all familiar because they were not the ones I expected to see. I was not lost in the same panic-stricken way I had been in Maine but felt just a little strange and disoriented until I realized that I was walking along the north side of the woods, not the east.

There are tricks to keep from getting lost in the woods. If you come to a creek, you can follow it. Most of the time following a creek will take you out to civilization eventually. If nothing else, it at least keeps one from wandering in circles. Creeks meander, but always the current runs downhill. If you are aware of the declination of the watershed you are in, you should know roughly where you will go following it upstream or following it downstream. If you are lost on a mountainside, going downhill will keep you from circling and generally take you to a creek.

The chance of getting lost in the woods or hit by a falling object are not as great as the possibility of a tree crashing down on your house if you live in the woods. The huge oaks that surround our place are a great comfort, both visually and for the cool shade they provide, but hardly a day goes by that I do not think of how high winds might hurl one of those giants down on the roof. But then I think about the odds. Life is dangerous by definition. Chances are probably greater that I will fall down the stairs and break my neck.

There comes a time when lovely big old trees near houses do begin to rot and die, and then they must be removed. If you live in town, city officials or your electricity provider will let you know, for sure, when one of these ancient trees needs to be removed or trimmed drastically, and you should be cooperative, not resistant.

Tree-trimming businesses now have the equipment and the skilled workers to take down any size tree, limb by limb if necessary, and although it seems expensive, the cost is a whole lot cheaper than a caved-in roof.

The bigger problem nowadays comes from trees or limbs falling on power lines. Electricity marched down our roads about seventy years ago, and enough time has now elapsed for many, many trees to have grown up and grown old under and over the lines. Even more thoughtlessly, we often deliberately plant trees under the power lines, thinking, incorrectly, that it will be ages and eons before such trees can cause a problem. When we moved to our woodland home, not satisfied with all those trees behind the house, I planted a row of evergreens out along the road, under the power line. Thirty-five years later, these trees all had to be cut down. The power company representative who came around to inform me of the bad news expected the usual anger and trash talk from the homeowner. Much to his surprise, I was overjoyed because I knew the trees had to come down and I didn't want to do the work. The utility company didn't charge me a penny. Whenever I start complaining about my electric bill, I remember that. Right now, in our village, some citizens are in an outrage because of the way the power company's workers butchered the trees along the road past our park. The city fathers should have faced reality and let the workers cut the trees down completely. You can always plant more, next time not under the power line. But our culture, in reaction to the wholesale destruction of vast acres of forest in the past, is overly reverential and protective about trees in the present.

Humanity's relationship with trees is a love/hate affair. Pioneer diaries reveal that early settlers often hated the trees because being enshrouded in deep shade day in and day out casts a certain gloom over the human spirit that can be very depressing. During our log cabin days when we lived among the trees, the environment around us in midsummer was on the gloomy side and the air in the house tended to be damp and musty. I can appreciate what it must have meant to live in the deep forest where it was impossible to look out on any kind of horizon and where you could never tell if a storm was coming your way. From our log cabin, we could at least walk a few steps and see grass and fields and skyline.

Much has been written about the theory that humans don't really like the deep forest but rather a savanna-type landscape, a sort of open, parklike environment dotted with trees, not totally gloomed over by them. The theory is that humans evolved in savannas, not thick forests. That seems likely, because the deep forest does not support nearly as many species of other plants and animals as a savanna, except maybe high up in the canopy of the colossal redwood forests of the West Coast where there is ample sunlight.

Whatever the truth may be in this regard, if you are attracted to the woods, as I have always been, put your house on the edge of it, or in the part of it that is more open. If you are gone all day at a job outside the forest, this might not be so important. But if you are leaving a wife or husband at home in the gloom, it is something well worth considering.

Clearing land by hand with an axe and a crosscut saw is one of the most arduous kinds of labor humans can perform. To think that millions of acres were so cleared in the 1800s and early 1900s bedazzles anyone who has done this kind of work. I think humans worked so hard at clearing because their natures rebelled against living in the deep forest. So-called forest gardening, becoming popular today, indicates that we could produce as much food from a savanna-like landscape as from completely cleared fields, and much more than from dense forest. So evolution argues for a savanna type of environment. But early farmers learned the hard way that trees are as relentlessly tenacious as any weed, and they wanted them completely out of the picture where they grew cultivated crops. Later, when we overdid land clearing—as humans overdo everything, it seems— society at large reacted by sanctifying the tree as a sort of icon or sacred monument to be protected at all costs. We still have a difficult time believing that cutting down trees is not evil. The real problem, though, is not allowing another tree to grow in place of the old one.

Another dark aspect of woodland life is the almost constant danger of an outbreak of some disease or insect infestation that might kill large numbers of trees. The worst case in American history was the death of the American chestnut throughout the Appalachian region. Then disease struck the black locust, although not with nearly the environmental or botanical impact. Then Dutch elm disease seemed to guarantee the end of elm trees in America. Then came the gypsy moth, causing great devastation to many tree species in the eastern forests, especially oaks. Now the emerald ash borer threatens to eliminate white ash trees from the woods. And even more recently, foresters worry about outbreaks of the Asian long-horned beetle, which can kill many tree species.

Although none of these threats should be minimized, I have grown calloused about them. I panicked when Dutch elm disease came along, and again when I drove through Pennsylvania and New York and saw vast areas of trees blighted or killed by the gypsy moth. But the forest is a whole lot more resilient than we usually give it credit for. Aside from the chestnut blight, which science has overcome somewhat by developing resistant chestnuts, the other diseases have not turned woodland into wasteland. Elm trees are now coming back in my groves. As the big ashes die, I see thousands of seedlings sprouting up and think that they will outlast their insect plague just as the elm trees seem to have done. Perhaps diseases and predator insects are nature's way of insuring that there will always be open places in the forest for new trees to grow.

Another grim aspect of woodland these days is the threat of invasive species. I am of the opinion that this fear is being overdone, but I wouldn't want to argue the point. A great new magazine that covers this problem well is *Woodlands and Prairies* (P.O. Box 713, Minona, Iowa 52159). To my surprise, even red maple is considered an invasive in some places like the oak openings in northern Ohio. The most dedicated owners or protectors of this rare kind of savanna try to keep red maples out. I don't blame them because red maples, or for that matter, all maples, can take over a woodland simply because they will grow in shade, whereas oak, hickory, and walnut will not. Red maples have been spreading in Kerr's Woods ever since the sheep were removed, but since they shade out other undesirables like multiflora rose, I rather favor them, and so far other species are holding their own.

But there are other plants whose invasive harmfulness is hardly debatable. Multiflora rose and autumn olive come to mind. The shade of trees growing up and over these two plants eventually kills or at least diminishes them, so they are not really an overpowering danger. And they do provide wildlife food. But we would be so much better off if the government had not funded and encouraged the planting of these two shrubs. What happens is that they weaken and die out over time in the deeper grove, but around the edges of the woods, where sunlight is ample, they proliferate to make an impenetrable thicket. In my earlier days, I battled them in my creekside grove with rotary mower and brush killer. One fall, I transformed the open parts of the grove into a wonderful little garden of paradise by cutting out all the multiflora rose and allowing clumps of goldenrod and wild purple aster to bloom in splendor. The multiflora is much diminished today, but alas, so are the goldenrod and aster.

An invasive plant you really need to worry about is oriental bittersweet. As I wrote earlier, American bittersweet makes clumps of berries out toward the ends of the vines and is not a problem in the woods. Oriental bittersweet has more or less single berries scattered up and down the vines, and does not make nearly as attractive a bouquet. Because I didn't know any better, I planted some of the oriental type at the edge of our grove. Fortunately, I began reading the magazine mentioned above and learned that this vine can literally take over the forest floor. We have cut the stuff back to stubs and are administering brush killer to the regrowth.

I have often wondered why there is so little bittersweet of either kind in our local woodlots as there was in the suburban wildwood outside Philadelphia. Then I saw what our sheep would do with it. They love bittersweet, and so our woodlots, all with a history of being grazed, were kept more or less free of it for a time.

Garlic mustard has become a scourge in many woodland settings. We learned, much to our delight, that sheep will graze it readily in very early spring. This will mean possibly sacrificing some early spring wildflowers for a couple of years, but in our experience the wildflowers come back faster than the mustard.

Japanese honeysuckle has become the scourge of woodland, especially in the states lying more or less within or adjacent to the Ohio River valley. But bush honeysuckle can spread in woodland too. Best not to plant them, no matter how gloriously the nursery catalogs describe them.

Deer ticks, which spread Lyme disease, are always a menace in our woodlots today. Wood ticks carry Rocky Mountain spotted fever, but rarely. As a lifelong magnet for ticks, I have developed what I can only call a sort of acquired sixth sense to defend against them. I can feel a wood tick almost every time before it bites into my skin. I find an average of a dozen ticks every year crawling on me, but in the last twenty years only one or two have successfully burrowed into my skin, and then only for a very short time.

I have never suffered a deer tick bite even though deer are around us constantly, but if you get a red pimple on the skin that is surrounded by a reddish circle, get it checked out. Deer ticks are much smaller than wood ticks and hard to see. Lyme disease is easily combated (when diagnosed early) with antibiotics, but so often the welts are not recognized for what they are because doctors see them so rarely. Check them out on the Internet, where there is ample information and pictures to help diagnosis.

In the seminary woods of so long ago, wood ticks were common, and woods rats like us lost our fear of them. We almost gloried in singeing them with a lighted cigarette (cigarettes were forbidden, of course) to back them out when they had burrowed their heads into our skin. Medical advice cautions against using this method of removal because the heat can cause the tick to release toxins into the skin, should any be present. Nor are you supposed to just grab the little blighter and jerk it out of your skin, although that is what I used to do many times. Use tweezers, says the latest advice, and pull the tick straight up out of the skin. The danger from disease-carrying ticks and mosquitoes (West Nile virus), not to mention poisonous snakes, wolves, wildcats, bears, and alligators (which, contrary to their movie persona do not prey on humans) is vastly exaggerated in the news, but the moment I say that, I realize I am tempting fate and could be the next victim. Just remember that you are far, far safer in the woods than on the road.

But the first lesson that needs to be learned in the woods is how to identify poison ivy and poison oak. Those of us brought up in a woodland culture learn to spot the three-leaved stuff at an early age and keep a wary eye out for it because our fathers lectured us strongly about its danger. But invariably everyone in the woods occasionally brushes into it anyway. I think I might really be a woods rat genetically because I seldom contract rash from poison ivy beyond a pimple or two. Sheep, by the way, eat poison ivy, so in our youth playing in Kerr's or Adrian's Woods, we didn't have to worry about contamination. Snider's Woods was full of poison "ivory." To country people, urban children who cross the street every day on the way to school are in much more danger than rural children playing in the woods.

CHAPTER 13

Your Own Low-Cost Wood Products

MY ALL-TIME FAVORITE EXAMPLE of using one's own low-cost wood to substitute for high-cost purchased products is a nineteenth-century smokehouse that once graced a farm in our county. It was a giant hollow sycamore tree. The owner simply sawed off the tree about fifteen feet aboveground, put a roof over the hollow opening, and cut a hole in the side, using the cutout portion for a door. It could have been used as a privy too, I imagine, or a garden house for the most upscale gated community anywhere (see figure 12). Sycamore trees often become hollow in old age but go on living for years. Such an ingenious use for a tree was common when flat-sawn boards were not easily available. Fast wood, in somewhat the same way as we use the term "fast food," could become common again as sawn lumber from the lumberyard climbs in price.

My second favorite example of low-cost wood is the chopping block in my sister's kitchen. Her son-in-law chainsawed a chunk off a large sycamore log and put legs on it (see figure 14). Traditionally, sycamore was favored for this purpose because it was thought not to impart off-tastes to food coming in contact with it and because the wood resists checking or splitting.

With the practice of pasture farming gaining ground, where livestock are allowed to graze for most of their food, there is a growing need for improvised shade for the animals or for a cheap covering for haystacks, as well as for fence posts. A few tall posts from six- to ten-inch logs, set in the ground with other slender logs laid across the uprights to act as roof rafters, serves the purpose very cost-effectively. In olden days, upright logs were selected that had a forked limb at the top to hold up the rafter logs. For shade, branches could be laid over the rafters and old hay or pasture mowings forked on top of the branches. For rain protection over hay, roofing tin or plastic panels will work okay, even used ones rescued from an old barn or shed being torn down.

In these days of cash grain farming and keeping livestock penned in buildings, fences are not as crucial to agriculture as they once were. But on today's growing number of pasture and garden farms, fences are again becoming crucially important, not only to keep farm animals in but to keep deer and other wild animals out. The cost of fence and posts, especially eight-foot-high ones to keep out deer, is prohibitive. If you have a woodland, you can supply your own posts, with startling savings. If you are a professional forest farmer like those in England, you can make entire deer fences out of split saplings.

On my grandfather Rall's farm, there was a most peculiar kind of orchard. Catalpa trees and only catalpa trees grew in it. His was not by far the only catalpa orchard in the county either. In a kind of agriculture where every farm had animals, fences were a priority, and every fence needed fence posts. Catalpa posts will last eighty years in the ground, and I know that for a fact because I am still using some of the posts that came from Grandfather's orchard that long ago. Grandfather used them a first time and, when he tore down the fence they were holding up, Uncle Carl used them a second time. As grain farming replaced husbandry on his farm too, he passed them on to me.

Catalpa has another advantage besides long life: the wood is soft and in demand now from woodcarvers. It takes a nail or staple easily, no matter how old the wood is, which is not true of black locust, another wood much prized for fence posts.

You can rarely buy a manufactured fence post today that will last anywhere near eighty years, and the ones you can buy that are tall and stout enough to hold cattle fencing will cost you about $8.00 each. This means that a catalpa orchard today could make you more money than an apple orchard.

The trick is coppicing, which I described in chapter 11. When the catalpa tree is about ten years old, it can be cut off at ground level for a post. Then several new trunks grow out from the stump, and in another ten years, or less, you have more posts. A catalpa orchard can be coppiced indefinitely for at least one farmer's lifetime.

Not having watched Grandfather actually harvest his catalpa posts, I have no notion of how many of them his orchard produced. I rely on Waldo Brown in his book cited in chapter 11, where he describes how he coppiced black locusts for fence posts just like Grandfather did with catalpa. (Brown said he preferred black locust over catalpa because on his farm catalpa grew slower and tended not to make as many straight, branchless posts as locust). Black locusts can be planted from cuttings, which is a great advantage. Catalpa is usually planted from seeds that are produced in long cigar-shaped pods. The seeds are very light and flaky and not easy to work with. I've started some just by broadcasting the seeds helter-skelter, but it would no doubt work better to plant them in compost or potting mix in a container and set them out later.

The yield of posts from an acre of locust trees as Brown described it is amazing. He tells of an acre of locusts planted at 8-by-8-foot spacing, giving 680 trees. At the end of ten years, when the acre was coppiced, there were more than 680 posts because some of them could be split to make 2 posts. When the acre was coppiced the second time, in ten more years, there was an average of over 4 trunks per tree, yielding, he says, over 2,000 posts and still leaving the original 680 trees to coppice again. Two thousand posts at $8 each today is a tidy $16,000. If, he projects, the 680 trees were allowed to grow just the best and straightest trunk for ten years more (continued coppicing would crowd the trunks too much), that would be another 2,000 or 3,000 posts or, if he allowed 1 trunk to grow tall enough to make 10 posts, then, at today's prices, that would amount to over

$50,000 more. Figures don't lie, even if liars do figure. In one farmer's working lifetime, an acre of black locust posts (or catalpa) might be worth something like $70,000, or $1,000 a year. Sure beats corn. If this kind of careful tree farming were practiced over millions of acres, there's no telling how much feedstock for electrical generation might be produced without diminishing the supply of wood.

Red cedar (which is really common juniper) makes a long-lasting fence post too, and millions of them are going to waste on hillsides in Appalachia that have been abandoned for farming or are used only for pasture. In this situation, fence post production can make a very appealing and low-cost savanna-type landscape. The trees plant themselves and spread like weeds. Cattle grazing the grass between them will not eat off the trees as they will hardwoods unless the animals are almost starving. Since you will probably need to mow the pasture at least once a year anyway, you can mow off unwanted cedar seedlings that are growing too thickly, and they won't grow back. There are few sights more appealing to the agricultural eye than cattle or sheep on a well-kept Kentucky pasture dotted with cedar trees. (You can see many such pastures traveling between Louisville and Lexington.)

Mentioning cedar, I must add that this pestiferous but very useful tree has many other uses, such as a substitute for mothballs, which I described earlier. In Texas, it has long been a tree favored for charcoal production. Charcoal is another fast wood product, although producing it is rather a slow process. Although I delight in charcoal broiling on our grill, I have an ambivalent attitude about it. Making charcoal—you can find tons of how-to directions on the Internet—is a rather polluting process. If you have your own woodlot, you don't really need the stuff. In our log cabin days, when we did not have money for such extravagances, I broiled any meal on our outdoor grill using strips of green hickory bark instead of charcoal. The taste imparted by the hickory was better than that from charcoal, and a relatively small handful of the bark, set afire with a few dry twigs, lights about as easily as charcoal and stays red-hot long enough to broil a steak.

You can use your coppiced black locust grove to produce fence rails too because this wood splits easily, compared to, say, white oak. Rail fences, once the common way to make a fence entirely of wood, still work just as well as they always did and are very attractive to many homeowners whether they have animals to fence in or not. Since coppiced locust trunks often grow straight and fairly clean-limbed, they work well for extra-long posts such as you need for deer.

I use a cheap temporary deer fence around my beans, peas, and other vegetables that deer seem particularly attracted to. Since I pull the posts every year and reset them to wherever I am planting those vegetables the following year, I use any saplings in the woods that have died, regardless of the kind of wood. If it is ash, for instance, it would rot soon in the ground but if pulled up every fall, rotting is delayed. I don't expect these kinds of posts to last but a few years anyway, and there are always replacements coming along.

A fence has to be about eight feet tall to keep deer from jumping over, but I've learned that you can cheat on that a bit. The posts need to be in the soil only two feet since they are not permanent and need to stick up in the air only six feet, not eight. I use old, used woven wire fence and thread it over the posts close to the bottom of the woven wire, then again through a panel close to the top, and slide it down to the height I want. The woven wire hangs about two feet above the ground and sticks one or two feet above the top of the posts. No tying, wiring, or stapling is necessary. The deer can't get under the fence, and since it sticks up one or two feet above the posts, they don't try to jump it. This is a very flimsy fence, but so far it has fooled the deer. Under the woven wire, I usually install two-foot-high chicken wire to keep out the rabbits.

For a more substantial or permanent deer fence that is still moveable if necessary, you can use the same kind of posts, or better ones like white oak or black walnut or black locust that endure in the moist soil, and attach cattle panels to them rather than woven wire fencing. Again, if you raise the panels so they are about two feet off the ground and the tops are about seven feet off the ground, the deer can't go under and won't jump over. A fence like this made two cattle panels high guarantees that the deer won't jump, but around gardens that are close to the house or where human traffic is frequent, the cheaper one-panel version works okay. Deer can jump over a seven-foot fence but in my experience seldom do. The deer's habit, usually, is to walk around the gardens nibbling here and there for something that tastes different from its usual fare (much like humans), and it will not bother trying to jump a seven-foot fence just to satisfy that kind of idle curiosity.

We are all more or less accustomed to think that, to make wooden structures of almost any kind, sawn boards are necessary. For sure, having flat-sawn wood makes construction easier, but nowadays you can carry $100 of flat-sawn wood out of the lumberyard under one arm. Many things can be made with what English forest farmers call "round wood" as in log cabin construction. (Anyone interested in round-wood construction will benefit greatly from reading *The Woodland Year* and *The Woodland Way*, both by Ben Law, from Permanent Publications in England, and distributed by Chelsea Green in the United States.) All or part of buildings, fences, hayracks, furniture, utensils like scoops, forks, and tableware, hangers for things like rope and clothing, and poles and stakes for a thousand uses can be made of more or less unfinished, unsawn wood.

Visiting an old homestead in Pennsylvania (the Karl Kuerner Farm near Chadds Ford, where Andrew Wyeth did so many of his most famous paintings), I noticed that the beams supporting one of the large sheds on the property were round-wood logs. Some of them were very long, at least fifty feet from one wall to the other and were about twelve inches in diameter, with the pillar holding up the skinnier end of the logs just a bit higher than at the other end so that the beams were level on the topside. Karl said, in answer to my question many years ago, that, yes, he just went out to the woods and selected trees that were the size and length he wanted, cut them down, dragged the logs to the barn and lifted them in place with a hydraulic front-end loader. I did a little rapid math. Fifty feet of 2-by-10-inch sawn board, spliced double to make a 4-inch-thick beam, would cost today about $200. That's good money for a young tree in the woods. Now that the Kuerner Farm is a living museum honoring the work of Andrew Wyeth, you can have a look at this old example of fast wood yourself if you are in the area. It is in seeing little things like this firsthand that the fertile human mind will say to itself, "Well yes, I could do that too if I had a grove of trees." The skill itself is not that complex or difficult. It is just that we haven't applied ourselves to thinking this way for generations.

Many kinds of structures that we now make with sawn boards can be made by using cloven saplings and branches. Cleaving a 3-inch-diameter sapling or branch of round wood is done by sliding or driving a billhook, froe, or even axe through its length, splitting it along the grain of the wood. Cloven wood is stronger than sawn wood, which cuts through the wood fibers indiscriminately. This kind of splitting is done mostly with green wood because the fibers will separate more easily then. Again, the skill of cleaving wood is not as difficult to master as it first looks. I used to save a lot of money making my own gates and hurdles this way. I used ash saplings because I had lots of them growing in the woods, and ash is a good wood for cleaving. You need a way to clamp the sapling down that you are going to split. English woodsmen in the two books mentioned above use a clever vise made of tree branches about four inches in diameter to clamp the sapling down. I often just nailed the ash sapling I was cleaving onto a big fallen log, using the log as a sort of work bench. Not having a froe, I used an old corn knife to do the splitting, tapping it along through a 3-inch-diameter sapling with a heavy hammer. The only trick involved comes into play when the split, following the wood fibers, starts to run out or away from the center, as it will often do. Then you must put prying pressure on the froe or whatever tool you are using, forcing the blade to cut through the grain back toward the center of the sapling. It is not possible, at least not for me, to describe the trick of doing that. You just must learn by doing. It really isn't that difficult.

So you end up with two lengths of wood, round on one side and more or less flat on the other. Cut to the desired length, nailing uprights to rails, flat side to flat side, and you have a serviceable hurdle, farm gate, or water gate over a creek. Another trick to make the gates sturdier is to notch holes into the uprights. This is very easy to do if you have become skilled with a chainsaw. Using the tip or nose of the blade, you can cut a notch through the upright and then shave the ends of the horizontals so they fit into the notches. Using a chainsaw this way can be dangerous because of kickback, and you must learn to ease the saw into the wood very slowly and carefully.

After you have done a few gates, all sorts of other possibilities where you thought you needed sawn lumber will come to mind: hayracks, chicken roosts, trellises of all kinds. Solid privacy walls can be made by placing the split cleavings up close to each other. Skinnier poles can be cleaved or used whole to make all kinds of bentwood furniture, not to mention beanpoles and pea trellises.

Some of the earliest plank roads were made by splitting logs nine to twelve inches in diameter into half planks. They were called corduroy roads until sawmills were plentiful enough to flatten the logs on both sides. It is interesting to note that in their day, wooden roads were considered better than any pavement. Eric Sloane in his book *Eric Sloane's America* points out that, in 1870, the New York State senate issued a report stating that plank roads were "more profitable than gravel or stone. They never break up in winter thaws or fall away in spring freshets the way paved roads do." That finding just might be true today, at least for secondary roads, if we had an abundance of wood. A plank road of oak was considered to have a lifetime of twelve years. That is about the amount of time it takes for blacktop or concrete to break up under the pounding of frost and traffic today. The road across the bridge on my home farm was made of loose planks like the old plank roads (they evidently lasted longer when laid loose), and every time a car passed over it, the rumble would wake us up in the night.

Until Google came along to more than complete my formal education, I did not know that hammocks were originally made of wood of the hamack tree. Columbus, stopping off in the Bahamas on his historic journey, was much enamored with the way the natives slept in their swaying beds and took a few "hamacks" back to Europe, where they became very popular with sailors sleeping on vessels lurching in the open sea. Other fabrics replaced hamack bark eventually, but as the champions of wood insist, hamack bark hammocks, being wider and less saggy, were more comfortable to sleep in.

Books like Eric Sloane's and the two others by Ben Law, cited earlier, or my favorite, *Forever the Farm,* by Marian Nicholl Rawson, are good reading for the woodlot owner intent on deriving low-cost wood from his trees. Drawings and photos in books like these show how skillfully pioneers used natural curves in the wood for bentwood construction, or natural crotches in log and limb timbers to take the place of sawn column and fitted brace. Once in seminary school, we wanted to make an arched bridge over a ravine in our school park. The easiest way to do this, we decided, was to find two naturally curved tree trunks that matched. (Remember we were just one generation removed from the students who had built the log cabins in the school forest, so we were still culturally prone to think that way. We could have also just used one curved tree and split the trunk down the middle for the two matching spans.) It was not easy, but over four hundred acres of woodland we did indeed find two trees growing curved trunks that matched fairly well. Manpower we had in abundance, and about twenty of us literally carried the logs of about twelve inches in diameter back to the bridge site. Once installed and braced with more fast wood, the curvature gave the bridge not just beauty, but all the strength it needed to bear the weight of human traffic.

Naturally bent or curved wood is the secret of making spoons, ladles, and other such utensils out of wood. You do not start out with a block of wood and carve a spoon out of it, but rather look for a piece of wood that has the spoon in it and cut away all the wood that is not part of it. A curved grain makes a spoon handle that is handy to use and strong. A straight handle cut or carved across the grain will be weak. For a ladle handle, you will want a curved handle too, a branch that is growing out of another branch large enough and at nearly a right angle from the handle branch to hollow out the ladle cup.

Cutting the ladle from the wood can be done with various handsaws, chisels, or, better yet, a band saw. You can't always clamp down a curved branch when you are sawing, but do so whenever possible. Otherwise move the wood through the saw very slowly so it doesn't jump if the saw teeth catch in the wood. I almost lost a finger that way. Finish up with a rasp, pocketknife, and sandpaper. Hollowing out the spoon or ladle can be done with a rasp in a drill press, but set the rasp so it can't inadvertently go all the way through the wood you are hollowing out.

The other secret to natural woodenware is to always make the utensil from one half of the branch. The very center of a branch or limb is its weakest place. A spoon or anything else carved from a whole branch will soon break. Carve out a spoon from one side of the branch, and another spoon from the other side.

Keeping an eye out for unusual natural forks and bends in wood enhances the enjoyment of walking among your trees. One year I decided to make the grandchildren each a walking stick. Doing this trained my eye to look for properly angled or unusually angled branches for cane handles. One tends to look at a fork of a tree limb as being at the top of the limb, when sometimes it is the branch above the fork that with the fork makes the angle desired. Turned upside down from the way it grows, such a fork makes a great hooked tool, or, in the case of walking sticks, a more serviceable cane handle. Such angled branches are also great to make hangers for clothes or tools or even a long-handled hook that with a little carving and shaping can be turned into a leghold shepherd's crook for catching sheep. I wanted one walking stick with the handhold sticking straight out from the stick, all one piece. I had to look quite a while to get the right-angled forked limb of ash that I wanted, but hunting for it was a pleasant preoccupation.

Around the barn there are scores of uses for low-cost wood, either round or split. Serviceable hayracks do not require much precision. I have just read about a Federalist-style farmhouse built in the latter nineteenth century where the stair steps are solid log pieces about 12 inches in diameter, squared on two adjacent sides. The owner said they never squeaked. I once built a corncrib out of sapling logs, laying them up as in log cabin construction but without notching, so that there was plenty of space between the logs for air-drying the ears of corn. In the early days, farmers would draw a young cedar or similar kind of branchy tree behind a team of horses like a harrow to level out plowed ground before planting. Now that's fast wood.

When our son was a little boy, he decided to make himself a golf club—a driver. Since he would grow up to make his living as a skilled woodworker, we probably should not have been surprised when he went out into the woods and found a straight branch about two inches in diameter and five feet long, growing at just the right angle off a bigger branch. He cut the stick off, leaving enough of the larger branch attached to shape into the business end of the club. He carved and scraped it into a fairly proper shape, then cut a flat face into it. It would actually send a golf ball flying quite a distance. He soon forgot about it, but I have kept it, one of the little treasures of my life.

Another kind of low-cost wood rapidly gaining in popularity is wood sculpture done entirely with a chainsaw. Early attempts at this kind of art were rather crude, and appealing for that very reason, but as human talent applies itself assiduously, it is amazing what can be done without any other tool (see figure 17). You can in fact make crude furniture with a chainsaw only, leaving a backrest of wood attached to a log section. Cut out appropriate spaces in the log seat, and you come up with four legs to make your low-cost wood creation look even more like a chair.

CHAPTER 14

The Living Architecture of a Tree

WHEN I LOOK AT A TREE, I find it difficult to think of it as a plant. It looks like pure magic to me. I can read over and over again the scientific explanations of how sunlight and photosynthesis and chlorophyll and cambium layers and all that work together to raise gigantic masses of woody fiber high into the air, but I still don't really comprehend it. I look at a big tree and think of the Parthenon. I wonder if the whole idea of propping up buildings with pillars began with propping them up with logs and proceeded on to stone columns when handy trees were all used up. If you have ever seen a photograph of the ruins of an ancient Roman city in North Africa, like Timgad, what remains looks like a petrified forest of stone columns rising starkly out of the desert, a sort of monument to what happens when soil erosion wastes the earth.

A tree is a marvelous architectural victory over gravity. With proper sunlight a trunk grows almost perfectly straight, tall, and comparatively slender considering the height involved. Yet it will resist all but the most violent winds while holding up living umbrellas of branches that with their leaves, seeds, and fruits literally save the earth from destruction.

Nature's ability to grow such a wonder defies belief. The redwoods of the Pacific coast can rise over 300 feet into the sky, held up by trunks 24 feet in diameter, and living more than 2,000 years. Wood giants flourished in other parts of our country too, even though not so celebrated as the redwoods. Early settlers found black walnut trees like one described in Forestville, New York, in 1841 that had a trunk diameter of 12 feet, a height to the first limb of 80 feet, and a total height of nearly 200 feet. There were 150 cords of wood in the tree, or 50,000 board feet of lumber. Black walnut sells for about $3 a board foot today, which means that a tree like that might sell today for $150,000. The age of the tree, which blew down in 1822, was not recorded, but it would almost have to be over 250 years old. (Eric Sloane quotes a description of the tree in his book, *Eric Sloane's America*, already cited, page 122.) Bob Chenowith, in his book *Black Walnut*, again previously cited, tells on page 30 of a black walnut tree in Ohio that became known as "the perfect walnut" when it was sold in 1976 along with seventeen other walnuts to a veneer company for $80,000. It alone was priced at $30,000. It was 57 feet to the first limb, 150 feet high overall, with a 38-inch diameter. It was estimated to be between 180 and 200 years old when it was cut down (it's not all that easy to count tree rings precisely). If 200, that tree increased in value by $150 every year it lived without one cent of human input. Show me anything in today's agribusiness world that could equal that.

The sycamore tree has been around for 100 million years. Dinosaurs nibbled its leaves some 65 million years ago. Individual trees are known to live as long as 500 years, often in old age becoming hollow with cavities forty feet in diameter—large enough for pioneer families to live in while they were building their log cabins.

The size of trees became a favorite subject of folklore. For example, so the story goes, a farmer, needing a way to get cattle across a river, felled a large hollow tree over the water for a bridge. That worked fine until a couple of cows fell through a knothole and drowned.

The architecture of tree branches alone is breathtaking. There is a giant sycamore that juts out into the Sandusky River not far from where I live. I used to walk out on one of its limbs that grew at nearly a right angle from the trunk, some 35 feet out over the water. It reached out that far because, of course, the only sunlight available for the tree in its earlier days was out over the water. I would hold onto another branch above me, reaching out too, and tightrope out over the water. I marveled at the strength of these branches holding me up. Even though the tree trunk was about four feet in diameter, I wondered how it could hold up such a massive superstructure of limb and leaf. I felt that if I moved out to the end of the branch too far, my weight would surely topple the whole tree into the water.

The tree's architecture has often applied directly to human architecture, not just in using straight logs for pillars, columns, and the masts of sailing vessels, but in ingenious ways to use crooked and curved limbs and trunks. Most of the examples of "low-cost wood" in chapter 13 are cheap and easy to make because they take advantage of the natural curvatures of wood. The English treasured their hedgerow oaks, which grew more or less out in the open and developed an assortment of curved, Y-shaped, and angled timbers. Without high-tech tools to cut desired shapes out of flat-sawn wood, or to make notched joinery, the carpenters used the natural bents and angles to brace their buildings and sailing ships. These natural curved and angled timbers were stronger than the later flat-board joinery of more modern construction. Indeed, the whole notion of reducing round wood to flat wood is contrary to nature since all wood formation is circular. The greatest headache for the woodworker is trying to keep his flat pieces of wood from warping.

Once a worker in wood grasps the idea of using wood in its natural shapes and curves, more possibilities will present themselves. One must, however, first cleanse the mind of the notion that all human activity must conform to straight lines. Humans insist on straightness, square corners, and flat surfaces because of an absolute adoration of the mental aberration called neatness. The shortest distance between two points is a straight line, and nothing else measures up to that perfection. Only daffy people "run in circles." Pillars of society strive always to remain square with the world. This habit of thinking in straightness runs counter to nature. Straight lines end; circles are forever. The earth is *round*.

Much is made of the height and girth of trees, but to anyone who has planted and cared for a woodlot, the more amazing part of forest growth is how closely together trees can grow even to large size in many cases. All my experience indicates that trees growing close together crowd each other until only about one every 15 to 20 feet reaches maturity. But when conditions are right, trees can proliferate more densely than that. Samuel Wilkeson in his *Notes on Puget Sound*, written in 1869 (quoted on page 52 of *The International Book of the Forest* published by Mitchell Beazley Publishers in 1981), complains of "endless" forests on Puget Sound so thick with large pine and fir trees that the only way to retrieve game from them was with a dog—the forest was impassable even to humans on foot.

Even hardwood trees are capable of unbelievably thick stands of more or less mature trees. I have seen photos of chestnut trees two to three feet in diameter as close as eight to ten feet from each other, growing in the supposedly poor soils of Appalachia before chestnut blight killed them all. When engineers say we can't grow enough wood to serve as a major source of energy, perhaps they are not thinking in tree time, in rotations of two hundred years, when the full capacity of a forest can be realized.

Think of the enormous energy in place in a forest, as carbon from the atmosphere and sunlight join hands in the wonder of photosynthesis to create wood, leaves, oxygen, soil, gas, oil, clean air, and clean water without any input on the part of human industry, without any waste. We say that today we don't need wood products so much as formerly because we can get them "cheaper" from metal and plastic, but we can only use metal and plastic by burning yesterday's trees, laid down as fossil fuel. Statisticians say that about two billion tons of wood are harvested from the earth every year, and half of that is used locally for fuel. Surely it is only common sense to conclude that another two billion tons' worth could be produced every year if we really tried.

Every detail of the tree's functions is integral to life on earth. A mature oak can lift one hundred gallons of water up through its woody veins in an hour. There is an efficiency involved here utterly above and beyond the scope of any mathematics or technology that the human mind can concoct. An oak doesn't just use up that one hundred gallons of water but, in the very act of using it, increases its usefulness. The tree draws that water in the first place from the reservoir of living soil of its own making beneath a forest floor, a reservoir of spongelike humus and organic matter built up of its own decaying foliage and minerals and sugars from its own leafy boughs. At the same time that some of that water is transpiring into the atmosphere to return again as rain, it is taking in carbon dioxide and releasing oxygen, another key ingredient of life. Every time a leaf or a tree trunk falls, the organic matter in the soil increases. The taller the tree grows, the more sunlight it can capture and so the more wood, soil, and oxygen it can produce and the more life-giving water it can sequester for the use of all living things.

The process of photosynthesis is about the same in all trees, but trees are wondrously diverse, one species from another, and so provide wondrously diverse products. There are hundreds of different species in our temperate forest alone. Worldwide, the diversity is staggering. Cork oak and bamboo are far apart in their woody makeup, yet both are trees. Conifers are often referred to as softwoods, although some of the broadleaved hardwoods, like basswood, have even softer wood. Trees produce such diverse products as rubber, turpentine, resin, dyes, tannins, and various commercial gums and oils. In many instances, of which cork and rubber are good examples, the trees that produce these products can, at the same time, support a stable decentralized agriculture around them. All this diversity comes to us without one erg of energy from human industry. Cork comes from the bark of cork oak trees that grow along the shores of the Mediterranean Sea, and in many instances this industry supports a stable, profitable, small family-farm kind of agriculture. We tend to think of rubber plantations as very large operations, but lots of rubber also still comes from plantations owned and operated by smallholders who are also producing food crops and livestock.

A permanent agriculture based on tree crops and pasture, not annually cultivated crops, is quite possible everywhere rain falls.

CHAPTER 15

Practical Wildwood Food

IF WE COULD HARVEST and process nuts from trees as easily as we can harvest and process corn from stalks, food trees would be our major farm crop and we'd be better off for it. Very little land would have to be cultivated every year, and the permanent agriculture that would evolve would induce enough stability and tranquility in society that we would have to try really hard to think up excuses to start wars. Can you imagine a line of trees down the center of all the superhighways from the East Coast to the West, from Canada to the Gulf, laden with fruit and nuts, all free to the public? The cost of maintaining this highway of food would be no greater than the cost of the fuel it takes now to mow those thousands of acres all summer.

The pecan plantations of the South, the almond and English walnut ranches in the West, especially those that combine tree farming with permanent pastures for grazing livestock under the trees, are examples of what can be done even without visions of giant helicopters vacuuming fruit and nuts off the trees like grain harvesters taking corn off the stalk. But of course almonds and pecans still would not be as cheap as grain to harvest. And almonds and pecans and choice English walnuts are not very acclimated to northern winters. English walnuts in the North often have a bitter taste, or at least the ones on my tree do. My two pecan trees have never produced a single nut in thirty years because late frosts kill the blossoms. Pecans that do produce in the North are usually small and not "commercially viable," as the learned economists would say. Even if that problem could be overcome, processing nuts—separating them from the shells—on a commercial scale is expensive. Partly because of that, nuts in our culture are eaten more as a delicacy than a food staple. If nuts were as easy to grow and harvest as grain, then even pine nuts would be more affordable and acorns would once again become an important flour and meal, as they were in earlier civilizations. The pity of it all is that nuts and fruits can provide, generally speaking, a more healthful diet than corn and corn-fed meat. The dietary pluses of nuts are well known. No cholesterol is involved for one thing. Nuts contain lots of protein—can take the place of meat in many instances. Although high in fats and therefore energy, most of the fats in nuts are of the so-called good kind, not the bad. Nuts are high in antioxidants too. New studies contend that walnuts contain more antioxidants than vitamin E. Adding to this kind of nutrition, what if (as I think quite possible) wildwood food growing on virgin wildwood soil contains nutritional values that have been lost in food grown on heavily cultivated farm soils?

That antioxidant discovery, above, was done with English walnuts, which are easier to harvest than wild black walnuts, but when I think of the millions and millions of black walnuts literally going to waste every year in the wildwood, I have to think that there is an opportunity knocking here. A neighbor of ours, who has educated herself in wild foods and gives classes in how to hunt and use them, told me once that if anyone were to starve to death in our Ohio rural county it would be due only to our pitiful ignorance of all the wild food that is available.

Given the way the world works, the wildwood is not going to compete with commercial agriculture as a source of food. But if we approach the subject from a noncommercial point of view, that is, as a personal, satisfying endeavor, then the food products of a home tree grove become very practical and add greatly to the value of a woodlot. My enchantment with wildwood food stems directly from the fact that it is beyond the pale of profit-and-loss economics. There is something sobering, even scary, about realizing that every decision made in commercial food circles hinges on financial profitability.

We try to make nature grow at the artificial rate that money grows, which leads to one fiscal crisis after another, not to mention food of questionable nutrition. When I remember that, during the Irish potato famine, Irish landholders were selling their oats to England because they could get more money for it while the Irish people starved, that's when I realize that business "models" ought not to apply to food. Nor do I see, in all this almost religious zeal over economic money models, any indication that the number of starving people worldwide is diminishing. So I rejoice that no one has found a way to commercialize many kinds of wildwood food production. My notion of a safe, secure economy is one that functions best when humans and nature join hands in individual effort that cannot be mass-produced. Mass production means mass manipulation too.

The hickory nut is therefore my favorite forest food because although cracking out the nutmeats is tedious work, the results per hour of effort are quite rewarding compared to harvesting most other wildwood foods. First of all, the taste is divine, if there is anything in this world that is divine. But even though archaeologists now theorize that humans may have spent almost as much time down through the ages improving their wild nut trees as they did in improving maize, there is no such thing as a commercial hickory nut farm as far as I know. If you want to enjoy this touch of divinity, you have to become a hunter and a gatherer. There are named hickory varieties available from nurseries, but by and large, the hickory nut is wild. May it ever remain so. It's one thing that you do not need Monsanta-Claus or the Department of Agriculture or John Deere or Walmart or the World Health Organization to enjoy.

Because my siblings and I practically grew up in a woodlot full of hickory trees, as I've described earlier, hunting and gathering the nuts have become yearly rituals. There surely are no hickory nut hunters in the whole wide world more accomplished than my six sisters. They have names for the best hickory trees in our Kerr's Woods. One sister, a respected artist locally, even did an artful sketch of one of them, titled "Long White," which hangs on another sister's wall. They say that Mom named that tree. For about seventy years (at least), Long White has been producing extraordinarily white-shelled nuts (usually a sign of quality) that are slightly elongated, sort of like a pecan, and easy to crack with a hammer into two "whole halves." The secret of efficient hickory nut processing is to be able to crack out two "whole halves" in one blow. My sisters, the professionals, disdain any tree that does not produce mostly nuts capable of "whole-halving." Picking out little fragments of nutmeat from the shells is too inefficient to mess with, they say. How long does it take them to pick out a pint of nutmeats? The length of a Cleveland Indians baseball game on TV. I've seen a pint of hickory nutmeats sell for $12, so maybe there is a bit of commercial possibility in them—especially if you can count the labor as recreation.

But someone has to crack the nuts before they can be picked out, which in our family is usually my job. I set a chunk of log on end as a bench out in the yard on a warm day in November, use a short length of iron train rail for an anvil on top of this bench, draw up a chair, have a bucket of nuts handy to my left hand and another bucket next to it to drop in the cracked nuts, and with a carpenter's hammer in my right hand, go to work. The log bench and train track are important to the setup. The more solid the cracking surface, the easier the cracking.

I turn myself into a sort of nut-cracking robot. Grab a nut in my left hand, set in on one of its edges (never the flat side) on the anvil, tap the edge with the hammer, maybe tap it a second or third time, drop the cracked nut into the other bucket, and repeat. After awhile, I can tell by the sound of the cracking whether the nut is rotten or wormy, in which case I can just toss it cavalierly away into the yard and reach for another nut without missing a beat. I wear a tight rubber glove on my left hand because sometimes when the nut cracks, it pinches the skin on my fingers. Because the nuts from different trees have slightly different shapes, sometimes I have to shift them around a little on the anvil to get a firm seating for cracking them open. When I get familiar with the different-shaped nuts and know which ones come from which trees, I can vary the way I strike down on the nut to crack open whole halves more often. I am learning from my sisters to discard nuts that break into many fragments. I just sweep them off into the yard with a masterful swish of my hand and grab another nut.

The work is quite pleasant and restful except when I hit a finger with the hammer. My biggest problem is growing sleepy, which is when I hit a finger. No, that's not quite true. The biggest problem is to discipline myself not to eat too many of the delicious morsels as I crack away. Hickory nuts are so rich in something, fats I suppose, that eating too many makes my tongue sore.

Then on winter evenings, my wife and I sit around the kitchen table and extract the nutmeats, using nutpicks and a regular nutcracker or a pair of pliers whenever a piece of cracked shell needs further cracking to get the meat out. This is a pleasant way to spend an evening if we can avoid talking about politics. We have not developed the knack of watching television and picking out nutmeats at the same time, even though, as my sisters point out, when watching the Cleveland Indians, there is often lots of time when nothing much is happening.

The actual hunting and gathering of hickory nuts is more fun than work. With thirty-five acres of woodland to cruise over and even knowing which trees have produced the best nuts in the past, we still hope for a new discovery. This is actually a possibility because hickories often produce only once every two or three years. One could conceivably overlook a certain tree for years if one passed under it for a long time only in its off years. If more than two out of five nuts are wormy or rotten, I move on to another tree. If the shells are thick or hard to crack open, I also move on. I check out thin-hulled pignut hickories too because sometimes the nuts are sweet. But mostly we gather nuts from shagbark hickories. Most of our shellbark hickories have nuts that are harder to crack than those from shagbarks. A nut of larger size does not necessarily mean more nutmeat. Some quite small nuts are very thin-shelled and bulging with nutmeat while some larger nuts have more shell than edible nut.

The interesting mystery about hickory trees is their remarkably wide variation even within the same species. No two shagbarks that I gather nuts from in our entire woodland acreage are exactly the same. The size, shape, shell thickness, taste, and even the size and tightness of the hull differ from tree to tree (see figure 1). On some trees, the nuts drop readily in the fall after frost. On others the nuts hang on into winter. Most trees bear only every other year, but there are exceptions. Even the way the bark peels off the shagbark trunks varies from tree to tree. On some the bark peels in long, loose strips; in others the strips are shorter and cling more tightly to the trunk.

Close to the gate from our lawn into our grove are two shagbarks hardly three feet apart that illustrate this diversity to an extreme degree. One has a trunk about twenty inches in diameter, with very rough, shaggy bark, producing an average-sized nut that falls easily out of the hull. The other's trunk is about fourteen inches in diameter, the branches partly overshadowed by the taller tree, with a nut larger than a Ping-Pong ball. The hull is extraordinarily thick too. We call these large nuts bull nuts and usually find them on shellbark hickories, not shagbarks. Usually bull nuts are more shell than nutmeat, hard to crack, and not nearly as desirable as smaller, thinner-shelled nuts. This one, however, has a very good meat-to-shell ratio and cracks fairly easily. The tree does not produce many nuts, unfortunately, and in fact it was several years before I actually noticed it at all. One would reason that since it is growing right in the shadow of the other, more normal tree, it is a seedling of that hickory. But if that is so, why is it so different from the other tree? And if it is not, why is it so different from all the other hickories in the grove?

I have started quite a few hickories, and one thing I've learned: they do not come true from seed, or at least they haven't for me. I plant only the most desirable nuts, and so far, the young trees that have grown from them have not produced nuts as high in quality as ones from the mother trees. On the other hand, on the back edge of our grove, a new tree that sprouted and grew on its own in the last twenty years, in the shadow of two big old trees, has nuts better than either of its elders. Obviously one can't conclude that either this tree or the one near the front gate are seedlings of the nearest tree. Squirrels could have started these trees with nuts from any hickory in the woods. But whatever the case, the variation in these trees of the same species in the same grove remains mysterious. It would seem that hickories have been hybridizing naturally for centuries. But even then, where did all that variation come from, and why does it seem to continue?

Archaeologists are suggesting that natural selection may not be the only activity in progress here. New evidence over the last twenty-five years suggests a startling idea. Possibly what we have customarily thought of as the forest primeval was in many instances agroforestry plantings managed by earlier civilizations. Pioneers to America came upon dramatic stands of oak, black walnut, and hickory. These trees will not grow up in the shade of the dense forest. There had to be clearings for them to get started. Fire, wind, and disease may have here and there made a clearing, but it is very problematical whether oak and nut trees would come up in these clearings after centuries of dense shade. Archaeological evidence is indicating that where a stand of nut- and acorn-producing trees is found in the forest, there were human villages and farming activities going on to insure open savannas where these trees could sprout and grow. Because nuts and acorns were so important to earlier civilizations, the people made sure that there was enough sunlight to nurture these tree stands.

One of the most remarkable sites that seem to bear this out is Cox's Woods in southern Indiana, which the book *Black Walnut*, already cited, describes in some detail. The stand is diminishing now as the ancient trees die, but in pioneer days there was a magnificent grove of black walnut trees at this site. Bearing in mind that such a stand could hardly have grown in the natural environment of the forest primeval, archaeologists went to digging and found that, yes indeed, next to the walnut grove was ample evidence of Indian settlement and activity—villages and various signs of farming activities. In the United States, this activity most often has been found in connection with large earthworks, which came to an end mysteriously around the thirteenth and fourteenth centuries. Since oaks and nut trees can live to be two hundred to four hundred years of age, stands of them in pioneer times could be only one or two generations removed from that civilization. Since these people were also improving corn over the centuries from a mere slip of a seedhead into comparatively giant ears of corn, it seems logical that they could just as well have been selecting bigger and tastier nuts and acorns to propagate. The lesson from the archaeological evidence is more significant than just this discovery. As time went by, annual corn production seems to have replaced perennial-tree food production, and that was followed, unaccountably, by a deterioration in environmental conditions and in health. Eventually this led to the downfall of the giant earthwork makers, just as it had done to the Mayan civilization in Central America.

After the hickory, I think that the black walnut is the next most practical wildwood food, all things considered. The black walnut varies from tree to tree too, like hickory nuts, but not as much. Because an individual nut produces more kernel than a hickory nut and because walnut wood commands a high price for fancy woodworking, there are some commercial black walnut farms around, especially in Missouri. In most Midwestern states, walnut processing companies will also buy nuts hulled or unhulled by the pound from homeowners. They not only process the nuts for the nutmeats but the shells for various abrasive processes. You are not going to get rich gathering and selling walnuts, but it is a way to squeeze a little more money out of a homestead.

Hulling black walnuts is messy work. Even if the harvester wears rubber gloves, brown-stained clothes and fingers are almost inevitable. With its fleshy hull on, the walnut is about the size of an apple. Old-timers sometimes use hand-cranked corn shellers to grind off the hulls, but I think it is far more practical to spread the nuts on a driveway, either graveled or paved, so that cars can run over them repeatedly. The husks are sort of squished off, the nuts dry considerably, and eventually can be picked up, hosed off, and spread out to dry completely under cover. But even if you wear gloves you will find that brown-stained clothes and skin are part of the job.

I rely on friends Andy Reinhart and Jan Dawson, mentioned in an earlier chapter, for detailed information on various wild foods. They operate Jandy's market farm near Bellefontaine, Ohio, sell at the popular farmers' market there, and have much experience with black walnuts. They are vegetarians as well as consummate organic market farmers (with lush lettuce plants that sometimes barely fit one to a bushel basket) and live on the edge of their tree grove, much as we do. They have a special interest in their many black walnut trees. When an acquaintance offered to pay them to remove the falling walnuts from his lawn in town, Andy thought maybe black walnuts offered a bit more opportunity than he had originally figured. (The take-home here is that you probably don't want to grow black walnuts in your yard because the mower will rocket the unhulled nuts into the nearest car fender or window. On the other hand, walnuts in the hull are ideal for throwing at loose-running dogs.)

Andy says that trying to make money with black walnuts is not very practical, but for those who really love the delectable taste and the nutritional value of the nut, it is a most gratifying food to harvest and eat. He is widely becoming known as the garlic king of the area, and what he enjoys most about his black walnuts is the pesto he and Jan make from their own walnuts, garlic, and basil.

Andy hulls his walnuts by hand. He smashes each one with a sledgehammer when the hulls are still firm and green. The nut more or less pops out and can be picked up and spread out to dry without too much mess. This kind of hulling needs to be done as soon as the nuts fall from the tree because, in just a few days, the hulls start decomposing, turn blackish and mushy, and ooze brown stain on anything that touches them. Nuts that fall from the tree with shriveled hulls usually are not good.

Cracking and picking out nutmeats is slow going, as with hickory nuts, but Andy purchased a mechanical nutcracker that he says makes the job easier. With hammer and anvil, he could crack and pick out at the rate of about a pint an hour. With the Kenkel nutcracker (www.kenkelnutcracker.com) he can do about a quart per hour, and the nutcracker, with an 18-inch handle, is easy to use—no smashed fingers. He finds the work sort of calming. "Time becomes irrelevant," he says. "It is kind of a Zen thing." He has tried cracking the nuts on the ends, on the flat sides, and on the edges. The last way is the best, he says.

Never one to waste anything, he throws the hulls to the chickens. The hulls often contain walnut husk maggots, which do no harm to the nuts and which the hens love. He notes that black walnut juice not only makes a great dye or wood stain (he and Jan use it to color the arty birdhouses they make and sell) but is considered by many to be an effective vermifuge for animals and humans. I put green hulls in a trough of water and pen the sheep away from any other water. I don't have much trouble with worms in sheep anymore but do not know if that can be attributed wholly to the walnuts. (Rotating pastures scrupulously may also be part of the reason.) Andy makes a traditional black walnut tincture, soaking clean green walnut husks in 100-proof vodka for a few days and taking a weekly dose of a spoonful or two to a glass of water.

My father-in-law advised us to store only walnuts that have a nice healthy white to light tan color. Dark meats, he said, won't keep. So far in my experience, that's true.

Black walnut sap can be boiled down to make syrup or sugar. So can hickory, and sometimes you can even find these delicacies for sale online. But of course nothing equals maple sap in this regard, which is why it has become an important commercial product.

Venison is wild food that should be considered more seriously, I think. At the moment, deer are overpopulating and causing environmental problems that the general public is not aware of or, more often, chooses not to become aware of. Ongoing studies as to the gravity of the problem are getting well-deserved attention. In experiments, a representative number of acres of woodland are fenced off from surrounding forest so that deer can't get into the area. Where deer population is high, in only a year or so the difference in the forest floor is profound. Whereas the woodland open to the deer is fairly shorn of all undergrowth, the fenced-off section is springing to life with new trees and wildflowers. Obviously, deer are destroying one or two generations of forest regrowth, just as sheep did here in the late 1800s and early 1900s.

Hunting regulations as now promulgated are not keeping deer populations at sustainable levels. Slowly but surely, the general public is coming around to understanding this and is bringing pressure to bear for laws that encourage bigger deer harvests. This is not easy to get done because today's hunters, surprising as it would seem, support strict regulations. They want to be able to go out on the first day of the hunting season, bag their deer from the thundering herds that are now roaming around in the woods, and get back home in time to watch the afternoon football game.

I see no sense anymore in arguing the pros and cons of deer population control. I have done that too long and know that people who want to protect deer completely are not going to change their minds until they start trying to raise a garden, or keep up the landscaping around their home in deer country, or suffer a serious car accident from running into a deer on the road. In your own grove, you can do something positive about the problem. Consider making venison a staple in your diet or, if you are a vegetarian, make provisions for hunters to harvest the deer in your woods and give the meat to hungry people who are not vegetarian. Already, a significant amount of venison is going to this purpose, not just from hunting but from the large number of deer killed in auto accidents.

Even two deer will supply you with a significant yearly supply of meat. I have hunters come in who are more than willing to share their venison with us if I let them hunt. They are what I call real hunters. They hunt for food, not trophies, and know that yearling deer, especially females, make much better steak than an old stag with a big rack of antlers.

Sometimes you can get permission from game wardens to take more deer than the law allows or take deer out of season if you can show that they are destroying your property. You can get permission to hire professional hunters to help you too. If you eat the meat, the cost is not prohibitive. I know from talking to them that wildlife officials are becoming more sympathetic about reducing deer numbers and so will generally be helpful. All indications are that because of the rising cost of grain, the price of meat from traditional sources is going to continue to rise. Take advantage of that free meat running in the woods.

We don't usually view domestic fruits—apples, pears, peaches, and so on—as wildwood food. But as I have suggested earlier, they can be. We have in our woodlot an apple tree that produces fairly nice apples without any spraying. Now it is being shaded by other trees, which I do not have the heart to cut down. But my thinking is that forest glades, where enough sun can get through, are a good place for fruit trees isolated at some distance from each other. The isolation from other fruit trees might keep such trees freer from infestations of bugs and diseases, as seems to be the case with our "wild" apple tree.

We have had good luck with peach trees grown this way—seedlings growing up in the little open glade in front of our chicken coop. Because this is virgin soil, never farmed, trees sprout and grow readily (see figure 2).

Although mulberry trees more often are considered weed-tree pests because they can spread rapidly in your gardens from seeds eaten by birds, there is a positive side to this forest food too. While the berries taste rather insipid to most of us, birds, wild animals, hogs, chickens, and children love them. So do Jan and Andy, the market gardeners mentioned above. Jan treasures the big mulberry tree on their property. The trick, she says, is to wait until late in the season, when a second crop comes on. These berries, blackish in some varieties, are sweet and ready to harvest, she says, when, by merely touching them, they fall off the branches.

I discovered my first mulberry tree when I was in first grade. There was one growing in the landscaped lawn in front of the school building—one of those grafted mulberries that allows the branches to grow down around the trunk in weeping form. Its berries were black and over an inch long, like Jan's. Though not as tasty as strawberries or raspberries, I could not resist them. Evidently, the lady who lived in the house next to the schoolyard liked them too, because when she spotted me eating "her" berries, she scolded me roundly and ordered me to stay on the playground on the other side of the school building. This was my first confrontation with adult dictatorship. The berries were obviously not hers. I am not known to bow to authority, especially that kind, and my tendency toward obstinacy was already present at an early age. I found that I could sneak inside the weeping branches where, unseen by the dictator, I ate to my heart's content.

I don't like to make generalities about mulberries because there's lots of difference of opinion about them. As far as I can learn, the white mulberry is the reason mulberries have so few friends. The white mulberry is the Asian species used to feed silkworms in the Oriental silk industry. It was brought to America by people with visions of fast bucks from producing silk. Silk farming is not, however, a product of fast bucks but of very slow ones, and consequently it didn't take hold here. The white mulberry, though, did take hold. It crossed quickly with the native American red mulberry and spread like a forest fire. So you can find lots of articles on Google about how to kill a mulberry tree.

However, that is still not the whole story. There is a red mulberry tree in our Kerr's Woods that has to be one hundred years old because it was already a mid-sized tree eighty years ago. I remember clearly when my cousin, Raymond, showed it to me. He prized this tree. It produces a dark red berry, not particularly tasty to me, but neighborhood children still eat them happily as we once did. For reasons I can't explain, new little mulberry seedlings have not grown up from it. There is a possibility that being a native tree, red mulberry is not as invasive as the Asian white species and the white mulberry crosses have not yet penetrated into Kerr's Woods.

If we lived in a culture that valued wildwood food, I am sure strains of mulberry would have been propagated by now to everyone's advantage. *Tree Crops*, J. Russell Smith's classic book on agroforestry, sings the praises of the mulberry as a potentially profitable farm crop. Farmers, particularly in the South where the blacker and sweeter mulberries don't winterkill, used to maintain mulberry orchards for chickens and hogs to fatten on. I once enjoyed a visit to author John McMahan's farm in Indiana where he was experimenting with all kinds of wildwood foods. He insisted (and reiterated in his interesting little book *Farmer John Outdoors* [Columbus, IN: CompuArt Designs, 1995]) that mulberry muffins taste just as good as blueberry muffins. He grew mulberries also because he said they drew the birds away from his cherries and strawberries. I think of John as one of the uncommonly innovative thinkers and pioneers of truly sustainable agriculture even though—or especially because—his newspaper column drew the ire of commercial agribusiness. He was at that time experimenting with an orchard of native wildwood foods that could take care of itself without spraying or pruning. Imagine an orchard of mulberries, persimmons, pawpaws, hickories, and black walnuts.

From what I've learned since those long-ago days, hackberry (the berries have a sort of datelike flavor), serviceberry, black cherry, crabapple, and maybe a juniper or two could be added to such an orchard. For sure it would be paradise for every bird around.

It needs to be said more than once that every species of tree requires some management to keep it from acting like weeds. For us, black walnut seedlings are almost as pesky as mulberry seedlings. Black walnut seedlings come up constantly in our gardens, and because the juglone secreted by their roots is toxic to tomatoes, asparagus, and apples, among other things, they need to be grubbed out. I would not on that account tell anyone that walnut trees are undesirable.

Acorns could be a practical source of woodland food as they once were. Even if not raised for human use directly, they will fatten livestock as effectively as corn will, just not as fast. *Tree Crops* has plenty of evidence on how practical acorn agriculture could be.

Plenty of information is also available on the Internet about how to process acorns into meal and flour for human food. But separating shell from kernel and leaching the tannin out of the kernels is tedious work. Some acorns have less tannin than others, even within the same species. Acorns of the white oak family are generally less bitter than those from red and black oaks. I have made it a practice to taste a white oak acorn from every tree in my grove. Some are less bitter than others. But oddly, as I have gone on at length in chapter 10, there are very few references to the food possibilities of the chinquapin oak, a member of the white oak family that has hardly any tannin at all in the acorns. The acorns are rather bland in taste, not at all bitter, and fine for making flour. Peeling off the chinquapin acorn shell is no more difficult than cracking hickory nuts. The problem here, I think, is that chinquapin oaks are rather rare, probably because wild animals will eat the acorns more assiduously than other wildwood foods.

Wild raspberries and blackberries, so often growing at woodland edges, are a practical wild food, which is to say that the hunter and gatherer can harvest enough of them in an outing to make it worthwhile. Many fungi, especially the morel mushroom, which I have already mentioned many times, are worthwhile to gather. Until you learn about the poisonous fungi yourself, take someone with you who knows which mushrooms are safe. Your teacher knows because he or she is still alive.

In addition to morels, there are other fungi that make practical woodland food. I will mention two others that are just as delectable as morels, are fairly easy to identify, and which almost always grow in sufficient quantity to make gathering worthwhile. The first is the giant puffball, which grows as big as a basketball in our woods, with a smooth white surface. The second is *Polyporus frondosus,* a fall mushroom, brown and grey in color and whitish inside, growing in bunches or tufts, usually around oak trees or stumps, but not connected to the stump or trunk. From a distance, this fungus looks like little clusters of dead leaves. Some mushroom hunters call them "sheepheads" because the color and texture does resemble the wool on a sheep's head. This current fall has been a very wet one here, and Kerr's Woods, Snider's Woods, and the grove next to our house are full of these mushrooms. One stump site I can see from my office yielded nearly a bushel of the tender, fluffy, fleshy tufts. The mushroom books call it one of the most delicious of them all. I like wild mushrooms fried in butter, but you can overdo it. Once we got sort of carried away with slices of puffball sautéed in butter and I didn't want to look at another mushroom for months. I've done the same thing with lobster tails, so I rather think the fault here lies with the butter.

Earlier I mentioned that the serviceberry (*Amelanchier* spp.) is another possibility for the wildwood orchard. Also called juneberry and many other colloquial names, it grows wild over most of the eastern part of the country. This small tree or large shrub is practical enough, in fact, that in rigorous northern climates, especially in Canada, where many fruits are hard to grow, it has been commercialized and is generally referred to as the Saskatoon berry. I found serviceberry bushes growing naturally in our grove and transplanted one of them to the yard so that it could get enough sunlight to prosper. It has endured quite well. The berries, which look like blueberries when ripe but are not as tasty, are loved by the birds, and I hoped the berries would keep them away from more preferred fruits. They did, but they don't last long enough so far to be of real help. The robins can wipe out the berries from my planting in a day if I let them. The berries sweeten when cooked, and they make a reasonably good pie or jelly.

You can find details about all kinds of less practical wildwood foods all over the Internet, but I will list some of them because if you don't know they exist, you can hardly hunt for them on a search engine, much less in the woods. Some of the following I have mentioned earlier.

- Young basswood leaves for salad mixtures. Surprisingly, not bad at all.

- I rather like pokeweed shoots in spring fixed like asparagus and understand why woodland dwellers seek them out, especially where asparagus is not available. Just remember that all parts of pokeweed except the flesh of the berry are poisonous once the plants grow out of the early shoot stage. Roots are toxic too.

- Roasted raccoon and groundhog. Coon hunters in our county used to hold a raccoon supper every year. My father often attended and said the meat was delicious. But one year he thought it had a bit of an off-taste to it—probably not butchered and refrigerated properly.

"Close to the bone, it looked a little green," he told me with a rueful smile. Raccoon recipes can be found in an old but still available cookbook, *Farm Journal's Country Cookbook*.

- Wild hazelnuts, if you aren't allergic to them. I think they taste better if roasted. Ditto beechnuts. Actually, hazelnuts might not belong properly in a list of not-so-practical foods since they are practical enough to encourage some commercial ventures in the North where it is too cold for other commercial nuts.

- Honey locust beans when still green from the pod. They taste sort of like peas when cooked, though garden peas are much better.

- After reading many herbals and wild food books, I am convinced that a tea has been made from just about everything that grows: spicebush tea, blackberry leaf tea, sassafras tea of course, wintergreen tea, on and on. But none I have tried tastes as good to me as regular tea.

- And from every berry and fruit known to mankind, someone has tried to make an alcoholic beverage. I think of elderberry wine since the elderberry often grows on the edges of woodland. My attempts at making it produced something that tasted a bit like kerosene. Save your elderberries for pie and jelly, I say. Persimmon cider has its fans and in pioneer times was a favorite, but I have not been brave enough to try it.

- A mountain dweller and writer in Kentucky (Nevyle Shackelford, one of the inspirations for this book) years ago gave me this recipe for persimmon pudding, which he said had been handed down in his family since pioneer times. "Take three eggs, one-half teaspoonful of salt, two cups of sweet milk, three cups flour, one quart of ripe persimmon pulp, a teaspoonful of soda, a cup of sugar, and a pint of water. Mix well with a spoon, pour batter in a greased pan, bake for an hour in a very hot oven, or until the pudding turns a dark brown. Serve with whipped cream."

- Wild grapes make a practical wine or jelly because it is usually possible to gather them in fairly large quantities. The secret is to wait until after a good frost or two to harvest them, when the foxiness or muskiness is not as pronounced, and they are sweeter. In my experience, some wild grapes are more flavorful than others. A farmer I worked for in Minnesota made fairly good wine from wild grapes and he was choosy about which vines he harvested.

- Hunter's stew is a name given to almost any hodgepodge of wild meats kettle-stewed with various vegetables and flavorings until tender. The ones I have enjoyed at open-air hunter gatherings irrigated with lots of beer were delicious, even when you might not really know what all was in the mix. One such recipe I repeated, with permission, in an earlier book, *Wildlife in the Garden* from *Farm Journal's Country Cookbook*. The stew was called "Squirrel Muddle" and seems most appropriate for anyone with a tree grove and an overpopulation of squirrels.

Squirrel Muddle

Ingredients (and I am not making this up):

> About 70 squirrels
>
> 2 stewing hens
>
> 6 gallons water
>
> 2½ pounds salt pork, chopped
>
> 2½ gallons butter beans or lima beans
>
> 3½ gallons peeled and cubed potatoes
>
> 4 gallons peeled and chopped tomatoes
>
> 1 gallon peeled and cubed carrots
>
> 2½ gallons freshly cut corn
>
> 1 gallon shredded cabbage
>
> 1 red pepper, chopped
>
> ¼ cup ground black pepper
>
> 1 cup soy sauce or Worcestershire sauce
>
> 2 cups honey

Clean, dress, and cut up the meat. Bring 4 gallons of water to boil in a 30-gallon iron kettle. Add squirrel and chicken pieces. Cook, stirring often, until meat comes off the bone. Add remaining water as needed. Fry salt pork and add pork and drippings to boiling mixture. Add beans, potatoes, tomatoes, carrots, cabbage, red pepper, and corn in order as each is prepared. Continue cooking and stirring in pepper, soy sauce and honey to your taste for one hour until stew is thick and flavors are well blended. Remove kettle from coals. Yield: 15 gallons.

CHAPTER 16

Jewels in Wood

SKILLED WOODWORKERS LOOK for pieces of wood with extraordinarily unusual and beautiful graining—jewels in wood—for their most artistic work. Such wood is often thought to come only from rare, exotic trees in faraway places, but actually it can occur anyplace, sometimes in wood that is not of interest to commercial timber markets. The renowned woodworker, George Nakashima, pointed out in his books that while the best wood for furniture usually comes from the bottom, clean-limbed log, the most precious treasures can occur in the secondary logs marred with crotch limbs. Or sometimes, the rarest of grained wood is in the big roots underground. He compared cutting logs to preserve rare and striking grain designs to cutting diamonds.

If the only thing I accomplished with this book were to persuade more people to read Nakashima's 1981 classic *The Soul of a Tree* (Tokyo: Kodansha International Ltd.) I would consider my effort well repaid. Not only did he become one of the most respected woodworkers in the world, but he saw in the woodland environment where he chose to live and work the necessary foundation for environmental and economic stability. Born in Spokane, Washington, in 1905, he spent his first forty years moving around the world, always at home in the woods, perfecting his architectural and woodworking skills. Then he homesteaded in Bucks County, Pennsylvania, in the 1940s, starting his own woodworking business from scratch on three acres he obtained in return for his labor. He and his family worked grueling hours building their home mostly by hand, growing their own food, and existing in primitive surroundings to attain independence and success by "bypassing the whole money system, having never had a mortgage and practically nothing in the way of loans" as he put it. Enchanted by the beauty of wood, he often said that every tree, every part of every tree, had "its one perfect use."

Another great woodworker, James Krenov, who just died in 2009, echoed that sentiment, carrying it almost to an extreme. He found jewels even in ash wood. In his book *Worker in Wood* (New York: Van Nostrand Reinhold, 1981—note that this was the same year that *The Soul of a Tree* came out), he discussed his reasons for preferring ash for cabinetmaking. Turns out, he had found a particularly unusual grain pattern for the back panels of the first ash cabinet he built. So sensitive was he to the sense of jewelry in wood, to his appreciation of the uniqueness of every piece of wood, that it was *ten years* before he found another grain pattern in ash that suited his demands for cabinetry.

I have dabbled in woodworking all my life, and adopted George Nakashima as one of my heroes along the way, but what I have actually learned comes mostly from members of my family who are particularly gifted in wood handicraft. When my son wanted a house, he built it himself, and what a beauty it is. When brother-in-law Paul wanted a large addition to his home, he built it himself. When his son wanted a log cabin to live in, he built it with Paul's help. When brother-in-law Keith decided to remodel his home, he did it himself, in his 80s, including knocking out a doorway in a thick concrete cellar wall. He used red elm for the inside window and baseboard trimming—unusual wood for this purpose, but with stunning effect. My son used red oak for his trimming and baseboard, again, not a wood generally used for this purpose. But the result was more wooden jewels in his house. Keith has won prizes at fairs with his jewelry boxes made out of cedar wood. Morrison, another brother-in-law, is known in the family and neighborhood for his furniture and carvings. Donnie and Jimmy, two other brothers-in-law, are undaunted by any kind of remodeling work and have made pieces of attractive and original furniture. My own brother has made exceedingly beautiful gunstocks out of feather-grained black walnut crotch wood.

Skillful work has a way of influencing everybody who comes in contact with it. People like me, without much talent, seeing what others have done, are encouraged to try themselves. This is the first move in getting back to a wood-based culture. There has been a remarkable increase in the number of hobby woodworkers over the past decade or two, and as each craftsperson generates more woodworkers, the result begins to look very much like a cultural movement. Under the influence, so to speak, I have made a jewelry box or two, a rather crude kitchen cabinet, a butcher block, a stool, and a hope chest for my daughter (my son helped on difficult details). My earliest "achievement" when we were first married and living, almost penniless, in a log cabin, was a rather ugly sofa for which Carol and her mother made cushions. The wood was walnut, some old boards moldering away in the basement that the landlord said I could have. My tools were a pocket knife, a handsaw or two, a homemade circular sander I rigged up to fit on an electric motor, and a ton of elbow grease. The sofa sits proudly here in my office, fifty years later. It is still ugly and needs a bit of repair, but now it's so loaded with sentimental value that I couldn't part with it.

When we first moved permanently to the woods, I was afraid I would not be able to make a living from writing. I decided that wood, marketed as fuel and furniture and timber, was the most logical alternative, along with a little farming income in case I could not continue to con editors into buying my prose. That's how I found out about jewels in wood. I was neither disciplined nor gifted enough to make fine furniture, but I learned about woodworkers who made part of their living selling pieces of wood that were in demand because of unusual graining or rarity of the wood itself—like persimmon, once used to make fine and beautiful golf club drivers. I learned that a maple log that might sell for $100 could bring four or more times that amount if it had bird's-eye grain in it. Once, watching a sawyer at work in a sawmill, I noticed that after he had made one pass with the saw along the side of a hickory log—a wood not worth much as lumber—he kicked it aside. Why? It showed on the sawn plane wood grain that looked very much like pecan, a close relative of hickory. Pecan wood does have value for furniture, and he knew where to sell look-alike hickory at a worthwhile price.

So I got all excited about the possibilities of finding rare and desirable wood, sawing it out with a band saw into choice blocks, and selling them to the growing army of amateur woodworkers. But then my writing market kept increasing beyond my dreams. I abandoned my scheme of agroforestry, as I called it, rather presumptuously, for agro-writing.

But that doesn't mean that there is not opportunity here wherever trees grow, as least for part-time income or as a hobby. Wooden jewels can be found even in nondescript little woodlots in the middle of the Corn Belt. My most sensational discovery came while leafing through a book titled *The Ultimate Band Saw Book*, by Donna LaChance Menke (New York: Sterling Publishing, 2006), about making boxes out of beautifully grained fragments of wood. One of the boxes illustrated had the most amazing streaks of marbled red grain coursing through it, surely some exotic wood from a tropical forest. But to my surprise, it was box elder (*Acer negundo*), a common tree of our area, one that some woodlot caretakers even consider invasive and undesirable. I grabbed my chainsaw and went back to the creek where a few box elders grew. I knew one of them was dying, so I cut a large limb from it. Sure enough, there was a ring of red grain running through part of it. If I were in the business of selling uncommon bolts of wood, I am sure I could have sold these red-grained segments of log quickly enough. That is the beauty of hunting wooden jewels. You need not be a skilled woodcrafter yourself. You just need to know what to look for.

Other common woods often hold jewels for woodworkers and furniture makers. The best-known example is called curly grain, most often found in maple, hence the term curly maple or sometimes tiger maple. When sanded smooth, the surface of such wood reveals wavy, sometimes almost quivering, ribbons of cross grain, breathtakingly beautiful when held at the right angle to the light. It can be found in many woods, actually, not just maple. Curly-grained wood is fairly easily to spot sometimes. The surface of the wood, especially on pieces split from a log, will look ribbed, like a washboard. Sand that washboard smooth, and the result is most pleasing to the eye. Whenever I am splitting firewood, I keep a close eye out for washboard surfaces.

Tiger maple, with cross-grain strips similar to the stripes on a tiger, is especially prized by gun makers. Early Kentucky rifles often have dramatically patterned gunstocks made from it. Often such wood comes from very unremarkable maples of gnarled and smallish size that have been stressed severely as they grew—perhaps on a rocky hillside. No timber buyer would give such a tree a second look. If you are a woodlot owner, though, take a second look before you split any such maple up for firewood.

Bird's-eye maple is another rare-grained wood usually found in sugar maples. The sawn plane of wood shows as a sort of speckled surface, a pattern of little brownish irregular circles across the usual plain yellowish color, the tight little swirls thought by some to look like birds' eyes. To this day, science isn't sure what causes this graining, and it is hard to recognize it without sawing into the wood. If you see a pattern of little dimples or pits in the surface of a maple log, or especially if a piece of bark comes off that has lots of tiny little pimples protruding on the inner side, it could be bird's-eye. In a standing tree, foresters look for a slight indentation or constriction in the trunk just above the soil surface. Above the constriction, the tree trunk grows normally. Maples, like most trees, are widest at the bottom, just above the root flare, and grow very gradually narrower as they ascend. A constricted trunk looks like some mighty giant grabbed the trunk at the bottom and squeezed it slightly smaller in his fist.

Other discoveries I made by accident or observation. Honey locust wood sometimes has pinkish grain lines in it. Mulberry is quite yellowish brown in color. The purple plum tree that just died in our yard shows wood at a fresh cut that has a quite unusual purplish brown cast to it. Pawpaw wood has a greenish color. Tulip poplar grain is wild with streaks of white and black and olive.

Trees in the woods occasionally develop big wartlike growths on their trunks called burls. Almost always the grain inside these burls is extraordinarily and beautifully patterned, making the wood very desirable for furniture or any decorative object. Black walnut burl is really awesome but rare. Part of the reason that the box elder box described above was so breathtakingly beautiful was that the wood came not just from rare red grain but from rare red grain encased in a box elder burl.

The larger the burl, the higher the price it will generally command. If you are going to sell it rather than using it yourself, resist the temptation to cut into it. Let the master woodworker who buys the burl do the diamond cutting. Better to cut the tree trunk above and below where the burl protrudes, rather than cutting the burl from the trunk. The precious graining in the burl usually extends into the trunk too.

Where large limbs meet the main trunk of a tree, the wood, if sawn across the main trunk and limb, reveals what is called feather grain sometimes—especially awesome in black walnut. The grain forms a sort of feather pattern across the face of the sawn wood. But even if not feather grain, the collision of grain between the trunk and limb almost always yields beautiful wood. And because the wood fibers of limb and trunk are so entwined with each other at their junction, the wood is especially strong and durable for carving out objects that have parts at more or less right angles to each other, like the handle of a cane. Knowledgeable woodlot owners save up larger pieces of black walnut crotch wood they find above the primary clean-limbed logs they sell to timber buyers. There is not generally enough money in them to interest the commercial buyers, but they will interest specialists.

This is true of lumber trees in general. A dead walnut too small to interest a timber buyer, or that has lain in the woods long enough to develop some staining in the wood that renders it undesirable to such buyers, still might have quite a bit of wood of interest to woodworkers. I am convinced that a woodlot owner with a chainsaw to cut the wood and a band saw to slice out boards and blocks large enough for woodworkers could make some worthwhile part-time cash. A chainsaw might work for both jobs, but a band saw wastes far less wood in the saw kerf. Try to cut out pieces at least four feet long by four inches square so that they are big enough to interest most furniture makers. Or if you know to whom you intend to sell, ask them what size wood they want.

Other jewel woods I learned about just from traveling the Internet. This is the beauty of the world we live in now. You can visit the most amazing people online. I found woodworkers there talking enthusiastically about the wondrous jewel-like characteristics of black locust wood when planed, sanded, and perhaps varnished. Just a few clicks down the Internet highway I ran into woodworkers describing in detail and with illustrations how to make extraordinarily beautiful bows out of Osage orange. I am convinced that for almost everything we use in our lives today, there is a wood equal to metal or plastic with which to make it.

It is fun to saw out blocks and boards of common woods rarely used for woodworking, just to see what they look like. I have done this with redbud, pawpaw, mulberry, pear, plum, and hackberry. All have beautiful color or grain if for no other reason than they are so different from what is usually found in worked wood. Even from small trees you can usually get enough wood to make a jewelry box anyway. Pawpaw is a somewhat soft wood and not particularly jewel-like, but it is fun to use it for little details like plugs or handles or inlays in a larger work. The jewelry box I made for Carol incorporates some unusual grain from wild black cherry wood with little pieces of redbud and wild plum and even a bit of wild grapevine wood. Such details give the woodworker something to point out and brag about, since hardly anyone would recognize such unusual details.

Another use for jewels in wood is for making musical instruments. In our metal and plastic culture, we sometimes forget that nothing can equal wood for guitars and violins and similar instruments. It is in the sound of music that we still know we belong to a wood culture. Violin makers sometimes search over the entire world to find just the right pieces of wood for their instruments. The jewelry inherent in a wooden musical instrument sometimes extends beyond the quality of the wood. An artist I know in West Virginia, John Fichtner, makes primitive Indian flutes and plays them. He teaches his high school students in forestry to make them too. Their beauty is in the simplicity of their design rather than the wood itself, and they remind me always of how nearly limitless are the gifts of the forest (see figure 18).

CHAPTER 17

Starting a Grove from
Scratch

WHERE YOU DECIDE to locate a new woodlot governs how you should
go about it more than the actual planting methods you use. Your
climate and geographical area will dictate which trees you can grow
with the most success. Native species are always to be preferred. The
easiest place to start a grove is right next to an existing woodlot,
because the trees already growing there will provide plenty of seeds
for new trees. In fact, in this situation, there will invariably be too
many new trees. The second easiest place would be in towns, suburbs,
and other residential areas where lots of mature trees are already
growing in yards and parks. All you have to do there is quit mowing,
and literally millions of new seedlings will spring up.

Obviously neither of these situations is where a new woodlot is
usually desired. But it is very helpful to observe the ease with which
trees can spread themselves in these situations. Trees in one sense are
just big weeds, and the idea that humans necessarily have to expend
a lot of time and money to plant them is an assumption that arose
because not many people live at home in the woods anymore. Just
provide the right environment and trees will come. I surely don't
want to criticize anyone who works hard at transplanting seedlings
into an open, treeless area because this is good work. But it is so much
easier to let nature, squirrels, birds, and wind do it, or for humans to

plant tree seeds, not transplant seedlings. I am amazed every year at the tenacity and persistence of native oaks, maples, elms, hickories, black walnuts, wild cherries and ashes seeking to engulf my gardens and yard with seedlings. Indeed, living next to woodland, we spend nearly as much time suppressing new trees as we do hoeing out regular weeds. Tree seedlings especially love raspberry patches and asparagus rows because we don't cultivate the soil in these areas, relying instead on mulch to control weeds. Tree seeds love permanent mulch. This year in the raspberries a mulberry sprouted. I whacked it off in May when it was about six inches tall and thought that was the end of it. In August, there it was again, growing vigorously—four little trunks from the original one, the biggest of which was eight feet tall! Think of that: eight feet of regrowth in three months. Five new ash seedlings that the raspberry canes had hidden from my view nearby were five feet tall. These have to be cut out below ground or sprayed with weed killer—and that won't necessarily kill them either. Black walnut, one of our most revered trees for its nuts and its wood, is especially bothersome. One of them came up inside a serviceberry bush in the yard where I did not notice it and where the mower could not reach it. By the end of the second year, it was seven feet tall, sticking brazenly above the serviceberry. Black walnut is an especially troublesome weed around the garden because after one gets established, the juglone in its roots (as pointed out earlier) can poison some garden plants. You don't want this tree growing close to tomatoes, apple trees, or asparagus, for example. It grows amazingly fast in its earliest years, especially if you cut it off at ground level after it grows about six inches tall. Then it fairly leaps back out of the soil.

The first deduction to make here is that if you are starting a grove next to an existing woodlot, or in a grassy or brushy lot surrounded by established residential landscaping, you will soon have trees growing there without doing anything at all. This is difficult for the workaholic American to believe. We want to set out new trees the way we set out tomato plants, everything neatly in rows and clean and proper, not weedy, brushy, sloppy areas for the new trees to grow in. But think of all the gas money you will not have to spend in mowing if you allow for some sloppiness. You may want to cut out undesirable growth like thorn bushes close to the new trees, but even that is rarely necessary. Native hardwoods will overwhelm brush in almost all cases. Softwoods—evergreens—need help getting established, but that is usually in areas where they are not native.

Most grove starters do keep mowed paths open throughout their stands of young trees in a new woodlot because otherwise walking through the undergrowth becomes almost impossible. Walking your paths and watching your trees and other plants grow is most enjoyable and interesting. I am amazed at all the kinds of bushes and weeds that will volunteer around the saplings—much more interesting than neat lawn swards of trees planted in straight lines, looking like grave markers in Arlington Cemetery. Some of the wild plants that come up might be rare ones from earlier eras. In our area, we never know when a native plant from the days before woodland took over our prairie areas might reappear, as if by magic. All the plants increase the bird and insect populations too, making your new young woodlot a paradise for wildlife watching.

In the suburb of a large city, I have been watching a four-acre plot of open land surrounded on two sides by established woodland and by suburban houses on the other two sides. For years, the lot was religiously mowed. I presume the owner planned to develop more houses there. One of the reasons this never happened was that a sewer line was laid right down the middle of this little acreage, making more houses less feasible. When the owner of the land passed away, mowing ceased. In just three years, little oaks, maples, and walnuts have appeared all over the lot, sticking up above the unmowed grass and weeds. If the owner had let this happen fifty years ago when the subdivision was new, there could be a pleasant woodlot on this plot and any lots sold off for houses would bring more money because of the trees.

The most difficult place to start new groves is where they most need to be started: open fields at some distance from established woodland, most often where heavy farming has eroded, compacted, or otherwise depleted the soil of organic matter, or where rubble is the rule in the deteriorating abandoned industrial sites of big cities. Whereas tree seeds sprout and grow easily in fertile woodland soils, even if just dropped on top of the ground, they do not do so as readily in soil depleted of organic matter and mycorrhizal fungi.

Even where the farmland soil is still fairly fertile, starting trees from seed is not as easy as I figured it would be when I started my new grove. The field I used was fertile bottomland next to the creek. It had been farmed by me and others for many years. Only a few of the first nuts and acorns I planted sprouted. My theory is that a farmed-out field needs several years to recover before trees will grow on it readily. It needs pioneer weed plants like ragweed to prepare the way. That's how nature usually does it: a succession of plants that starts with weeds and thorns and ends in trees. Also, high populations of mice and deer took their toll on the tree seeds I planted. Where nature is expanding forestland, it drops thousands of tree seeds per acre, not just a few hundred as humans do, so wildlings can eat their fill and enough seeds still remain for forest expansion.

To counteract wildlife like rabbits and mice and deer grazing on young trees, the usual practice is to grow them inside transparent plastic tubes, four inches in diameter and about five feet tall. John Gallman, who used to head up Indiana University's publishing house, was an enormous influence in my life, not only because he championed and published some of my books, but because he bought a hill farm in southern Indiana and transformed nearly the whole thing into a forest. It was a marvelous thing to watch worn-out farmland turning into a forest. John used plastic tubes to start hundreds of trees. It seems improbable that the little seedlings will grow up inside the narrow confines of the tubes, but they do. But by the time I decided to follow his example in one of my fields, I just didn't have the kind of energy to grow trees that way—each tube had to be staked. I decided I could get enough trees to grow without them.

I made several mistakes at first. I was too careless in my transplanting methods. Maples are fairly shallow-rooted; I can unceremoniously pull them out of the soil of established woodland in early spring and plunk them down in the new location of similar soil. But in old farm soil, or vacant lots in city ghettos, they need to be moved in a big clump of woodland soil so the roots are not much disturbed. In other words, in these situations the seedlings should be started and handled just like growing a tomato plant in a pot. But trying to plant several acres of trees that way was too much work for an old man, or so I figured.

Also in the first year, I transplanted seedlings in April and early May, and because the field is in a lowland location, late frost hit hard there and killed the new, tender leaves of the transplants. Now I put out transplants only after the last frost date, around May 15 here.

But more and more I plant only seeds because that is so much easier. I have had particularly good luck with white ash. I gathered a bucket of ash seeds after they matured on the mother trees and simply scattered them over the new grove in the fall as if I were broadcasting clover seed. In one area, the trees actually came up too thickly but will thin themselves if I get too old and lazy to do it myself.

I am fond of white oaks and learned that planting their acorns takes special knowledge. Planting the acorns right after they fall from the tree is best, but the window of opportunity is small. White oak acorns, unlike black and red oak acorns, sprout in the fall even if lying right on top of the ground. They often do this before I have time to gather them for planting. The acorn splits open and a white sprout, almost as alive as a snake, burrows into the turf to a depth of several inches in a matter of days. Then the acorn sits there through the winter looking as if it is not rooted, and when warm weather comes, a little reddish-green set of leaves quickly appears. Here again, as in so many instances, the white oak shows its tenacity. Even some of the acorns that have been parasitized by worms or otherwise show a bit of decay or desiccation, will sometimes grow a plant so long as that sprout from last fall is stable in the soil.

To transplant acorns that have already put that white sprout down, lift them gently before the sprout grows any deeper in the spring, which it will do rapidly. Then it is too difficult and time-consuming to dig them loose for transplanting, and they are not as apt to survive. In any case, at the planting site, I open the soil with a shovel and slip the sprout into the slit with the acorn just at soil surface, then tramp the soil firmly around it. Sometimes it takes, sometimes it doesn't.

For unsprouted acorns, hickory nuts, and walnuts, I jam the shovel into the soil just a couple of inches or so, push forward with the shovel handle, opening a slit in the ground, and drop a seed or two from my pockets behind the shovel blade no more than an inch or two deep, withdraw the shovel, and tamp the slit closed. You can plant fast this way. Again, sometimes it works and sometimes it doesn't. I plant lots of seeds, hoping that one in twenty grows. I carry a pocketful or two to the site whenever I have time in fall or spring. I can plant thirty acorns faster than I can plant five little seedlings. Likely, two of the little transplants will survive compared to maybe six of the seeds, so seeding is more efficient than transplanting. Also trees from seed invariably grow faster and more vigorously than transplants and so survive and push up through surrounding weeds better.

Hickory and walnut seedlings are very difficult to transplant because, like the oaks, they put down long taproots in the first year. It's much better to plant the nuts. Small seeds, like those from maple and ash and wild cherry, do well enough if broadcast like grain on top of the soil, even if the survival rate is poor. Apple trees will root and grow easily by spreading the pomace from cider making on the soil surface.

I think that watching a woodlot grow is even more enjoyable than watching a garden grow, so grove starters get rewarded even if they die before the woodlot matures. And you don't have to spend nearly as much time with weeding. At least along your paths, you will want to cut back or spray the multiflora rose, European bittersweet, autumn olive, and other invasive plants that sometimes threaten to destroy the trees or other native plants. A good source of information to guide you is a new magazine, *Woodlands and Prairies*, not only because it describes these invasives but also acquaints you with some rarer natives that you might not know about or overlook. If you object to poison sprays, you can cut back "bad" plants until the "good" ones shade them out, but that isn't always effective. There are cases when you need to decide which of two evils is the greater, the plant or the spray. The greater evil may be the invasive plant when there is no other practical way to eliminate them except by poison sprays. Just don't spray on windy days, and even on still days be very careful that you apply the poison only to the plants you want to kill.

Sometimes tree species come up in my new grove that I have not planted. Pin oak is one. For a while this was a mystery to me since there are no pin oaks close by. Then I learned that blue jays—maybe other birds too—were planting them. A blue jay likes the little pin oak acorns and has a habit, whatever it is eating, of stuffing its gullet full when it gets the chance, then flying back to its favorite perch, disgorging and eating them one at a time. As the jays fly over the fields, they sometimes drop an acorn here, there, and everywhere.

A grove of wild fruit trees like persimmons and pawpaws might be most intriguing, as I have suggested in earlier chapters. Because both of these species spread by root shoots, a grove of either can develop from one original tree. Not far from our place, a Civil War soldier brought back home from Georgia a handful of persimmon seeds (according to local folklore), which he dutifully planted in the pasture on the home farm. One of them grew. By the time his great-grandson told me this story, that one tree had spread out into a large and most unusual grove for Ohio, around which and among which the pasture grass continued to grow as long as livestock were present. Cows, unless they are starving, will not eat the slightly toxic persimmon leaves so did not graze them as they would other trees that might have shaded out the persimmons. Livestock won't eat pawpaw leaves either, for the same reason, which accounts for similar pasture groves of this species. Pawpaws will tolerate a little shade, but if native large hardwoods are around, they will move in and shade out these wild fruits.

This bears repeating an earlier caveat. All trees are weeds in some respects, especially those that can spread by both seed and root, as in the case of pawpaw and persimmon. A small woodlot should be viewed, I think, much like a garden. The caretaker must realize that whatever he plants requires management—time spent making sure one species doesn't dominate other species. Small home woodlots, which are what this book is mostly about, make it possible to have a variety of trees, including weedy ones, because the total acreage is small enough to manage in what I call the handcrafted mode. You can even add mulberry if you are willing to do the hard and constant work of containing and controlling them. Otherwise they might march all the way from Georgia to Ohio without any help from folkloric tales of Civil War soldiers.

When starting a softwood grove, as, for instance, a planting of Christmas trees to sell, weeds need to be controlled, especially where the evergreens are not native and don't reseed naturally. Plenty of books and manuals give complete instructions on starting a Christmas tree plantation. I will not go into it since Christmas tree plantations are strictly commercial operations, which are not the focus of this book. My idea and ideal of a Christmas tree grove would be a block of red cedars because the trees spread like weeds; don't have to be trimmed since they grow naturally in a thick, pyramidal shape; and don't have to be sprayed unless bagworms get bad. I have never been able to win this argument because most people are culturally predisposed to spruce and fir and pine, trimmed properly, for holiday decoration, which means tons more work and expense. But I am stubborn and keep repeating it, as I did in a previous chapter: being cultural misfits, we use red cedars for Christmas and think them just as pretty as any tree. And they fill the room with a heavenly scent.

Hardwoods and softwoods grown for a timber sale some far-off day should be allowed to grow thickly to make long, knotless trunks for lumber logs or for easy splitting into firewood. I have covered this in other chapters. But while forestry management does not encourage it, there is no reason not to develop a more savanna-type grove if that's your penchant. Then, when the trees grow beyond the reach of livestock, they can be combined with pasture farming or hay farming. Growing pecans or other nut trees this way and introducing sheep or cattle after the trees get too tall for the animals to graze might be a way to make a little money as well as lots of nutritious food and enjoyment. I think that combining livestock and fruit trees might be especially interesting because the animals gather under the trees for summer shade and concentrate their manure there, which is good fertilizer for the trees. The livestock also eat all the fruit that falls, and I have seen incidences where such trees don't need nearly as much spraying because the animals, by eating the fallen apples, eat the worms (larval insects) in them too, breaking the pest's life cycle. The fruit can also be an important part of the animals' diets. The trees, being dispersed in a savanna-like landscape with other kinds of trees, are also less likely to spread disease from one to the other.

Grove lovers might want to think about starting a woodlot based almost entirely on fall color, just as homeowners do around their houses. This is why so many villages and city residential areas have nearly as much fall color as the landscape of the New England mountains. Homeowners have always looked in nursery catalogs for shade tree specimens noted especially for unusual leaf and trunk color. A grove starter can do the same. The maples and oaks in our village put on a show in October the equal of any state park or mountainside. My grandson and I used to play a sort of game to see who could find the prettiest tree in town. There are several street-side maples that are even more brilliantly red than the pictures in the catalog, if you can imagine that, and yet they don't seem to be red maples, or scarlet maples. Where they came from I can't find out because they are quite old. But someone knew something when those trees were planted. When I was an active member of the North American Fruit Explorers (NAFEX) I became acquainted with other members who maintained that tree leaf color could vary considerably within a species, and they would collect seeds from trees with outstanding leaves and try to propagate them. Unfortunately these "accidents" do not usually continue true to type from seed into the next generation. But it can turn your walk through the village into an exciting treasure hunt, and no one objects if you collect seeds from exotic trees to plant in your own grove.

You can use nursery catalogs to guide you in planting a grove for fall color or for summer blossoms. You will find glorious pictures of sugar maple, red or scarlet maple, scarlet oak, glowing yellow ginkgo, copper beech, sunburst locust, and others. But of course, catalogs sort of exaggerate the color sometimes. Better to walk the streets and gather your own seeds.

We like to think we have the most beautiful woodlot in the world in terms of fall color, and it happened totally by accident. The sugar maples are filling the woodlot and dominating the other trees. They blaze orange-gold in the fall (see figure 8) during the last two weeks of October, sometimes lingering into November. When the sun slants in late afternoon or early morning, it almost seems that the trees are on fire.

For color, the sugar and red maples perhaps are the champions, but white oak, scarlet oak, and red oak sometimes take a backseat to none. The weather seems to have some effect on oak coloring in the fall. Some years their red to purple hues are more noticeable than others. Nothing can beat sassafras for fall color (see figure 5). Wild black cherry leaves hang on yellow into November. I love shingle oaks not because of their fall color but because they stay green well into November, providing variety to the browns, reds, and yellows of the other trees.

Of our native trees, ash and walnut are the least desirable for fall color. White ashes do turn purplish but are soon gone. Walnuts shed their leaves quickly and without much celebration of color at all.

Another option for a grove is to plant hardwood trees that stay greenish longer into the fall, stretching the appearance of summer further into winter. Shingle oak, already mentioned, is the best for this. Weeping willow holds to greenish leaves into winter and then stays yellow, sometimes until snow falls. So does Norway maple, the best northern tree for putting off the look of winter. Peach leaves hold on green well into November here in Ohio. Tamarack or larch trees are evergreen well into November, and then the needles turn golden brown before shedding in late winter or early spring.

In addition to leaf color, some trees add contrast and color with their bark. The sycamore is the most outstanding in this regard, not to mention silver birch and river birch. Sometimes the sun adds unpredictable color and contrast without any help from botany.

When there is a red sunset here, it turns the trunks of winter white oaks on the west-facing hillside of our neighbor's woodlot a glowing orange color.

Starting a tree grove is a work of love. The planter of such groves will likely not live long enough to enjoy all the beauty he or she is creating. But it can be very fulfilling just to glory in the anticipation of what will come. It can keep a person living longer, I think. I once knew a man who started a grove of pear trees when he was seventy years old. He happened to love pears. Everyone had a good chuckle at his seemingly naïve optimism. But he lived well into his nineties to enjoy, literally, the fruit of his labors. And he lived longer than a lot of the people who had laughed at him.

CHAPTER 18

Keeping the Sanctuary
Lamps Burning

My woodstove is my sanctuary lamp. As it burns, it symbolizes the presence of the life force of nature keeping my family alive through the cold death of winter, keeping us safe—or as safe as life can be, despite civilization's determination to destroy itself. By keeping my sanctuary lamp burning, I celebrate the possibility of everlasting life right here on earth.

Burning wood will only be practical, however, when the keepers of the flame learn how to burn wood efficiently. I am embarrassed when I remember how ignorant I was when we started heating with wood in 1979. And I do not claim to know it all, by far, even nearly forty years later. Much of the lore and learning about wood heating has been lost and is only slowly being relearned. Some of it, I suspect, is not yet known and will only be discovered if and when more and more people turn to wood for lack of other handily available fuels.

Keeping the sanctuary lamps burning properly involves three divisions of efficient labor and technology: the kind and condition of the wood itself; the stove or other vessel in which the wood is burned; and the circulation system that transfers the heat through the house and smoke out of the house. I am going to start with that last category because the exhaust systems for heating stoves and furnaces are what most of us are most ignorant about. Certainly I was. When we built our house, I assumed that the masons who had laid up the fireplaces and chimneys knew what they were doing. Not so. They knew all about laying brick; they knew only a little about proper wood heating systems. Today the situation is much improved because many more people are putting in woodstoves or fireplace inserts for backup wood heat, but in the beginning we made several mistakes simply because traditional knowledge had been forgotten.

First mistake: our builder said that a chimney need not have a cover on it because updrafts would keep rainwater from running down inside most of the time, and what water did get in would be channeled away in the masonry foundation below the chimney. We learned that this was a mistake, especially if you install steel fireplace inserts. Water inevitably gets down the chimney and rusts anything metal it comes in contact with. If the cover is not removable, it needs to allow space enough to get cleaning equipment into the chimney. Chimneys can be cleaned out from below, but there are times when you will want to do it from above. We now have removable covers for our two side-by-side chimneys, although we can actually clean them by sliding a log chain up and down the chimney without removing the covers completely. The opening of the chimney should also be screened to keep out birds, bats, and raccoons.

Second mistake: side-by-side chimneys must not top out at the same height, the way ours did in the beginning. If they do, inevitably when smoke is issuing from one chimney, downdrafts will suck it down the other chimney if it is not in use and fill the room below with a tiny but discernible bit of smoke. Make sure one chimney sticks up above the other by at least a foot. We had to add on that much to one of our chimneys.

Third mistake: It is better for a chimney to have a crook in it rather than run straight up from the fireplace. Almost all old houses have such chimneys, and I have heard people make fun of them, believing that the builder made a mistake and had to correct it by angling it to its proper position. Something about putting an angle in the chimney about halfway up discourages downdrafts. I don't know the physics involved, but I do know the results. One of our chimneys has a crook in it, the other runs straight up. The one with the crook, fortunately the one we use all winter, almost never has a downdraft. The other does puff out smoke from the fireplace occasionally. This is not a problem with a woodstove, because the stovepipe has a right angle in it after it issues from the stove and is connected to the chimney.

Fourth mistake: beware of improperly shaped or designed fireplaces or a chimney too short or positioned above the roof where it can cause downdrafts. To draw well, they must have the proper ratio of height to depth and of chimney diameter and height to the fireplace opening. All inserts I know about today have these proper design ratios, but where the fireplace is handmade with firebrick or other masonry, the mason in charge may or may not know how crucial these ratios sometimes are. Nor is there a particular set of numbers that covers every situation. There are several kinds of fireplaces, including very shallow, tall ones that are designed to throw more radiant heat into the room. What you must do is find a builder who constructs fireplaces that really do draw the smoke up the chimney, not puff it out into the room. The only sure way to do that is to look at fireplaces that work and hire the people who built them. But keep in mind that during weather changes, when the barometric pressure is falling, any fireplace might occasionally back-puff.

If you are really interested in the most efficient and effective wood heating system, you will avoid fireplaces and fireplace inserts of all kinds in favor of cast iron or soapstone stoves that sit out in the room with stovepipes that rise straight up from the stove a few feet then through the wall into the chimney. Many experts will no doubt disagree with me on that, especially if they are selling fireplace inserts. It's a free world, so go ahead and believe them if you wish. Or if you just like watching a fire burn in a fireplace and are not particularly interested in the most efficient setup, fireplace inserts are fine.

We built our house with a fireplace in the living room before we understood that a woodstove was far more efficient and effective, so when we installed a stove, we had to run the stovepipe from the back of the stove into the fireplace and then up the chimney. This works okay and avoids putting a hole in the living room wall for the stovepipe to enter the chimney, but the draft is not as strong as it would be if the stovepipe went straight up from the stove sitting out in the room, where the pipe could be acting as a radiator too, and then into the chimney through the wall.

Metal stovepipes are easier to clean than masonry chimneys. Eventually, we extended stainless steel pipe up into the lower part of the chimney about ten feet high, the part more likely to collect creosote. The pipe needs to be stainless steel because the moisture that comes down the chimney, even with a cover on it, will rust out a regular stove pipe. I can shove a wire brush up the pipe in the fireplace opening quite easily where it goes up into the chimney, cleaning out any creosote in one fairly easy pass. But again, it would be easier to remove a stovepipe when it rises directly above the woodstove, carefully carry it outside, and clean it there.

Sometimes creosote forms in a blob right at the very top of the chimney where the hot smoke meets the cool air. It is easy to remove, but not a place you'd expect blockage to occur.

Fireplaces lose more heat up the chimney than stoves or furnaces and so are less efficient. I won't get into the numbers involved because BTUs can be manipulated just as imaginatively as biblical quotations and end the same way: in more argument. But there are ways to cut down on the fireplace heat loss. If the fireplace is in a room that is somewhat separated from, or can be closed off from, the rest of the house, it can't suck warm air out of more than that one room where it is located. That room is benefiting from the radiant heat from the fireplace so the loss is not as significant. If you love to watch wood burning in the fireplace, and who doesn't, you can draw your wing-backed chair up close to the fire so you can hardly feel the room air rushing past you and up the chimney and know that at least you are not drawing air from the whole house.

We use our open fireplace on the lower level of the house for holiday time. It is more efficient than a regular fireplace because it has a heavy steel insert in it with its own air ducts below to draw in air and ducts above to direct the heated air out into the room again.

The insert has its own electric circulating fan built into it, which is supposed to enhance the air movement, but we hardly ever run it because convection alone pulls in cool air below and emits warmed air above quite strongly. It is especially important to us that the fireplace, like the woodstove upstairs, can operate entirely without electricity because our main objective is to have heat and sustenance when the electricity goes off. Because the fireplace is on the lower floor, convection increases efficiency even more. The radiant heat can rise up through the entire house. If you stand in the kitchen at the top of the stairs, which are about ten feet from the fireplace opening below, you can easily feel the warm air coming up the steps. We figure that the amount of warm air so distributed about equals the warm air being sucked up the chimney. We can also close the fireplace doors to further slow the inflow of air up the chimney, but this cuts the radiant heat from the fire into the room, so not much is gained, if anything.

Makers of woodstoves, made of metal or soapstone or whatever, often boast about the internal design of their appliances, which circulate the heat through various chambers, thus seeming to take advantage of it longer. The increase in efficiency of such stove designs is somewhat exaggerated in my opinion, although again experts might disagree with me. A woodstove really warms better than a fireplace insert because it stands out in the room a little and radiates heat all around it. You can snuggle up next to it. No matter how many internal tubes or chambers the heat moves around inside it, the unit as a whole is the bulk or mass which soaks up the heat and radiates it into the room. Our Defiant, from Vermont Castings, has a built-in damper that can direct the heat straight into the stovepipe, or route it around to the end of the stove and back to the stovepipe before it exits the stove. The distance of the reroute is hardly two feet, not enough to make much difference in delaying the hot air on its way to the chimney. The main advantage of this rerouting, I think, is that the hottest air from the fire does not go directly into the stovepipe unless you want it to for increasing draft and so minimizes the chance of a chimney fire. Cast iron will "hold" more heat than steel and soapstone more than cast iron, but whatever, the bulk of the stove is more important to heat output than the internal recirculation design. Friends of ours, Dave and Pat Haferd, have only a very simple, cheap old Franklin stove, but one with a fairly long length of stovepipe involved, and they not only heat the house with it most of the time but cook their meals on it too. In this day and age if that is not remarkable, I don't know what is.

The most efficient heaters in terms of requiring lesser amounts of wood to heat a house are usually referred to as masonry heaters. They are large, even massive, walls or formations of stone or masonry which soak up the heat from a hot, quick fire within them, then slowly release the radiant heat absorbed by the mass over the next twelve to twenty-four hours. The more massive the heater, the more heat it will retain and the longer it will keep a house warm on one charge of wood. A masonry heater might take up, or actually be an integral part of, a whole wall of a room, or be built as a highly ornate stone formation in the center of a room or house. In fact the heater can conform to any size or shape an artisan builder desires, so long as it has a pathway inside for the smoke and heat to make its way out of the house. Since its heat output is closely related to its size, masonry heaters are almost always found in larger-than-average homes. Always they are beautiful beyond words but can cost the price of a new car easily enough. That is the only reason they are not more in vogue. (A good book on the subject is *Masonry Heaters: Designing, Building, and Living with a Piece of the Sun* by Ken Matesz [Chelsea Green Publishing, 2010.]) According to the author's figures, a house with a masonry heater needs only two cords of dry wood per winter for every one thousand square feet of room space to stay comfortably warm if the house is well insulated and designed to take some advantage of direct solar heat from the sun. I don't know of any more eloquent testimony to the practicality of home heating with wood for a significant part of our population than what Matesz writes in chapter 10, "Fuel to Burn." As he puts it: "Whenever I go to my woodshed, I marvel that nature not only sends all the free energy to the earth [by way of the sun] but also provides the free batteries [wood] for its snowy-day storage. Each air-dried pound of wood stores 6,400 BTUs of solar energy. A single oak log contains over 30,000 BTUs. Holding a 5-pound oak log is like holding 60 square feet of sunshine in hand because that one log when burned efficiently, will release about 1,000 BTUs per hour through an efficient masonry heater."

Most of us, alas, do not believe we can afford massive masonry heaters, although in hindsight, I think that if we had built our home with one in mind, working the extra cost into the very design and structure of the house, it would have been affordable, even on our limited income. This would be especially true in locations where plenty of fieldstone is available on-site for free, and the owner-builder had some skill in masonry. In the future, surely, masonry heaters will become more common.

Another kind of heater gaining in popularity is the outdoor furnace or outdoor boiler. These units stand alone at some safe distance from the house, and the heat is piped into the house. The big advantages are that the danger of fire in chimney or house is removed and the heat is transferred to the house, not the smoke. Most outdoor furnaces are advertised as needing to be filled with wood only once a day, but I wouldn't take that as gospel. These furnaces have the ability, so owners tell me, of burning quite large pieces of wood, hay bales—in fact anything combustible. Some of them also heat water for the house. Most outdoor furnaces are now made to comply with EPA pollution regulations, removing the main objection to them. Expect to pay around $5,000 and up. You can find tons of information about them on the Internet. Owners respond to my questions enthusiastically most of the time, but lukewarmly some of the time. Like all technologies, there are pluses and minuses. The remark I hear often is that you have to be prepared to go outdoors in cold, nasty weather to put in more wood.

Although outdoor furnaces are supposed to burn wood even if it is not well cured, in all other circumstances make sure your wood is very well dried. Heating with wood requires menial, everyday tasks. Making sure these tasks are easier to perform takes the drudgery out of the routine and encourages more people to heat with wood.

As I have said earlier, wood ought to be split and dried for at least two summers before use. In the winter it is to be burned, make sure there's a good supply under cover close by so you don't have to fight snow to get it into the house. We line the walls of our attached garage with ricked wood.

There is one detail, never mentioned, that can mean cooperation or opposition to burning wood if you have a wife who is as persnickety about dirt as mine. We have tried all sorts of carriers to bring wood into the house, most of which dribble dirt and bark on the rug. That will never do in our house. There are wood carriers now that resemble a sort of large satchel. They will hold about six pieces of wood completely enclosed and so do not dribble. I just set the satchel of wood next to the stove, and when it is empty, I go get another satchel full. The pieces of wood never get the chance to let loose that awful stuff called dirt, except right close to the stove where it is easy to sweep up. And of course, you must have a little shovel and broom right there handy to make that little bit of dirt disappear before "the missus" sees it.

Having really dry wood not only means more efficiency and less creosote, but it makes lighting fires much easier. Every day, sometimes more than once a day, one must rekindle the fire. The more easily that can be accomplished, the better. There is an art to it, especially in arranging the pieces of wood that are about to be set on fire—what the old-timers called "laying the fire." Like all art, there is more than one way to do that, but the principle involved is that two or three pieces of wood together will kindle faster and easier than one. The pieces should be very close to each other, but not touching, so that air and flame can course up between the pieces of wood.

Our stove has no grate, so, after years of experimenting, I now lay two pieces of wood averaging four inches thick side by side in the ashes of the previous fire to act as a sort of temporary grate. Our Defiant will take lengths of wood to about eighteen inches long, which is better than dinking around with little twelve-inch pieces. Between the two pieces I lay in maybe three or four very dry twigs. Then I place a third log piece and maybe a fourth, slightly angled, on top of the lower two and over the twigs. I place a wad of paper in front of the twigs. I light the wad, and the draft draws the flame into the twigs, which ignite readily. The flame then advances through the twigs and upward, lighting the log pieces. Until the flame strengthens, I leave the stove door slightly ajar so that there is plenty of draft to spark up the flame, but not open enough for sparks to jump out onto the floor.

Sounds simple enough, but any deviation from that method will often result in a flame that smolders out rather than igniting the wood. Not until the wood is crackling well do I close the door completely. When the temperature on the stovetop thermometer gets to 300 degrees, I close the damper and set the thermostat opening about medium.

Cooking on a woodstove is a skill learned only by experience. We keep a kettle of water for tea on the stove and cook only stews and soups or, most often, warm up leftovers. Our stove has a griddle for pancakes or frying meat, but we rarely do this kind of cooking on it.

In childhood days my parents had a big wood-burning furnace in the basement, which fed warm air by convection through big ducts to all the rooms on the first floor. I still think that is the most efficient way to heat a house entirely with wood. We children would fight for space to sit on the registers in the floor out of which the heat rose on cold mornings. That big old furnace would take enough wood at one filling to keep the house fairly comfortable nearly all night. I was describing it to Rick and Suzie Roth, a couple I met at a book signing recently. They nodded knowingly. They still heat with one just like it. Suzie, after a pause, casually added: "I got my pencil out the other day and figured that in the last twenty-five years, we've saved $88,000 heating with our own wood."

Woodstoves can be very temperamental creatures. Each one has its own personality, so to speak, in the strength of its draft and the way it has to be babied to get the best operation. That is why it is difficult to generalize a set of directions. But always they will behave better if the barometer is rising than when it is falling. When the weather is very cold and the wind is blowing briskly, mine will draw more strongly than in warmer, calmer temperatures. In a January blizzard, it can almost suck the cat right off the hearth, but in March, when the weather is warming, I must open the thermostat vent wide, maybe even leave the stove door slightly ajar, to get a good draw, at least until the stovetop warms up to 300 to 400 degrees.

The trick here is to always set the stove to burn hot so that combustion is complete and the smoke leaving the chimney has only minimum pollutants in it. The whiter the smoke and the lesser the volume, the better. Black, billowing smoke means you are not burning the wood completely and therefore are losing money while at the same time coating the inside of the chimney with creosote and irritating your neighbors.

Our stove, like so many built in the 1970s, is an airtight model, the idea being, back then before we knew better, to burn the wood with limited oxygen so that a charge of wood would last longer. An airtight stove operated in this mode is an excellent way to start a chimney fire because a low draft builds creosote in the chimney. Keep a thermometer on top of your stove to make sure that the fire is burning hot—in the 500- to 700-degree Fahrenheit range. Your situation might dictate an operating temperature a little higher or lower than that, but I get nervous if the stove heats up to more than 700 degrees. On the Defiant, the thermostat vent will automatically start closing in that case, which keeps the temperature from getting excessively higher than that, but I try to avoid that situation by never putting more than three or four pieces of wood in the stove at one time. (It will hold six easily.) First of all, more means wasting wood in my estimation, since three will keep the stove plenty hot enough in most situations. Then when the three pieces burn down to the equivalent of one and a half, I add a chunk. By adding pieces at just the right stage, I can keep the room warm with about a fourth less wood than I used to burn. Burning this way is just as saving of wood as using four or more pieces with the draft closed down, and it actually keeps the room warmer. Of course this means that at night the fire will go out before morning. I have to get up at night to go to the bathroom anyway, so I can at the same time add wood to the stove. The only real advantage of an "airtight" stove is that, if you do get a chimney fire, you can close the stove down completely and snuff out the fire.

Of course neither my wife nor I can always be right there by the stove to add pieces at the right time. My office is just a few steps away, however, so I can take a break from writing when I need to stretch my legs and usually keep the fire going. What I want to avoid, but don't always, is letting the fire go out during the day. Then I have to go through the whole ritual of starting it up again.

Since starting the fire inevitably becomes more than a once-a-day chore, I make it as easy on myself as possible. In the fall, I gather up a woodbox full of tree twigs from windblown branches in the woods. There is a little know-how involved, even in this. It doesn't make much difference which kind of tree I gather from, but to make the job easy, I snap twigs off various downed branches till I find some that are just at the right age of decay, where the twigs are old and dry enough to break easily but not so old as to be starting to rot. Such twigs kindle almost as easily as any of the products on the market for starting fires and of course are free.

I think it is wise to have another kind of heat as backup, particularly for older people. This is especially handy in late fall or early spring when the weather is almost warm enough to do without any heating. On such days, younger people can do without; old folks need to raise room temperature just a few degrees.

Laying a fire in a fireplace so it will start easily and burn well is more of an art than laying a fire in a stove. A grate is not at all necessary, but I use one because it makes starting easier in my estimation. First I put a big chunk of wood in the back of the fireplace, behind the grate, for a backlog. Here is where I use knotty wood that I can't split with the maul. I always think of my father-in-law, who used to regale me with stories of his mountaineer aunt and uncle in the hills of Kentucky who bragged that they used only one match a winter to light fires. Into a big yawning open fireplace they would roll a backlog in the fall way too big to lift. It would keep hot coals glowing all winter long.

Then, in the bottom of the grate I lay a fistful of dry twigs. Over the twigs I put two or three very dry sticks maybe three inches in diameter. On top of them go a couple of splits or log pieces about five or six inches in diameter, sometimes more. Here is where I use wood that won't split easily or that is partly moldy or greenish stuff that I wouldn't use in the woodstove. A fireplace has almost unlimited draft, and if there are a few good, dry pieces of wood at the base of the fire, this less-than-ideal wood on top will dry out and burn okay. Sometimes it will sizzle for a while. I would rather burn all dry wood, but this is one place where I can get rid of the less-than-ideal stuff. I pay for it, though, because it won't burn nice and crackling like really dry wood will. I usually mix in pieces of dry wood after the lower dry pieces burn up to keep a bright flame going.

The secret of a good fireplace fire is to lay the wood pieces in with about half an inch to an inch of space between them. The fire needs that space for the flame to climb up through the logs to give you that picturesque fire you always see in the movies. If you love fiddling with fire like I do, you can spend lots of time making sure space remains between the burning embers when you add new pieces of wood. This is my favorite activity of the Christmas season.

I have a sentimental attachment to our fireplace. In 1978 during the Big Blizzard, it literally kept us alive. I did not yet have a woodstove, so all of us, including the two families next door, huddled around the fireplace for three days waiting for the electricity to come back on. The wind was howling and the snow piling up even over my woodpiles outside (this was the very last time I did not go into winter with plenty of wood in our garage for storms like this). The temperature bottomed out at twenty below. Fortunately, since our lower floor is below ground level on three sides, the fireplace could keep the room warm enough to be almost comfortable. Carol kept a big pot of stew on the fire crane over the fire, and I spent nearly all of the daylight hours swimming and digging through snowdrifts to find the wood I had ricked up in the woods. Nothing melts so slowly as snow on wood or in a bucket in front of a fire, but we managed to get enough water that way to drink and enough fairly dry wood to keep the fireplace going. That was the day of my enlightenment, the biggest milestone of my life. I promised myself that I would never again be without wood heat, at least for emergencies. So far I have kept that promise.

INDEX

ci refers to color insert figure numbers

INDEX

INDEX

About the Author

BEN BARNES

A PROLIFIC NONFICTION WRITER, novelist, and journalist, Gene Logsdon has published more than two dozen books, both practical and philosophical. His nonfiction works include *Holy Shit*, *Small-Scale Grain Raising*, *Living at Nature's Pace*, and *The Contrary Farmer*. His most recent novel is *Pope Mary and the Church of Almighty Good Food*. He writes a popular blog, *The Contrary Farmer*, as well as an award-winning column for the Carey, Ohio, *Progressor Times*, and is a regular contributor to *Farming* magazine and *Draft Horse Journal*. He lives and farms in Upper Sandusky, Ohio.

the politics and practice of sustainable living

CHELSEA GREEN PUBLISHING

Chelsea Green Publishing sees books as tools for effecting cultural change and seeks to empower citizens to participate in reclaiming our global commons and become its impassioned stewards. If you enjoyed reading *A Sanctuary of Trees*, please consider these other great books related to food, gardening, and sustainable agriculture.

GROWING, OLDER
*A Chronicle of Death, Life,
and Vegetables*
JOAN DYE GUSSOW
9781603582926
Paperback • $17.95

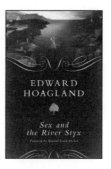

SEX AND THE RIVER STYX
EDWARD HOAGLAND
9781603583374
Paperback • $17.95

THE HOLISTIC ORCHARD
*Tree Fruits and Berries
the Biological Way*
MICHAEL PHILLIPS
9781933392134
Hardcover • $39.95

THE RESILIENT GARDENER
*Food Production and Self-Reliance
in Uncertain Times*
CAROL DEPPE
9781603580311
Paperback • $29.95

the politics and practice of sustainable living

For more information or to request a catalog,
visit **www.chelseagreen.com** or
call toll-free **(800) 639-4099**.

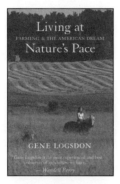
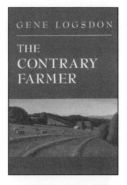

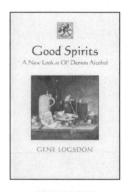